ScreenPlay

What are young people really doing on computers at home? Computers feature heavily in the lives of today's young people, and this book sets out to question commonplace assumptions about the use of technology by children at home. Bringing together research from the perspective of psychology, sociology, education and media studies, the authors ask whether we are really witnessing the rise of a new 'digital generation'.

Drawing upon the results of their in-depth research project, the authors filter and assess their findings accessibly, offering fascinating reading on:

- how computers are used in the home;
- how parents and children negotiate access to and use of the computer;
- what role the computer plays in the day-to-day lives of families.

This book makes use of illuminating case studies, and highlights key areas of concern around issues of equality and access in a wider social context. This truly interdisciplinary perspective will be instrumental in reshaping the understanding of teachers, ICT advisors, policy makers, and all involved in ICT for children.

Keri Facer is Head of Learning Research at NESTA Futurelab. **John Furlong** is Director of the Oxford University Department of Educational Studies. **Ruth Furlong** is Senior Lecturer, School of Art Media and Design, University of Wales College in Newport. **Rosamund Sutherland** is Head of Department and Professor of Education, University of Bristol.

ScreenPlay

Children and computing in the home

Keri Facer,
John Furlong,
Ruth Furlong and
Rosamund Sutherland

RoutledgeFalmer
Taylor & Francis Group

LONDON AND NEW YORK

First published 2003
by RoutledgeFalmer
11 New Fetter Lane, London EC4P 4EE

Simultaneously published in the USA and Canada
by RoutledgeFalmer
29 West 35th Street, New York, NY 10001

RoutledgeFalmer is an imprint of the Taylor & Francis Group

Typeset in Times by
HWA Text and Data Management Ltd, Tunbridge Wells
Printed and bound in Great Britain by
Biddles Ltd, Guildford and King's Lynn

British Library Cataloguing in Publication Data
A catalogue record for this book is available from the British
Library

Library of Congress Cataloging in Publication Data
A catalogue record for this book has been requested

ISBN 0–415–29842–3 (hb)
ISBN 0–415–29843–1 (pb)

Contents

Tables

Pictures

Acknowledgements

The ScreenPlay project (1998–2000) was made possible by a grant from the Economic and Social Research Council (ESRC) (R000237298) and we are indebted for that support. Individuals who have helped in making suggestions, reading drafts and in other ways have included Toni Downes, Susan Groundwater Smith, Mary O'Connell, Roger Jenkins, Tim Rudd, Craig Anderson and Ian Sutherland. In every case we have benefited from their contributions though the responsibility for the ideas presented in this book remain our own. We also acknowledge the help given by our eight schools, particularly in the early stages of our project. However, our greatest debt of gratitude goes to our case study children and their families. They welcomed us into their homes on numerous occasions and all gave generously of their time; without their support, there would have been no project.

Abbreviations

2D	two dimensional
BECTA	British Educational Communications and Technology Agency
CA	California
CAD	computer-aided design
CLAIT	computer literacy and information technology
CUP	Cambridge University Press
DfES	Department for Education and Skills (formerly DfEE – Department for Education and Employment)
DTP	desktop publishing
ed.	editor
eds	editors
ESRC	Economic and Social Research Council
HMSO	Her Majesty's Stationery Office
HTML	hypertext mark-up language
ICT	information and communications technologies
Int	interviewer
LEA	Local Education Authority
LSE	London School of Economics
MASS	Massachusetts
MIT	Massachusetts Institute of Technology
MUDs	Multi-User Dungeons
NLG	New London Group
NSW	New South Wales
PC	personal computer
QCA	Qualifications and Curriculum Authority
UCL	University College, London

Part I

Introduction

Chapter 1

The ScreenPlay project

In homes today across much of the developed world, young people are growing up with computers. In living rooms, bedrooms, hallways and landings, computers are an increasingly familiar sight in the public and private spaces of the home. This phenomenon raises important questions for educators, for policy makers, for parents and for children, and it is in response to these questions that this book has been written. In it, we explore the implications of young people growing up with, living with and learning with computers as a familiar part of their day-to-day lives.

The trigger for this book, and the research upon which it is based, was the argument in academic and public arenas that we are beginning to see a new generation of young people emerging whose social identities, styles of learning and interactions with the world have been radically altered by prolonged and frequent use of computers in the home. On an almost daily basis, we see newspaper articles and academic research suggesting that young people are 'digital natives' compared with the adults of today who can, at best, be considered 'digital immigrants', belatedly attempting to incorporate new technologies into their existing lives.[1] In the field of education, a rallying call has been made to researchers, policy makers and teachers to recognise that we are now seeing the emergence of 'aliens in the classroom', children whose interactions with digital media mean that they are now psychologically and socially different from the teachers teaching them every day.[2]

At the same time, outside the academic arena there are increasing calls to equip young people for a world of work in which computers and associated technologies are seen as likely to saturate even the most menial of occupations. Major government initiatives around the globe see millions poured into initiatives to ensure children learn to use computers in schools. At the same time, the home is increasingly seen as a site for learning with technologies as parents and children are bombarded with advertisements urging them to buy home computers. Alongside these injunctions to use computers, however, is a sense of unease about how our young people are growing up – there are concerns about 'over-exposure' to technologies, about disturbing content, and safety issues surrounding the Internet and computer games. Any study of children and computers today, then, needs to remain mindful of the complex position of children in our society; they are at the centre of a network of concerns, praise and rhetoric which offer a powerful association between young people and technology as natural bedfellows.[3] This book is an attempt to move beyond some of these sweeping assumptions in order to understand, through detailed research, how families and young people are themselves shaping the role of computers in their daily lives.

The need for diverse perspectives

As we have indicated, the debate surrounding young people's use of computers takes many forms: there are articles in daily newspapers on children's safety, political initiatives concerning education and the economy as well as highly theoretical discussions on, for example, the changing nature of existence in a digital world. Often, these debates draw on different theoretical perspectives, if only implicitly. For example, some have a psychological focus, asking how young people's learning might change through interaction with these new tools; others are more sociological, looking at emerging patterns of social inequality in the access to and use of these tools. In the research that formed the basis for this book, we too drew on a range of different perspectives. Our research strategy was to 'follow the child', to explore how, from their own point of view, young people were living and learning with computers in the home. In so doing we had to recognise that young people's daily lives don't fit into neat sociological or psychological boxes labelled 'impact on learning' or 'social consequences'; we could not simply say that the most important question was how children's learning might change, or how social factors determine which children get access to computers and which do not. Rather, in working with and watching children and their families over the 18 months of the study, we needed to call upon existing research from a range of theoretical perspectives to enable us to ask the right questions about what we were seeing.

One source of questions has been research in the field of media studies that has looked at how other technologies – television, video and radio – have, in the past, become 'domesticated'. From this literature we came to recognise that we cannot assume that it is the technologies 'themselves' that determine how they are used in the home. Rather, the environment into which any technology is introduced is likely profoundly to affect the ways it is perceived and used by the people in that setting.[4] To talk about 'the computer' in the home, then, may be misleading, as what 'the computer' actually comes to mean to a family is likely to be shaped by the existing values, practices and interests of the family itself. For example, earlier studies on the way in which television or radio fit into family life highlight how existing gender patterns of behaviour can be projected onto any technology; as a result new technologies are often used in ways which reinforce the family's (and society's) views of appropriate activities for boys and girls, men and women.[5] Previous studies of the introduction of computer games into the home also highlight the ways in which different families' 'moral economies' – their views of the appropriate values and practices within the home – shape whether these games are encouraged, valued or rejected within the family.[6]

Research in cultural studies is also useful in that it alerts us to the fact that the computer is a 'consumer good'; as such it is brought into the home for a wide range of reasons. Families will have different views about what it is that a computer is supposed to 'do' for the family. For example, as a consumer good it may be intended to demonstrate something about the family's wealth, about their values and aspirations for their children, about their relationship with the modern world that the computer often seems to represent. At a time when we see computers being sold to families on the basis that they will 'give your children a head start' (as though the technology 'itself' and alone is responsible for any and all educational benefit that may come from owning it), we need to remain sensitive to the fact that the 'meanings' of computers within families may be very diverse.

In understanding how young people interact with computers, we have also drawn on questions from the contemporary sociology of childhood which recognises that there are changing and increasingly complex 'geographies of childhood'.[7] Young people occupy the streets and spaces of their local communities, navigate routes to school, to friends' houses, and, with changing patterns of family life, often live in more than one family home. However, growing concern about children's safety in the outside world means that there are increasing attempts to constrain their unsupervised occupation of the streets and parks of our cities and towns and, instead, to create 'digital playgrounds' of safe spaces in their homes and schools.[8] Within that world, however, they live in an increasingly global culture which enables them to become as familiar with a high school in Los Angeles or Melbourne as with Grange Hill, with Japanese

Manga Art in computer games or with the all-powerful information resources of Microsoft Encarta. At the same time there is increasing concern that these technologies, in particular the Internet and computer games, are bringing the 'outside' *into* the home, reshaping the traditional boundaries and borders of childhood geography, bringing the threats of the 'real' world into the apparent security of the family space.[9] Modern children therefore occupy a range of different sites, both physically and virtually, that cannot be constrained simply to the home or school and, as a result, identifying the 'location' of childhood today is ever more difficult.

Another source of questions has been contemporary socio-cultural psychology[10] which alerts us to the complexities of how we as humans interact with cultural tools such as the computer. The computer that we see in homes today is capable of supporting a wide range of different practices – we can design and make things with it, we can write and animate, we can calculate and quantify, we can communicate, and we can look things up, combine information, images and sounds and send these halfway round the world to friends or colleagues. However, in trying to understand what we, and young people, learn from using a computer, we cannot separate the learning from the activity itself. When we write this book on the computer, for example, we cannot simply say that we 'alone' are writing it. Socio-cultural psychology highlights the fact that it is us 'plus' the computer that is involved in the writing; the technology *affords* different ways for us to write – it offers a range of possibilities that we come to see in the technology.[11] For example, as we as authors are based in different locations from each other, one of the key *affordances* of the technology for writing is that we are able to send drafts to each other via email, and comment on them digitally without having to meet face to face. This is evidently not the same thing as saying 'the computer *makes* us write differently', nor is it the same as saying that we write the same way we always used to, except that we now do it on computers. Rather, we would want to say that the way we write is now a product both of our needs and interests and their intersection with the possibilities offered to us by the new tools available.

But how does this relate to understanding children's learning with computers in the home? What this perspective has meant is that we have not assumed that there is only one way of using computers; rather that we need to understand how different young people work *with* different aspects of the computer system. We need to think of it as the young person *plus* the technology and study this interaction. Only through understanding how the individual and the tools interact in particular activities can we understand *what* is being learned and *how* that learning takes place.[12] This is a very different perspective from some of the more enthusiastic statements on education and technology, in which it is argued that computers necessarily 'make' people learn better, learn faster, learn smarter. Rather, we have adopted a position that necessitates understanding how the individual and social life stories of the children using computers intersect with the possibilities offered by the technology itself to create specific learning experiences.

And yet, as we see society increasingly dependent upon technology, as we see government services, education, health, legal and welfare information increasingly disseminated via the Internet, as we see community groups and activists increasingly mobilising technologies to find a voice within the public sphere, we do need to ask broader, more sociological questions as well. We do need to ask whether these technologies are simply providing an additional barrier to social participation and educational attainment for those who are already socially excluded. We do need to consider how, if society is increasingly organised to assume that computer skills and resources are open to all, those people without access or without interest in computers might come to participate in social and civic life. While learning to use computers might need to be approached from a detailed understanding of how individuals and technologies interact, the wider questions of social equity remain.

These are the questions driving recent government policies around much of the developed world. In the UK, for example, we have seen over £1bn invested in information and communications technologies (ICT) in schools, both in the form of infrastructure, and in content provision and teacher training. If we cannot provide a level playing field in schools for all of our children to come to terms with and understand digital technologies, then the patterns of social exclusion are likely to be perpetuated. And yet, as schools continue to provide, in the main, only sporadic access to ICT, we need even more to understand the implications of *not* having a computer *at home*. We need to ask what young people with computers at home are coming to learn and know about how they might use these technologies, and therefore what children without computers at home may be missing out on.

The ScreenPlay project, upon which this book is based, therefore aimed to map out the field in response to these complex questions: to explore what it is that young people with computers at home are coming to learn and know through home computer ownership, to examine how these processes emerge, and to understand how they are played out within the context of young people's day-to-day lives. By bringing together researchers with backgrounds in psychology, education, sociology, media and visual culture and cultural studies, we hoped to gain some purchase on each of these issues and how they interrelate.

The ScreenPlay project

The project itself began in 1998 and ran through to October 2000. At this time, the Internet was only just beginning to take its place as an everyday technology in the home; the rhetoric about a future 'information society' was at its height; the Internet bubble had not yet burst; and, in the UK, a New Labour administration had been elected which placed education, and in particular the role of new technologies in education, at the centre of its agenda. At the same time, we were approaching the millennium and the fears of the 'millennium bug' stalked many a conversation with young people and their families throughout the project. The project, then, is coloured by its timing; despite this, we are confident that our findings about how young people interact with, make sense of and use their computers in the home remain pressing today.

In designing the project, we set ourselves five questions, each of which was informed by the theoretical perspectives described above. Our questions were:

- Who has access to what screen-based technologies at home, in school and in other social contexts?
- Under what social/physical circumstances do young people engage with screen-based technologies?
- What is the significance of screen-based technologies in young people's lives as a whole?
- How do young people learn to use computer technologies?
- In what ways do computer technologies enhance and transform children's capabilities?

In order to answer these questions, we carried out our research in three phases:

1 A detailed questionnaire on home and school computer use to 855 young people in four sites in south west England and south Wales;
2 Case studies of 18 young people's[13] use of computers in the home, conducted over an 18-month period, including interviews with the children, parents and siblings, observations of their computer use, interviews with some of their teachers and with selected friends;
3 Group interviews in school with 48 young people who described themselves on their questionnaire as low users of computers.

The research sites

The research was conducted in four locations in south west England and south Wales. These sites were chosen to provide diverse locations in terms of nationality, geography, ethnicity, employment and local industry. In each of these sites, we initially worked with one secondary school and one primary feeder school.

Pen-y-Bryn

This ex-mining town was located adjacent to a motorway in Wales. It was a small town with little in the way of amenities for young people; the nearest large town with cinema and shopping facilities was approximately 10 minutes away by car. Locally, there were areas of outstanding natural beauty – the coast, the Welsh Valleys. Young people in the town were able to get out into the countryside to visit a local park with ancient, ruined buildings and wide open spaces. The town itself was rather 'down-at-heel', suggesting that many people now chose to shop elsewhere, either in the new discount designer park a short way up the motorway or in a major city only 20 minutes away. Pen-y-Bryn had one secondary school which most children in the town went to and a number of primaries; we selected the primary school closest to the secondary school. In terms of intake to the schools we worked with, we ascertained from the postcodes children included on their questionnaires that approximately three-quarters of them were from middle income households, with approximately 11 per cent from both low income and from high income homes.

Deanbridge

This dormitory village was located 20 minutes by car from a city in south west England. It was an affluent village with families living in a mix of executive homes, cottages and small estates built in the 60s and 70s. In the village itself there were a few pubs, a bank and a scattering of small shops. Most of the shopping was done elsewhere, mainly in the nearby city. In the vicinity, there was rolling countryside, with easy access to walks in the hills and fields from the village. Through the village, however, ran a very dangerous main road with heavy traffic. In working with the local secondary school, we became aware that many of the children in the school were bussed in each day from a variety of smaller hamlets, and even from the city itself. The secondary school was highly desirable and competition for places was intense. The primary school we chose was also in Deanbridge and mainly served the village children. The primary and secondary school here had the highest percentage of high income households (23 per cent) with the remainder predominantly middle income homes.

Saxingham

This chocolate box village was in the heart of the English countryside; it had a duck pond and a bustling high street that saw antiques shops sitting next door to charity shops, hotels and a small supermarket. The village was on the main train line to a major regional city, but by road, the city was approximately an hour away. The village residents were a mix of locals, incomers looking for a good country life, and agricultural workers. Indeed, the village was surrounded on all sides by working farm land and the local agricultural show was a major event in the calendar. As would be expected, the secondary school saw large numbers of children bussed in from the surrounding areas – from small farms and from other villages in the area. The primary school we selected was the village primary school and mainly took children from Saxingham itself; the majority of these children went on to the secondary school though a few regularly transferred to independent schools elsewhere in the county. In terms of income make-up, this village was probably the most diverse, including nearly 20 per cent of children from low income backgrounds as well as around 14 per cent of children from high income backgrounds; rural poverty and rural affluence co-existed in this area.

Pandy

This research site was an inner city residential district in a city in Wales. The large multi-cultural secondary school we chose accepted children from across the city though the majority lived near by. The school had mixed intake with children from Asian and white working class families plus children from middle class households living in the leafier streets near the local university. Because most children were locally based, they were able to see each other as they walked to school, at evenings and on weekends; they were also able to take advantage of the amenities of the city centre. The primary school we selected was close by and served the same community. The children from these two schools had the least numbers of high income backgrounds in our sample, only 5 per cent, and a high number of children from low income backgrounds (20 per cent).

The case study families

The case study children were chosen from these four communities, using the questionnaire as a sampling frame. One boy and one girl were chosen from each of the 4 primary and 4 secondary schools, and as we had inadvertently selected two children who had twin siblings, we extended our sample to 18 rather than 16 children. These children were not chosen to produce a 'representative' sample of any notional UK population, but rather to include in our sample children from a range of different backgrounds selected in terms of factors that might influence computer use. We chose the two children from each school using the following criteria:

* presence of a computer in the home
* equal numbers of medium and high users of their home computer
* one boy and one girl from each school.

In addition, we wanted to ensure that our group as a whole included families demonstrating:

* a representative range of socio-economic backgrounds
* a representative range of family structures (including extended families, single parent families, occupation of two households, and nuclear families)
* a representative range of geographical locations
* a representative range of different levels of connectivity and media ownership.

Table 1.1 summarises the key features of each family that we worked with over the 18-month course of the case studies.[14]

In summary, then, this book is based upon questionnaire surveys of 855 children, detailed case studies of 16 families, and interviews with over 130 young people conducted between 1998 and 2000. In addition, in order to update our evidence in this rapidly changing field, in Chapter 2, we supplement our own questionnaire data with evidence from two more recent surveys which we have conducted.

Table 1.1 Key features of case study families and their computer use

Name, school and age at beginning of project	User type	People living at home	The home	Computer(s) and locations	Child's main use of computer	Mother's main use of computer	Father's main use of computer
Alistair Deanbridge Primary Aged 9	High user	Lives with mother, (marketing and sales) and older sister	Three-bedroom cottage on busy road in Deanbridge	DOS PC in Alistair's bedroom; mother's partner brings portable computer into the home	Writing basic programs; used word-processor to produce a major project on electronics at the end of primary school	Occasionally uses databases within her work	An airline pilot, but we have no information on his computer use
David Deanbridge Comprehensive Aged 12	Very high user	Single parent family; mother hospital doctor; one younger sister	Two-bedroom bungalow on 1970s estate in large commuter village near Deanbridge	Multi-media computer with colour printer, and Internet connection; located in dining room; second older computer in living room for games only	School work, writing, production of teenage magazine (CO2) and entertainment; regular use of Internet, chatrooms, email; downloads music, images and some software	Recently learning to use computer to support her work; mainly administrative	An ICT teacher, but has little regular contact with family
Emma and Rebecca Pandy Primary Aged 10	Low users	Live with mother University Union Rep, and lodger; stay with father in same city every week	Large three-bed Victorian semi in Pandy near university	Mother's laptop (from work) in her study; Playstation in girls' room	Games, typing	Learnt basic ICT skills through work – mainly administrative; use at home only for work	No information on father's ICT use

Faezel Pandy Comprehensive Aged 12	Moderate to high user	Lives with mother (housewife) and father (cook), older brother and twin sister	Inner city Victorian terrace in Pandy	Multi-media computer and colour printer located in bedroom on 3rd floor	Constructing images with clipart, playing strategy games	Does not ever use the computer	Does not ever use the computer although he has expressed a desire to learn
Heather Deanbridge Comprehensive Aged 12	Moderate user	Two brothers, one older, one younger; father – engineering company; mother an administrator in small local company	Four-bedroom 'executive' home in small commuter village near Deanbridge	Pentium PC in children's playroom with Internet access, Commodore in Heather's bedroom, two Playstations	School work, looking up information, typing up course work; games	Mainly secretarial experience learning complex financial packages; used the computer to complete English A Level course at home	Uses pre-set programs, which he modifies, within an aeronautical engineering environment
Helen Deanbridge Primary Aged 9	High user	One older brother; lives with mother (ICT assistant in secondary school) and father (systems engineer)	Detached 60s/70s house on small estate in Deanbridge	Children's multi-media PC, Internet connection, in dining room; three other computers (all networked) in house; varying numbers of laptops	Games, school work – writing up, information seeking; web design, designing posters	ICT assistant, high level of understanding; teaches CLAIT classes, used PC to complete Open University Degree	Systems engineer; high level of interest in programming; main user in the home
Huw Pen-y-Bryn Comprehensive Aged 12	High user	Lives with mother, stepfather and two younger brothers	Four-bedroom house on modern housing estate in Pen-y-Bryn	Own multi-media PC and Internet in Huw's bedroom; his older computer now for family use in living room	Games; school work, information seeking, web design, email	Games and uses PC with youngest brother (aged 2)	Low interest at home but some work-based use

(continued…)

Table 1.1 (continued)

Name, school and age at beginning of project	User type	People living at home	The home	Computer(s) and locations	Child's main use of computer	Mother's main use of computer	Father's main use of computer
Jamilla Pandy Comprehensive Aged 12	Moderate user	Father (taxi driver) mother (housewife) – five children – one older sister, one younger brother and two younger sisters	Inner city Victorian terraced house in Pandy	One Multi-media PC purchased for all five children placed in children's room downstairs	Mainly for school work and occasionally for games and 'lifestyle' software	No experience or use of the computer	No experience or use of the computer
Maria Saxingham Comprehensive Aged 13	Moderate to high user	Lived with parents, two younger brothers in grandparents' home; towards the end of the project moved from grandparents' home; had previously lived in Ghana (father was Ghanaian)	Grandparents' home – small rural cottage several miles from Saxingham; later a small semi-detached rented home	Initially, family laptop (from work); then PC in Maria's bedroom; after moving house, then in sitting room	Writing, exploring information-based CD-ROMs, homework	First computer had been brought home for mother to write Open University assignments; mother was also learning to use spreadsheets for her work	Very reluctantly used at work for administration
Karen Pen-y-Bryn Primary Aged 9	Moderate to high user	Lives with mother and father and twin younger brothers; mother works in sales from home;	Three-bedroom house on modern housing estate in Pen-y-Bryn	Multi-media PC with printer, scanner, Internet in downstairs study	Mainly educational software and educational games	Used at home for secretarial purposes in connection with family business	Highly technically competent but largely self taught;

						administration	father ex-army technician
Nick and James Saxingham Primary Aged 10	Moderate to high users	Live with mother (teacher) and father (computer consultant) and younger sister	Three-bedroom large cottage in rural hamlet near Saxingham	Multi-media PC with printer, scanner, Internet connection; on landing outside bedrooms	Primarily games; also writing stories and poems, designing pictures; looking up information	Uses PC to complete adult education course, and for outside interests; also ICT co-ordinator for her dept at school	regularly upgrades systems and supervises children's use
Paul Saxingham Comprehensive Aged 12	Moderate user	Lives with mother (administrator) and father (electronics engineer); older sister now living locally with husband	Two-bedroom cottage in small village near Saxingham	PC (updated during project to multi-media with colour printer and Internet) in living room; Playstation in bedroom	Games, designing and making cards, pictures; writing stories; looking up information	Learnt to use computers through administrative work; little use at home	Used computers as part of degree; now advises on major international computer systems projects
Samantha Pen-y-Bryn Comprehensive Aged 12	Moderate user	Mother and elder sister both part-time shift workers in local electronics factory; father deceased	Ex-council house in Pen-y-Bryn	Multi-media PC; bought for Samantha two years previously, based in her bedroom	Mainly for homework and occasional games	No experience or use of the computer	Learnt to use computers in the military; no use at home

(continued…)

Table 1.1 (continued)

Name, school and age at beginning of project	User type	People living at home	The home	Computer(s) and locations	Child's main use of computer	Mother's main use of computer	Father's main use of computer
Simon Pen-y-Bryn Primary Aged 9	Moderate user	Lives with mother (administrator) and father (RAF engineer); and younger brother and sister	Three-bedroom 60s/70s house in Pen-y-Bryn	Multi-media PC + peripherals and Internet connection in dining room; Multi-media PC in boys' bedroom	Primarily games; also history research, homework, looking up information	Uses PC for administrative work, and personal interests	Uses computer systems at work for engineering; also hobbyist with keen interest in use at home
Stephanie Saxingham Primary Aged 9	Low user	Lives with father (herdsman) and mother (dental receptionist); one older sister	Semi-detached three-bedroom 'tied' house on farm in rural location near Saxingham	Multi-media computer with (broken) printer; located in under-stairs cupboard	Games – demos and educational; occasional letter writing and information seeking	Taught herself basics of computer at home	No use or experience of computer
Tim Pandy Primary Aged 9	Moderate user	Lives with mother (programmer) and father (sales manager) and older sister	Large Victorian terrace in Pandy	Multi-media PC + peripherals in family living room; Playstation in Tim's bedroom	Primarily games; also information research for school	Trained in administrative uses of computer; now involved in local council computer systems programming	Little or no use at work: primarily administrative and delegated to his secretary

The structure of this book

Chapter 2: Setting the scene

In the second chapter of this introduction we go on to 'set the scene' for the remainder of the book by providing an overview of current statistical evidence of children's use of computers in the home across the UK. The overview summarises results from our initial survey of children's home computer use in 1998 and reports on more recent surveys, conducted by ourselves and others, looking at levels of ownership and use of computers in the home.

Chapters 3 and 4: The domestic context

This part of the book is dedicated to exploring the role of the computer in the domestic context. Picking up some of the questions raised by research in media and cultural studies, we explore how the computer came to be introduced into the families we studied and the different interactions around the computer within the families. In Chapter 3 we map out parents' histories of computer use at home and at work, examining how these different 'technological biographies' shaped the ways in which different families came to use the computer to mediate their relationships with each other. In Chapter 4 we deal more directly with questions of how families negotiated children's use of the computer and how space and family practices changed and were changed by the introduction of the computer into the home.

Chapters 5 and 6: Young people's computer use in the home

This section of the book focuses specifically on how the young people in our case study families were using computers in the home. Drawing on research into new digital literacies, it examines the types of interactions that characterised children's use of the computer, examining how notions of interactivity, of knowledge, of creativity and of literacy are being transformed through home computer use. In Chapter 5 we focus specifically on children's use of the computer for games play and information navigation. In Chapter 6, we widen our focus to include children's use of the computer for writing, drawing, designing, programming and Web design and conclude with a discussion on the merging of different practices as children's own interests shape interactions.

Chapters 7, 8 and 9: Digital cultures

In this section, we broaden our focus to provide an overview of how the young people themselves were using computers as part of their daily lives and interests, examining how computers are implicated in children's ongoing identity formation and exploring how computer use enables different forms of interactions with peers, adults and a wider community. Chapter 7 focuses specifically on how different children use computers in their personal lives for a range of different purposes, exploring how notions of 'consumption' can be used to understand different children's 'digital identities'. Chapter 8 examines how wider societal structures such as gender, class and culture impact on these personal identity projects, and asks how questions around the 'digital divide' might be reformulated to take account of these factors. The final chapter of this section, Chapter 9, explores the nature of children's occupation of 'space' and knowledge, the blurring of boundaries between work and play and between adult and child, through children's interaction with computers.

Chapters 10 and 11: Learning with computers in home and school

This section sharpens our focus to explore how children are learning with and from computers in the home. Chapter 10 takes a detailed look at children's interactions with the computer and with family and friends and asks how young people are learning to use computers and learning from computers in the home environment, and how these processes are linked with their wider personal and social identities. Chapter 11 explores how these processes are different from children's reported experiences in schools. In particular, this chapter examines children's comparisons of school and home experience with computers and raises questions about how we might want to reconsider the role of computers in the school setting in the light of children's home computer use.

Chapter 12: Conclusion

The final chapter of the book reflects on these different aspects of children's computer use to answer questions of current concern. In it, we discuss what conclusions this research has led us to reach about current notions of a 'digital divide', of the view of children as a 'digital generation', and of debates on whether children's learning is being transformed through computer use. The chapter goes on to argue that children's home use of computers requires serious consideration by policy makers and the educational establishment, and outlines some of the implications of our research for these constituencies and for parents.

Chapter 2

Setting the scene

Patterns of computer use in the home

In this chapter, we set the scene for the rest of the book by drawing on four recent surveys which provide statistical evidence of young people's use of computers at home in Britain today. In so doing, our aim is to provide a framework within which our qualitative research can be read and to identify certain key questions that will be explored in more detail in later chapters.

As we described in the last chapter, the initial ScreenPlay questionnaire was administered in 1998. However, since that time, we have used the findings from our research to refine and develop a questionnaire on children's home computer use and have employed it in two further projects with different communities. The first of these was an evaluation in 2000 of the National Grid for Learning in 10 Pathfinder Local Education Authorities (LEAs) across the UK for the Department of Education and Skills and the British Educational Communications and Technology Agency (DfES/BECTA).[1] The second was the ESRC InterActive Education survey conducted in Bristol in June 2001.[2] In the discussion below, we will also include results from a relevant recent national survey, *Young People and ICT*, conducted for the DfES in Autumn 2001.[3] The dates, samples and locations of the different surveys are described in Table 2.1.

Taken together, the findings from these four surveys allow us to answer a range of basic questions about children's ownership, access to and use of computers at home today, which provide a wider statistical context for the detailed qualitative case studies we carried out between 1998 and 2000. They also indicate how patterns of access to and use of computers in the home are changing, and how the initial ScreenPlay results provided a good indication of later results both across the UK and locally.

Table 2.1 Key features of cited surveys on children's use of computers in the home

Survey	Date	Age range	Sample size	Survey location
ScreenPlay	June 1998	9–10 and 13–14	855	South west England and south Wales
InterActive Education	June 2001	9–17	1,818	Bristol and south Gloucestershire
Pathfinder	June 2000	10–16	2,280	England
Young People	Sept/Oct 2001	5–18	1,748	Nationwide

Young people's access to computers outside school

In 1998, the ScreenPlay survey reported that 83 per cent of children were using computers outside school and the Pathfinder survey reported that, in 2000, 88 per cent of secondary children and 83 per cent of primary children were using computers outside school.

In principle young people might be using computers in a wide range of locations – at home, in friends' houses, libraries, science centres, Internet cafés or other commercial outlets. However, according to these surveys, *the home* was the key site of regular computer use. In the InterActive survey (2001), for example, only 4 per cent of children reported using computers on a weekly basis in Internet cafés, only 10 per cent in science centres or museums, and 26 per cent in friends' houses. In contrast, 78 per cent reported using a computer at least once a week at home.

In 1998 our initial survey reported that 69 per cent of young people had computers at home. At the time, this figure was received with some scepticism and indeed we ourselves were concerned that it was much higher than national figures. Since then, however, we see even higher reported levels of home ownership amongst families with school aged children. The latest figures reported in 2001 by the nationwide Young People and ICT project and the InterActive study based in the South West are 76 per cent and 88 per cent respectively. Again, these are above national levels, suggesting that the presence of young people in the home is a significant factor in encouraging home computer ownership. An early poll by MORI suggested that children were a key driver for home computer purchase, indicating that as far back as 1996, 90 per cent of parents felt under pressure from their children to purchase a home computer.[4]

Internet access is similarly substantially higher amongst this age group than amongst the wider population, and seems to be increasing at a fast rate. When we consider that our initial scoping survey in 1998 reported only 25 per cent 'modem'[5] connections, the figures of nearly 75 per cent of children now reporting Internet connection in the InterActive survey and 64 per cent in the Pathfinder survey suggests a rapid increase in connectivity in this age group.

These figures suggest that only 24–12 per cent of young people now do *not* have a computer in the home, reinforcing our need to understand what these technologies afford young people both in their leisure and 'schooled' lives.

Socio-economic status, gender and ethnicity

Home computer ownership is, however, patterned according to socio-economic status. In 1998 we found 80 per cent of children from high income areas reporting home ownership, compared with 54 per cent from low income areas. Both the InterActive and Young People and ICT surveys have also identified clear differences in levels of ownership of technologies according to socio-economic status. The Young People and ICT survey, for example, reported 91 per cent of households in social grade AB with a home computer compared with 78 per cent at grade C2 and 58 per cent at grade DE.[6] The InterActive survey used a different method of determining social class,[7] but nevertheless reported similar differences, with 92 per cent of children from areas of high socio-economic status reporting computer ownership, compared with 76 per cent in the low socio-economic areas in the sample.

In terms of gender, there is little reliable evidence to suggest major differences in home computer ownership, although the recent InterActive survey does indicate that boys are more likely than girls to report having their 'own' computers (50 per cent boys compared with 37 per cent girls).

Finally, the only reliable data on patterns of computer use and ethnicity is found in the Young People and ICT survey. This survey did find significant differences in terms of access to computers in the home along lines of ethnicity. The report states, for example, that Black/Other households were less likely to own most of the sources of ICT than other ethnic groups. For example, 67 per cent of the Black/Other group owned a PC or a laptop, compared with 77 per cent of the Asian group and 79 per cent of the White group.[8] Similarly, Internet access in the home is reported in this survey to be patterned along ethnic lines, with 61 per cent of White respondents reporting home access, compared with 52 per cent of Asian and 53 per cent of Black/Other respondents.[9]

The ways in which gender, socio-economic status and ethnicity are 'played out' in terms of computer access and use in the home are discussed in detail with reference to our case studies in Chapters 7 and 8.

Location and access to computers in the home

In our 1998 survey, we found that 53 per cent of home computers were located in family spaces (such as dining rooms, hallways, computer rooms etc.) and only 43 per cent in bedrooms, which may also have been used by other members of the family. Only 6 per cent of the children responded that 'no one' was likely to be using the computer when they wanted to use it.

More recently, in the 2001 InterActive study, 24 per cent of children reported that the computer they used most of the time was in their own bedroom, 12 per cent in someone else's bedroom, 24 per cent in living rooms, 27 per cent in attic/computer room/kids' room/study and 7 per cent in kitchens/halls and landings. Again, only 6 per cent of children reported that no one else used the computer in the home, with over half (57 per cent) reporting at least three other people also using the computer they used.

The significance of computer location and of negotiations around access to the computer for children's computer activities in the home are discussed in more detail in Chapter 4.

Activities on the computer in the home

The home computer, as we shall go on to discuss in the remainder of the book, is essentially a multi-purpose tool which can be used for a very wide range of activities, from writing, to designing, to programming, to communicating with others, to games play, to looking up information. There are, accordingly, many different ways in which we might begin to ask what activities children are using computers for in the home.

In the original ScreenPlay survey in 1998, we asked respondents to report how often they played 'computer games' at home, how often they used the computer for homework, and how often they used the computer for other things, with the following results:

- Computer games (including console games): 71 per cent reported at least once a week

- Homework on the computer: 36 per cent reported at least once a week
- Other things on the computer: 29 per cent reported at least once a week.

In the InterActive survey in 2001, 84 per cent of children with home computers reported using it for 'fun' and 64 per cent reported using it for 'schoolwork', at least once a week. This suggests that school-related work with computers in the home is much more prevalent now than in 1998, although, as we shall discuss in Chapter 10, it is also arguable that our category of 'fun' may include many activities of relevance to children's learning in school.

These results do not, however, provide much insight into the actual activities that young people are using the computer for in the home. Given that the surveys were administered to different groups and ages of young people, and that they used slightly different categories of activity, it is impossible to compare between them in terms of asking questions such as: how many more children are using computers for writing in 2001 than in 1998?

What we can do, however, is look at how different activities were ranked in each of the surveys, looking at what was most popular in each of them. If we do this (Table 2.2) we find a high degree of consistency across the surveys, with games, writing and what we might call 'information seeking' all persistently high; the use of the computer for making Websites, films/animations, mathematical activities such as spreadsheets and programming ranked relatively low. There are however some interesting changes in ranking between these different surveys. Email use seems to have become relatively more popular over time, as does using the Web rather than CD-ROMs for information seeking, changes that reflect the growing numbers of young people with Internet connections in the home. At the time of the ScreenPlay survey, Internet ownership was still relatively rare, though as the study progressed, we saw Internet connection amongst our case study families rise from only two out of 16 households to eight. As we have already mentioned, by the time of the InterActive Education survey in 2001, nearly three-quarters of young people sampled reported using the Internet at home.

What these 'rankings' of popularity do not show, however, is the wide variation in popularity between the different activities. In the 1998 ScreenPlay survey, for example, 66 per cent of children reported recent games play, compared with only 12 per cent reporting making Websites. In the 2000 Pathfinder survey, 60 per cent reported games play once a week or more, compared with 12 per cent reporting making Web pages

Table 2.2 Relative rankings of computer activities over ScreenPlay, Pathfinder and InterActive surveys

	ScreenPlay 1998 rankings	Pathfinder 2000 rankings	InterActive Education 2001 rankings
Most popular			
	Games	Writing	Web for fun
	Writing	Games	Games
	Drawing	Looking up info on the Internet	Writing
	CD-ROM		Fiddle around
	Educational software	Looking up info on CD-ROM	Emails
	Internet	Drawing/designing	CD-ROM
	Spreadsheets	Email/chat	Draw/images
	Make music	Educational software	Educational software
	Email		Chat rooms
	Films/animations	Spreadsheets	Make/design
	Program	Making Web pages	Organise computer
	Make Websites		Make charts/graphs
	Powerpoint		Program
			Watch DVDs
			Make Websites
			Make films/ animations
Least popular			

once a week or more; and in the 2001 InterActive survey, 69 per cent reported weekly games play compared with 13 per cent reporting making Webpages once a week or more. What this ranking also does not show is quite how close games play and writing are in terms of frequency of use amongst young people in the home, with, for example, 69 per cent reporting games play at least once a week, and 68 per cent reporting writing on the computer at least once a week.

When identifying patterns *within* these surveys then, it is clear that there are activities (writing, games play, information seeking) we might now consider commonplace and others we might consider rare (Web production, numerical practices, moving image production). When we take these 'exotic' activities in isolation, however, it remains remarkable that the home computer is, in fact, being used by 12–13 per cent of young people on at least a weekly basis to produce Webpages, by 30 per cent (Pathfinder) and 54 per cent (InterActive) of young people for email, and so on. We could argue then that even while use at home may be *dominated* by particular activities, even the most exotic activities represent large numbers of young people engaged in practices that might previously have been considered part of adult professional domains or that represent emergent practices developing in homes alongside the growth of this technology.

The types of interactions that characterise these activities are discussed in detail in Chapters 5 and 6, and the implications of these uses of the computer for changing notions of 'childhood' are discussed in Chapter 9.

Activities at different ages

It is clear from all these surveys that age is a key factor influencing activities on the computer in the home. In the first instance, this is inevitably shaped by levels of computer ownership. On a basic level, the older the child, the more likely they are to have a computer in the home. The Young People and ICT survey reports 67 per cent of children aged 5–8 reporting computer ownership compared with 88 per cent of post 16-year-olds. The InterActive and Pathfinder studies report similar results. There are, however, also age differences in what young people use the computer for. For example, Table 2.3 shows age differences in the percentages of different age groups using the computer frequently for schoolwork at home.

A more exaggerated pattern emerges in the Young People and ICT survey, with only 4 per cent (Key Stage 1) and 7 per cent (Key Stage 2) of primary school pupils reporting ever using the computer for homework/study compared with between 78 per cent and 89 per cent of secondary school pupils (age 11–18) (Table 2.4).[10]

Differences in activities across different age groups, however, are not only related to school work. Internet access and use, for example, increased in line with age, with only 4 per cent of Key Stage 1 compared with 49 per cent of post 16 reporting email use in the Young People and ICT study.[11] In contrast, games use, in both InterActive and Young People and ICT surveys, seems to decrease with age (Table 2.5).

Working with visual media also seems to decrease with age, as making or designing things and playing with images and photos are reported by more children in Years 5 and 7 than in Years 10 and 12 in the InterActive

Table 2.3 Schoolwork on the home computer by age group

	Yr 5	Yr 7	Yr 10	Yr 12
	n = 148	n = 655	n = 566	n = 216
Use of home computer for school-work at least twice a week or more	21%	32%	39%	46%

Source: InterActive Education survey, n = 1,818, Facer (2001), p33.

Table 2.4 Activities on the home computer by age group

	Key Stage 1[a,b]	Key Stage 2	Key Stage 3	Key Stage 4	Post 16
Base: all children using a computer at home	n = 220	n = 372	n = 266	n = 220	n = 168
Playing games	89%	88%	69%	55%	49%
Homework/study	4%	7%	78%	88%	89%
Internet	13%	27%	42%	52%	65%
General purposes/typing letters	20%	26%	16%	24%	39%
General info/CD-ROMs	23%	24%	16%	21%	35%
Emails	4%	9%	19%	35%	49%
Drawing pictures	60%	45%	–	–	–
Playing CDs	–	–	27%	30%	29%
Writing stories	15%	30%	–	–	–
Chat rooms	–	–	9%	16%	19%

Source: DfES 2002[a], p15.

Notes
a   Key Stage 1 = 5, 6, 7; Key Stage 2 = 8, 9, 10; Key Stage 3 = 11, 12, 13; Key Stage 4 = 14, 15 (ages at start of school year).
b   Key Stages 1–2 prompted, Key Stage 3 and above not prompted.

Table: 2.5 Games use by age

	Yr 5 (9–10)	Yr 7 (11–12)	Yr 10 (14–15)	Yr 12 (16–17)
	n = 148	n = 655	n = 566	n = 216
Use of home computer for games at least weekly	78%	83%	65%	40%

Source: InterActive Education survey, n = 1,818, Facer (2001), p33.

survey. A similar pattern also emerges in the Young People and ICT survey, with no respondents above Key Stage 2 freely offering 'drawing' as an activity on the computer.

Given these differences in use at different ages, could it be conjectured, then, that the meaning of the home computer changes for children as they grow older? In order to answer this question we need to turn to more detailed qualitative research with children and families and, in Chapter 4, we discuss how notions of 'childhood' are negotiated by parents and children in the home and, in Chapters 7 and 9, how children's developing identity projects and their experiences at different ages inform their interactions with and around computers.

Conclusion

To summarise, then, we can say that the majority of young people now have computers and the Internet in their homes and that, indeed, the home is the key site for young people to use these technologies. We can also say that young people are using computers in the home for a wide range of activities, from the 'commonplace' such as writing, games and information seeking, to the more unusual activities such as Web design and programming. From these surveys, at least, we might want to argue that we are witnessing major changes in the prevalence of computer use in young people's lives, both for leisure and for schoolwork. Importantly, however, there remains a persistent group of young people who do not have access either to computers or to the Internet at home, and these young people are disproportionately likely to come from lower socio-economic groups.

While providing a useful *context* for discussions of children's computer use, however, these 'whole population' figures serve to mask major differences in patterns of use by individual children. We could in fact say that this method of quantifying behaviours serves to reinforce the impression we are trying to challenge, namely, that there is a 'typical' child computer user or a 'uniform' digital generation. The remainder of this book takes a different approach and, through detailed descriptions of our 18 case studies, maps out the diverse ways in which individual children are making sense of and using these new tools in their daily lives and learning. In so doing, we hope that this book begins to explain why we need to look beyond the headline numbers heralding the digital generation and engage with the lived reality of children's experiences with computers in the home.

Part II

The domestic context

Chapter 3

Computer histories, computer roles in the home

'… children are at the epicenter of the information revolution, ground zero of the digital world …'

(Katz, 1997)

It is well established that the generation of young people who are the subject of this book are the first to grow up with computers both at home and at school.[1] Consequently, we often talk about them as though there were no history of interactions with computers in the home or elsewhere until they were born, as though they emerged, fully formed, as the first generation of computer users. Adults, in contrast, are often presented as naïve newcomers to the digital age in comparison with their children.

And yet, the techno-popular cultures of this new 'Net generation' have arguably been forged within the context of a series of inter-connected histories: the histories of technological change over the last thirty years and the rapid transformations in the presence and role of technology in schools and workplaces.

Histories have been written before about the gradual penetration of computers into our homes. Researchers have documented the introduction of the personal computer (PC) into the domestic context, mapping the shift from the early 'hobbyist' assemble-yourself micros of the 1970s, to the multi-media, networked PCs of the 1990s.[2] Other commentators have focused on the changing discourses of computer manufacturers, from the days when it was conceived that there would be a market only for three computers in the world, to the concerted onslaught of computer manufacturers and government in arguing the case for the computer as an essential aspect of any family's educational and entertainment needs.[3] These histories take the emergent technology and its surrounding discourses as their focus and thus concentrate almost exclusively on mapping the history of the computer *itself* within the home. The computer, however, is not exclusively a domestic artefact: indeed, for many it remains primarily a technology associated with the workplace. If, rather than mapping the history of the 'home computer', we instead attempt to follow the *user*, to track how today's *parents* have come to know about and engage with computers over the last thirty years, a picture emerges of radically divergent biographies of computer use into which, rather than a blank canvas, today's 'Net generation' are being born. In this chapter, then, we provide a brief 'pre-history' of parents' computer use and go on to examine how these different experiences in the workplace and at home converge to create radically different contexts for children's computer use in families today.

Parental biographies of computer use

The age of the abacus

Sitting in living rooms and kitchens surrounded by the familiar electronic detritus of cable television, Playstations and computers, the school experiences of the parents in this study do seem to belong to a different age, an ancient pre-history of technological innocence recollected now by parents with a degree of humour and astonishment at the speed of change and the difference between their own experiences and those of their children:

Interviewer:	Let's say at school, did you have any experience of computers at school?
Paul's mother:	No, no. I'm afraid I'm too old for that. They didn't have computers at school.
Paul's father:	The nearest thing to a computer was an abacus wasn't it?
Stephanie's father:	Well when I was at school you weren't allowed to take the beads in [to exams].
Simon's mother:	(Laughter) Were there computers in school, Mike, when we were at school? Not for children's use anyway.
Simon's father:	We had a 10 foot by 10 foot big box called a calculator.
Karen's mother:	I left in 1976 and I did O Levels but it was all no computers, just books and blackboards and pens and things.

Indeed, all but three of the parents in the 16 families in the study had no recollection of seeing, knowing about or using computers in any form during their school years. The exceptions were a series of vague recollections by the younger parents, of computers being used by other children for 'computer studies'.

Bringing work home

For many of these parents, it was in the workplace that they first encountered computers. The workplace, however, provided a diverse range of introductions to the world of digital technology. Five of the mothers in the study, for example, first came across computers as an 'office tool', a next generation up from the electronic typewriters they trained on in secretarial college or at school. Two of the fathers (of Tim and Maria), in managerial positions, attempted to avoid computers for as long as possible by delegating responsibility for computer-based tasks to their secretaries. Three mothers (of Nick and James, Emma and Rebecca, and David), in educational and medical professions, had only in the last few years been required to use computers as, prior to this, computers were marginal to their main focus of looking after patients or students. Three of the fathers came across computers in a more technical capacity: one, a computer consultant (Nick and James' father), was designing computer systems for major multinational companies, another was using programs to run engineering trials (Heather's father), a third had taught himself to program and worked in telecommunications (Helen's father). One father (Paul's) had a unique introduction to computers through his experience in the military:

> My first contact was in the 80s. [...] In the military [...] for fire control. [...] Well I look at a map and I say 'I'm here' and I look at the map and say 'The enemy's there', punch the figures into a little computer and it's saying he's pointing from that direction at that angle and land there. But you're also trained to bypass that technology and use it as a human being.
>
> (Paul's father, Saxingham)

Importantly, however, these workplace experiences also impacted on the home setting, as parents with access to outdated computer equipment at work were able to bring it home, to keep topping up supplies of paper or toner for printers. At the same time, the presence of these 'second-hand' computers in the home, and of individuals with expertise in computer use through the workplace, also enabled some parents to first start to use computers in the home. Several of the mothers in the study, for example, had used the home computer to gain qualifications – two had taken university degrees, one had taken an A Level, while others had studied for professional qualifications from the National Childbirth Trust, in IT literacy and in counselling (Helen, Nick and James, Heather, Maria). These activities in themselves often led the family to upgrade their computer equipment.

Another group of parents (Samantha, Faezal and Jamilla), however, had no experience of computer use in the workplace. In these families, the parents left school early, often with no qualifications, and took manual jobs, which did not require computer use. In two of the families (Faezal and Jamilla) the mothers also stayed at home to look after the children and in all three, the parents' first experience of computers was as a result of the decision to purchase the computer for their children.

The role of the computer in family life

The computer in the home then, does not enter into a 'blank slate' of technological innocence. Our case study parents' histories and experiences of using computers were highly varied and these histories were necessarily influential in how the technology came into the home in the first place. But, once the computer had arrived, how was it regarded by parents; how did they construct its meaning in family life? Our aim in the second part of this chapter is to explore this question, drawing out significant differences between families. What becomes apparent is that parents' own personal histories of computer use at work and at home were highly influential; they helped to produce a range of different metaphors for the role of the computer within family life.

The computer as 'children's machine'

While most, if not all, of our case study families described computers as an intrinsic part of children's future leisure and working lives, in some of our households it was clear that the computer was seen as the 'child's machine', as a key symbolic representation of the aspirations of parents for their children's future welfare. That this construction of the computer was dominant in households where parents had little or no experience of computer use within the workplace is not surprising, given that their main access to cultural constructions of the computer was via the marketing campaigns of computer manufacturers and the dominant discourses within the media.

In these households, the computer was usually located in a room either 'belonging' to the child, or used exclusively by the children, such as a playroom, or a previously unused space in the house. This is not to say that the computer had no 'meaning' for the parents; it was simply that as an object, the computer was constructed within the household as having significance primarily, if not exclusively, in its relation to the children in the family and their future.

Samantha was a case in point. The youngest by two years of two sisters, she lived with her mother in Pen-y-Bryn, an ex-mining town in south Wales. Her mother, a shift worker at the local factory, with no experience of computer use either in work or in school, had bought the computer specifically for Samantha when she was 10. Samantha had been using a computer at school since she was six and had been asking her mother to buy one for some time. However, her mother had been uncertain about whether she should spend such a large amount of money on something that Samantha might, as she had with other things, lose interest in very quickly. A major family event, however, triggered the purchase:

> But she'd asked for the computer for about 3 years previous to when he died. 'Oh yeah, Samantha, yeah Samantha' because it's like my own keyboard, played with it for a week, chucked it in the cupboard. My own guitar, played for a week, chucked in the cupboard. And I thought I'm not spending all that money to have it wasted. And then when her father died she said, 'Mum, I still want a computer,' so right, do it for her. It's the best thing I ever did.
>
> (Samantha's mother, Pen-y-Bryn)

Even before the computer came into the home, then, it was 'for her', for Samantha. The computer was brought home and installed in Samantha's bedroom and one of her first uses of the computer located it firmly within the family history as both specific to Samantha and tied up with her father's death:

> And I think she'd had it, must have been about a week, and she was busy finding out and, you know, I wouldn't see her for hours on end. And I sat in the bath and I thought, right I'm going to shut the door and stay in there for an hour, you know, you like just chill out in it. When I'd come out I had eight pages on the type of cancer that my husband died of because she'd found everything on this particular cancer on the computer. So she'd printed it all out for me, 'Mam, go on have a read of that.' Well she even had a picture and she printed

the picture out of a tumour and … I think it helped the both of us really. And from that day on I haven't looked back. She's really into it, like.

(Samantha's mother, Pen-y-Bryn)

This exchange located the computer firmly for this family as a tool almost of salvation for the child and the family. This 'salvation', however, was not restricted only to Samantha's family and emotional life, but to perceptions of her future working life. Samantha's mother and Lynsey, her sister, always talked about the computer as 'something other', something that was Samantha's alone. They viewed the computer as a 'way out' for Samantha, in comparison with their own lives:

I mean I'd prefer to see Samantha using a computer for a job than stuck in a dead end job like I am. You know, I'd prefer her to do something better.

(Samantha's mother, Pen-y-Bryn)

This view of the computer associated it specifically in opposition to the types of factory work both Lynsey and her mother did. The computer was seen as part of the world of 'white collar' jobs and well paid work. It also specifically linked Samantha and the computer together as survivors of the family's past trauma, unlike her older sister Lynsey whose education had suffered throughout her father's illness, and who finally dropped out of school with no qualifications and joined her mother working in the factory. This view of the computer as a 'way out' also impacted on the uses that Samantha's mother supported on the computer in later years. She did not, for example, approve of the use of the computer for games. Rather, she encouraged Samantha's existing interests, identifying what her daughter already enjoyed and providing resources to support this:

She got one game. Monopoly I think she got. She plays that with Lynsey now and again or she'll play against the computer or whatever. But I wouldn't go … I mean I bought her the CD for Xmas, but it was the medical one. I preferred her to find something … she's got an interest in things like that. She was always up the garden as a kid, cutting up worms or chasing woodlice or something.

(Samantha's mother, Pen-y-Bryn)

Gradually, over the years, Samantha had been identifying aspects of the computer that expanded on this family 'meaning', she had been regularly using it for school and had even chosen ICT at General Certificate of Secondary Education (GCSE) level. While she did play some games to pass the time, her main interests continued to be in finding things out on the computer or making things as presents. Within the family, her sister and mother continued to see the computer as 'Samantha's' own; it stayed in her bedroom, with the single chair in front of it, covered in her cuddly toys and drawings and managed and maintained as a source of pride by Samantha (Picture 3.1).

It was not only in Samantha's family that the computer was constructed as primarily the 'children's computer', as an opportunity and way out for the children in the household. In both Jamilla's and Faezal's households the computer was seen as a key route by which the children could gain a 'leg up' economically and educationally through their computer use. Notably, in these households, the computer's meaning as the 'children's machine' was reinforced by locating the computer in a space used primarily by the children. In Faezal's house it was located in his bedroom; in Jamilla's, it was in the children's front room. Alongside this spatial construction of the computers as belonging to their children, came the explicit statement by their parents, that this machine was actively 'not for them'.

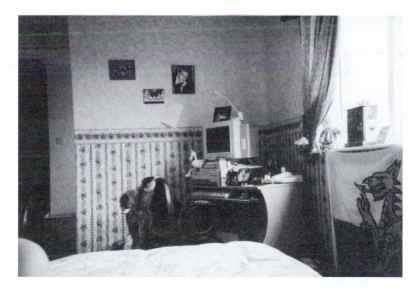

Picture 3.1 Samantha's computer in her bedroom

Because I didn't know myself what it was, computers, you know. I
used to think I wish I could do it, but I felt it was a so difficult thing
to get into. But once they were able to show me, they could write
their names in the computer, they could draw things, they could use
the keyboard on the computer, they were getting quite good at high
school, you know, and they were talking about it a lot. So when they
go to a shop they fiddle about with the PC. I said to myself, I wish I
was that young and I could learn myself. So I would encourage them.
So that's why I bought it.

(Faezal's father, Pandy)

In these households the computer signified escape from low paid jobs,
signified again a white collar world of high incomes. We are not arguing,
however, that the symbolic meaning of the computer to these families
determined what these computers were used for, although it did impact
on who was expected to use it. Rather the computer was drawn into a
more complex set of family relations and histories, serving visually to
underline parental aspirations for their children and as physical
embodiment of the support provided by the parents in encouraging their
children educationally and financially towards the world of work.

Computer as 'interloper'

In contrast, in other households the computer was never fully 'incorporated', in Silverstone and Hirsch's terms,[4] into the household. While
the computer was seen, in principle, to represent many of the educational
and economic advantages described in the previous case studies, when it
was brought into the home the computer was found, to some degree, to
be in conflict with the dominant family culture. In Paul's family, for
example, there was substantial family disagreement about the 'meaning'
of the computer. Paul, who was fanatical about animatronics and computer
games, loved the computer. In contrast, Paul's father, a scout master,
survival specialist and ex-soldier, viewed the computer as completely at
odds with his priorities for parenting and his worldview as a whole. Paul's
mother retained some sense of anxiety about the computer's effect on his
health but tolerated Paul's use of the computer for educational or artistic
purposes. Indeed, it was his mother's anxiety about Paul's 'falling behind'
at school, because of not having a computer at home, that triggered the
family purchase. Within this household then we saw a constant tug of
war between the views of the computer as valuable educational resource
and its function signifying the dangers of a modern world overreliant on
technology. Paul's father's military training, for example, was

instrumental in shaping his view of computers as something that ultimately should not be relied upon:

> Well if a big mushroom cloud appeared there'd be no computers, no telephones, no radios, no radar, nothing in Britain like that. The electromagnetic pulse would knock everything out, screens and everything. So you've got to take over manually when the screens get knocked out.
>
> (Paul's father, Saxingham)

As Paul joked: 'The only time Dad would ever use the computer would be to go on the Internet to find the best type of fungus that you could eat.' The computer, within this household then, was a necessary 'fact of life', brought reluctantly into the home because the family felt that Paul simply wouldn't be able to compete without one. Looking at how the family organised the computer within the household, this discourse of 'managing' and constraining the computer was very much in evidence. The reason given for keeping the computer in the sitting room, for example, was: 'The thing is at least it's in the room with us. So we have got control over it.' Similarly, Paul's mother was concerned that the computer should be used for school, but not to the exclusion of other tools and ways of working:

> And that's why a lot of the time when he does homework it's not always done on the computer and I know a lot of the boys do do it all on the computer. But I think it has to be something to help you, not something that you have to rely on.
>
> (Paul's mother, Saxingham)

Importantly, however, Paul also had access to a wider family culture – his sister and her husband lived nearby and both were heavily involved in using computers both for work and leisure. Paul's sister had, in fact, used her computer recently to publish a book of poems, and was expert at making and dismantling computers. On our final visit, after 18 months of interviewing the family, the computer seemed to have been 'accepted into' the family. Paul's father proudly showed us work that Paul had produced on the computer for his local scout troop, and said that Paul had been teaching the local scout leaders how to use the computer as part of scouting activities. Arguably, the 'meaning' of the computer as interloper was undergoing some revision as its potential uses to support approved family activities were emerging.

While Paul's household may seem unique, there were similarities between his family and those of two of our other case studies. Stephanie's family, for example, viewed the computer as an irrelevance to their daily outdoor lives on a farm (we will discuss Stephanie in more detail in Chapter 7). In Emma and Rebecca's home, in contrast, the computer was brought reluctantly into the home by their mother for her work as a University Union representative. Within this household the mother, as all others, was concerned that the girls should learn to be confident around computers, a concern based upon her previous experiences with computers:

> But I had come across it in university, and I can remember the first time I came across the Web when I was looking for something for an essay I was doing. And I was just 'Oh!' by it all. And I don't want them to feel like that.
>
> (Emma and Rebecca's mother, Pandy)

This was tempered, however, by a concern that the girls should not be distracted by the computer, and in particular computer games, from more 'approved' pursuits, in particular reading and spending time with the family.

> I mean Emma and Rebecca, certainly in my opinion, are quite bright. They're doing fine, you know, they can read, they're interested, and I'd rather keep their interest in books actually. Once they get to secondary school and they're doing homework then I'll get them the reference stuff that they need for the computer. But when they need it.
>
> (Emma and Rebecca's mother, Pandy)

The computer was kept in their mother's study and was flagged up as definitely not belonging to the children but to her workplace. Later, when she finally gave in to purchasing a Playstation for the children, she did not buy a television on which they could play for several months.

> I've only just bought them a Playstation, they've been nagging me for some time for a Playstation, and I made a deliberate decision not to get them one because I'd seen the way other children are around them, and I didn't want them getting sucked into all of that, but having said that I gave in at Christmas and bought them one at Christmas. Having said that, they haven't got a television to play on yet, so ...
>
> (Emma and Rebecca's mother, Pandy)

Interestingly, these households in which the computer was viewed as an interloper tended to be ones in which parental expertise in computer use was not well developed, and in which computers were marginal to, or simply a necessary fact of, parents' working lives. Moreover, family relationships were not maintained through the computer. Rarely, if ever, in these families, did family members gather around the computer and share tips and strategies for using it. But this was not because the parents did not know how to use the computer at all or viewed it as the 'children's machine', as in the earlier examples. Rather, it seemed to be because the parents were actively constructing their relationships with their children through *other* activities, such as reading, going to football, climbing. The computer, until it had proven its worth in supporting and maintaining these relationships, was generally relegated to a grudging place within the household.

Computer at the heart of the home

In contrast, the computer in other case study households played a significantly more central role in the interactions between family members and within the life of the family as a whole. Through using the computer, interacting around it and discussing it, certain families reinforced existing relations and developed new ones between individual members. Nick and James' family were a case in point. In this family, the computer had been brought into the household as a 'by-product' of their father's work. Their father, a computer consultant, had brought home an old computer with the vague idea that the children might enjoy using it. Similarly, he used to find things for the children to do on the computer that he thought would entertain them: 'And he used to bring things home for them to try out. Sometimes when he went abroad he would buy something and bring it back for you. He brought a few games back for you.' (Nick and James' mother, Saxingham.)

The computer in this household was located very centrally, on a landing on the first floor outside the family bedrooms. From this position the children could see down the stairs to people entering and leaving the house and moving between rooms downstairs. This location actively encouraged family interaction around the computer as people passed each other while they were playing on the computer and often stopped to offer comments and advice (Picture 3.2).

Although the children's mother had initially been wary of computers, her children's interest in them was instrumental in encouraging her to engage with computers as a way of maintaining her relationships with her children.

Picture 3.2 Nick and James' computer on the landing

> And Jim started bringing laptops and PCs and things home from work now and again and playing games with the kids and so on and I got interested in that and I could see the value of that and doing things with the children.
>
> (Nick and James' mother, Saxingham)

In this household both parents also used the computer for their own devices. The father used it for work and for composing his own music, the mother for her work as a teacher and as an advisor for a charity. Importantly, both parents also saw the computer as a 'playable' machine, not only in terms of computer games, but in terms of their own interest in 'fiddling around' with the computer to explore different ways of doing things. In this household the computer had not been brought in burdened with a pre-existent 'meaning' as either an educational device or a route to the future; rather it was given a range of different possible meanings for both parents and children – a machine to play with, to work with, to collaborate around. Importantly, however, the children's father seemed to construct the virtual space of the computer in the same way that other households might construct their physical space – by designating different areas of the computer for each family member and personalising this to meet their needs:

> When I set up the accounts I thought well, I'll change it so it's all different for them. It was just I thought I'd set it up differently for each of them so it becomes more like their space, so that they would do their own things with it. I started scanning in some other photographs and things to have as different backgrounds and things.
>
> (Nick and James' father, Saxingham)

Just as in other families where parents show children how to enter the world of particular hobbies, in this household, the parents were using the computer as a means to bring their children into contact with new experiences:

> And now and again if I'm feeling really brave I'll get on the Internet and look for things and I'll print stuff for them. When they do their stories as well if they're printing stories off like that, I mean they can do it themselves now, but to begin with they couldn't and because I was having great fun with the Clipart I showed them how to do that.
>
> (Nick and James' mother, Saxingham)

This sort of view of the computer, as a multi-purpose tool, which afforded the opportunity for parents to discuss and learn with their children, was in evidence in other households as well. In Simon's household, for example, the computer was seen as a *tabula rasa* on which to inscribe the family's interests:

> To be honest with you, when I got the computer I didn't have anything in mind at all because I didn't have a clue what I could do with it. Everything that I've done on that computer's been a surprise really.
>
> (Simon's father, Pen-y-Bryn)

As a very competent 'DIYer' and Royal Air Force (RAF) engineer, able to build a new washing machine from two battered and old ones, to Simon's father the computer was the latest in a long line of technical challenges to be overcome. To his children, Simon's father was 'mister fixit', the man who could find out all manner of things. The computer, and his relationship with it, simply extended these skills into a digital world he could share with his children without the health and safety risks involved in some of his other activities. Using the computer in this household, then, would often be a 'family affair' as Simon's dad found new and entertaining animations and Clipart to show his children, or helped them when they were stuck. On visiting the home it was usually impossible to interview the children alone as their father always wanted to be on the computer with them. The computer's location, in a dining room, by the side of bookcases, in full view of the kitchen television and alongside the sitting room where the family watched television, surrounded by family photographs and topped off with a pot plant, was also important in supporting this ongoing production of the computer as a key resource in mediating and embodying family relationships (Pictures 3.3 and 3.4).

In these households with the computer at their heart, parental experience of computers at work, their networks of support in the workplace and community and their home uses of computer were intertwined. Within these households, the parents' enthusiastic interest in the computer and their sense of collaborative use of the computer as being a valuable activity located the computer as an important medium for developing and sustaining relationships between family members.

Conclusion

Having mapped these parental biographies of computer use we can see that our case study children's computer use at home was informed by a series of intertwining histories, some of which had been in play since before they were born, dating back to parental experiences in education, at work and at play. It is undeniable that the children's experiences of computer use in home and at school were radically different from those of their parents. What we cannot say, however, is that nothing had gone before, that they were entering an arena divorced from pre-existing notions of what a computer is, or might be, used for.

Arguably, we can see these different histories of computer use playing themselves out in the home: parents' experiences of computers as technologies grudgingly to be accepted, actively exploited or enthusiastically played with seemed to shape the models they presented to their children of computer use. Importantly, we can see that these models were themselves embedded within wider patterns of social inequalities and gendered workplaces, as we shall go on to discuss in Chapter 8.

It is interesting, however, to conjecture that we might never again see such a generation gap in experiences of computer use. Within this group of families, for example, we saw children who were the first cohort to experience 'mass' and sustained schooling in computer 'literacy', rubbing up against parents who had come to learn about and understand computers in a widely diverse range of contexts. The next generation of children may be born to a group of parents with a much more homogeneous experience (at least through school) of computer use. It is interesting to speculate as to what will be lost and what will be gained from this change.

Pictures 3.3 and 3.4 Simon's dining room with computer and bookshelves

Chapter 4

The computer in family life

In the previous chapter we mapped out parental biographies of computer use and began to discuss how these shape particular roles for the computer within the home, along the lines of the computer as 'children's machine', as 'interloper' and as at the 'heart of the family'. In defining these roles, however, we need to recognise that the 'family' is not simply a pre-existing and unchanging entity, but rather one that is constantly being shaped by its members, and through its use of the technologies in its midst.

When exploring young people's computer use in the home, for example, we need to recognise that children themselves bring into the family, from their school experiences, from their peer group cultures and from their media cultures more widely, potentially different views of what a computer might 'be'. Views which may at times rub up against, even challenge, parents' aspirations for their children and for family life.

Previous studies of media technologies in the home also alert us to the need to recognise that the computer 'itself', as a media technology, brings with it connections to the outside world, problematising our ideas of the family as a private, bounded space.[1] 'The computer [...] potentially and actually extends and transforms the boundaries around the home [...] and can threaten to shift or undermine what is taken for granted in the routines of domestic life' (Silverstone *et al.*, 1992, p20).

Moreoever, as Silverstone *et al.* (1992) and more recently Holloway and Valentine (2003) have argued, domestic media technologies such as computers act as medium through which a family represents its values to itself and the wider community: through establishing boundaries with the outside world, through negotiating differential access for different family members, and through maintaining or challenging the established routines of family time and practices.

While we need to recognise that the computer enters into already existing practices within the family, that 'however transformative and innovative [technologies] are, they work on what is already there, what already gives shape to people's lives' (Strathern, 1992, p.viii), we also need to recognise that the 'family' is itself in a state of constant transformation and negotiation by its members. As Ehrenrich has argued, 'the family so long reified in theory looks more like an improvisation than an institution' (cited in Furlong, 1995, p178). Just as the family 'works on' the meanings of the computer in its midst, so, too, does the computer function as a site around and through which families come to define and shape themselves.

This chapter is an attempt to explore how our case study families 'improvised' around the computer, how it was exploited to maintain or frustrate routines of family life, how access to the computer functioned as a site for negotiating family identity, and how uses of the computer sustained or challenged the emotional and physical boundaries of the family home.

The domestic technological landscape

Managing a shared resource

First, we need to recognise that our case study families had different levels of computer resources to draw upon in their improvisations. As we outlined in the previous chapter, the parents in these families had widely divergent experiences of computer use themselves, and different levels of access to economic and cultural resources. As a result, some households were on their third, fourth or fifth computer in the home, with the earlier models dotted around the house or gathering dust in attics, while others had only recently purchased their first computer. The highest level of technology saturation amongst our 16 families, for example, was in Helen's household. There, the family had seven functioning computers in their four-bedroom house, several networked to a printer, with Internet connections on three computers. In contrast, at the beginning of the study, Maria's household had only one ageing computer and no Internet.

Our case study families, and our wider surveys, both suggest that in order to understand family negotiations around computers, we need to recognise that computers are often *shared resources* within homes. In contrast to a view that home computers are predominantly driving children towards a private and individualised media world in their bedrooms,[2] in both our original ScreenPlay survey and our more recent Interactive survey, only 6 per cent of children reported exclusive access to their own computer. In the two surveys, 53 per cent and 64 per cent of children respectively reported that the computer they used was located in a family space within the home.

These patterns of ownership, location and access are replicated in our case study families, where only Alistair and Samantha reported exclusive access to a computer in their own bedroom. In the remainder, the children were required to share the family's main computer, and to negotiate access to it in a range of different sites.

If the computer was usually seen as a shared resource, however, different families had widely divergent views of how that resource should be managed. In those families where the computer was seen primarily as a children's machine, the computer was located in spaces that were mainly used by the children in the house – a child's bedroom, or the front 'children's room'. These decisions both reflected and helped to reinforce the view of the computer as belonging to the children alone, as any parent

Table 4.1 Computer ownership and location at halfway stage of the project

	Location of the computer the child usually used at start of study	Who else uses it?	Other computers
Alistair	His bedroom	No one	Sister's
David	Dining room	Sister and mother	One older in living room
Emma and Rebecca	Mother's study	Mother	One defunct
Faezal	Bedroom	Siblings	None
Heather	Children's/ Computer room	Siblings and parents	One in Heather's bedroom
Helen	Dining room	Brother	6 (various)
Huw	His bedroom	Brothers and parents	One in living room
Jamilla	Front 'children's room'	Siblings	None
Karen	Computer room/ study	Siblings and parents	4 (various)
Maria	Laptop	Siblings and parents	None
Nick and James	First floor landing	Sister and parents	Dad's work laptop
Paul	Living room	Mother	None
Samantha	Her bedroom	No one	None
Simon	Dining room	Siblings and parents	One in Simon and brother's room
Stephanie	Understairs cupboard	Sister and mother	None
Tim	Living room	Sister and parents	None

wishing to use the computer in these households would not only have to negotiate access to the computer, but also access to the 'children's space' in the home.

In other households where the computer was seen as an interloper, marginal to family life, it was located in spaces where it could be monitored, or to which access could be restricted. The most notable example of this was in Stephanie's household, where the computer was placed in the understairs cupboard giving on to the living room. In this family, the computer was seen as marginal to the family's interests in outdoor activities and, over time, the computer was gradually hidden beneath laundry and ironing board, thereby further providing a discouragement to use it.

In those households where the computer was seen as a resource at the 'heart of the home', however, we saw greater diversity – where resources permitted, space was allocated that was neutral and accessible by all family members, often landings, spare bedrooms, extra downstairs rooms; in others a previously private space, such as a bedroom, was allocated to which others were then required to have access.

The decision to locate computers in specific areas of the household, however, also reflected and reinforced different family views about how time should be spent within the home. In certain families, it became clear that the computer was viewed as potentially 'disruptive' to other family activities, such as watching television or talking. The computer was seen as something against which the family needed to erect barriers in order to protect other activities. In particular, the association of the computer with computer games activities, or shared activities amongst the children and their friends, often lay beneath the decision to place the computer in spaces away from the main public rooms in the home.

> Well because it's the other side of the house at the back so you don't have to hear it. So if you were in here watching television and we've got company then they're out the way. And also they have their friends in … There's a backdoor that goes into that room, so if they have their friends in to watch telly or play on the computer it doesn't interfere with our privacy.
>
> (Heather's mother, Deanbridge)

At the same time, computer use was also seen in most households as something to be protected from distraction by other activities. In all the homes, for example, the computer was placed on a desk and given a single chair in front of it – never located next to a comfortable sofa, or placed on the floor – suggesting that its use was envisaged as requiring concentrated, usually isolated activities. Computer use was seen as something that both required protection from other distractions *and* as an activity that needed protecting *against*.

This ambivalence reflects a degree of uncertainty as to the 'meaning' of the computer – as games machine, as social resource, as individual educational tool. Unsurprisingly, then, we saw the computers often located in sites within the home of similarly 'ambivalent' identities – spare bedrooms, landings, understairs cupboards, extra rooms that became 'children's' or 'computer rooms' through the location of the computer within them, dining rooms, or bedrooms that previously had little 'daytime' identity.

Mother: Then it moved into the spare room.
Int: Why did it go in the spare room?
Father: Because it was a spare room.
Mother: There was room in there and we could just let everybody else use it. It's a sort of spare room cum office.
Steve: It's not as private as your bedroom.
Helen: Cum junkyard.

(Helen, aged 9, Deanbridge, family interview)

In these families, the computer, unlike the television or radio,[3] was not being brought into the home to supplement and replace previous technologies, or to adopt a role familiar within the home; instead the introduction of the computer required families to (re)define household space to incorporate a new and sometimes confusing technological resource.

Over the course of the study, however, it was evident that this spatial organisation, and the concomitant role of technology within the family, was constantly being revised. In Simon's household, an increased interest in the entertainment potential of the computer led to the purchase of a new computer. This meant that the older one was located in Simon's bedroom, separating his homework activities (conducted in his bedroom) from his and his family's entertainment activities (carried out on the new computer in the dining room). In Huw's household, the older computer, used primarily for games, was kept in the main family space while the newest was located in his bedroom for him and his brother to share for schoolwork. Arguably, the ambivalence of the home computer as educational or entertainment device was in these cases being managed

Picture 4.1 The computer in Helen's 'spare room'

Picture 4.2 Nicolas, Huw's brother, using the family computer in the sitting room

Picture 4.3 An old computer in hallway in David's house

Picture 4.4 David using the main computer in dining room

through a process of *specialisation* of the computer technology through the spatial organisation of the home. Even if each computer 'itself' remained in principle a multi-purpose technology, the decision to locate multiple computers in specific places within the home was beginning, in some households, to lead to a specialisation of use and activity according to location.

Claiming 'ownership' of the computer

In those households where there was competition amongst individuals for access, however, families had to develop specific rules about the duration and frequency of their children's computer use, based on a range of different strategies. In Helen's household, for example, the family relied on specific timetabling of access to ensure that both of their children were seen to have equal claim to the computer.

… Steven normally gets in first you see, so he would always get the opportunity of going to the computer first. So we said, 'That's not fair'. So Mondays and Thursdays Helen has first choice. She can decide whether she wants to go on the computer or watch television and on the other … I mean it tends to be just the Tuesday and Wednesday because Friday you're quite often not here or doing other things.

(Helen's mother, Deanbridge)

In other households access to the computer was granted on the basis of activity – with homework taking priority over other uses of the computer. In other households again, however, the children were encouraged to negotiate their own access within an overall quota of computer time:

Int: What about … if either of you wants to go on it […] do you do that together or do you do that on your own?
Nick: Well we do it on our own but if we're doing it at the same time we race each other up to the computer. Whoever gets there first …
Int: Is that right?
Nick: Then we have 15 minutes, each of us has 15 minutes and then … […]
Nick: It was either, I think it was either half an hour or 15 minutes and we decided on, because of our time restriction on the computer, 15 minutes.

(Nick and James, aged 10, Saxingham)

The shared management of access between children according to allocated clock time or by activity, was not, however, the only way in which individual family members negotiated access to and claimed ownership of the computer. Indeed, particularly keen computer users, for example, would snatch any opportunity that presented itself, as Helen's brother Steven demonstrates:

Helen: And I was having a go at that and I couldn't get past this particular bit and I called Steven …
Steven: I did it in 30 seconds.
Helen: He did it in 30 seconds.
Int: Right. So if Steven shows you something …
Steven: He normally does it.
Int: He normally does it and then you carry on.
Helen: And then I carry on. Or he normally does it. He pushes me off and he goes the rest of the game. He does that a lot of the time.

(Helen, aged 9, and brother Steven, Deanbridge)

This opportunism was a response to the high level of competition for the computer in this family, in which access was only ever temporary and transient. Because Steven was unable to claim ownership of the computer through location (it was in the family dining room) and because his parents scrupulously observed timetabled access where possible, he had to grasp the opportunity to claim temporary ownership of the computer not through an appeal to the clock, but through his demonstration of superior games expertise.[4]

This assertion of 'ownership', and the rights to claim time to use the computer that accompany it, was evident on a number of other fronts. While Steven was able to claim ownership through games expertise, individuals in other families claimed metaphorical ownership of the computer through their expertise in managing the hardware. In many families, for example, one person took responsibility for the set-up of file-management systems, installing shortcuts, de-installing software and freeing up memory for authorised or 'preferred' practices. This expertise afforded the individual the opportunity to control both the uses of the computer and, to some extent, other people's access to the computer. They were able to decide, for example, whether games software should be allowed onto the computer or whether Internet access should be password protected – thereby actively determining whether the computer could be seen as a 'games' machine or a communications device, and consequently shaping the types of interaction with the computer that other family members would be allowed.

Different managers of the computer within the home adopted different 'metaphors' for this process. Maria, for example, conceptualised the computer primarily in terms of memory – accordingly, text files and other similarly small files were allowed to remain on the computer, while larger picture files were often summarily eradicated. In contrast, Huw simply wanted to 'keep it tidy' – files that were left scattered around in the wrong folders or left on desktops would be reorganised into the appropriate locations. Nick and James's dad, and Simon's dad, as we described in the previous chapter, conceived of the computer in terms of space. In Nick and James's case, children would open the computer up using a password to access 'their own' computer space. In Simon's case, his dad drew lines on the desktop and located software the children could use in specific sections of the screen.

Those within the family who did not have this access to the computer as an organisational system (either through lack of knowledge, inclination or more explicit prohibition), however, could only occupy the computer tactically and temporarily, as the files, documents, shortcuts or bookmarks they had installed might be removed at any time by other members of the family.

Int: So what package do you normally work in? Is it Word?
Heather: Normally yeah, but I can't seem to find it. Because my mother works on the computer at home now. [...]
Int: So what's changed since your mother started working on it?
Heather: They put that bar up at the top where normally they would have it in the documents. And you go into File Office.
Int: So you know your way in normally and now they've changed it?
Heather: Mm.

(Heather, aged 12, Deanbridge)

The development of one individual's expertise within the home at times frustrated attempts to define a shared 'meaning' for the computer, as individuals able to develop the expertise to manage the computer were able to define, to a much greater degree than other family members, the meaning and uses of the computer in the home.

A lower-level attempt to claim ownership of the computer was also in evidence in the families: in some cases the screen functioned as territory onto which family members could inscribe their ownership by leaving traces of themselves and eradicating traces of others' occupation. An activity in which many of the children in our case studies participated, for example, was the process of changing the settings of the computer – the desktop layout was changed to lurid greens and purples, menu bars and icons were altered and relocated or the screen saver was changed to read 'kids computer, keep out' or to represent images of favourite places, pets or pop stars. There was frequently a rapid turnover in screen savers and settings as different children eradicated the traces that signified previous habitation of the computer space and imposed their own images and settings in their place.

In these families the installation of the game, creation of a shortcut, and establishment of files or folders had its impermanence inscribed within it. In this digital landscape the alteration of desktop settings to greens and purples or the installing of a screen saver could all be theorised as sorties into contested terrain, a transient victory of time over space in which, like graffiti on city walls, the inevitability of eradication provides the justification and necessity for the action. This poaching of the computer space was derived from the role of the computer as a shared resource, but could also be seen as a negotiation to fix the meaning and, subsequently, the function of a technology that had the potential for multiple uses. The different family members danced around the computer, negotiating access, claiming temporary ownership and marking their terrain.

Negotiating childhood through the computer

Managing childhood 'time'

> ... [the computer is] a site of struggle between contending discourses, notably those emanating from government and the education system on the one hand and from the entertainment industry on the other. This struggle is regularly played out in conflicts between parents and children as to the proper use of the machine.
>
> (Murdock, 1989, p233)

As we have already pointed out, it needs to be acknowledged that the computer 'itself' is not an easily definable object. The home computer today, with its graphics cards, scanners, printer, CD-ROM and Internet connection, affords the possibility of a range of different activities. It could be a communications device, an entertainment medium, an information resource, a production tool or all four at the same time. It can be used for homework, for games play, for correspondence, for publication. As has been argued by previous commentators,[5] not only does the computer have a range of different possible identities within the home, but parents and children are subject to widely divergent discourses around the computer. Parents are often the focus of marketing and government campaigns emphasising the computer's educational potential, and children the focus of campaigns emphasising its potential for games play and leisure activities.

This slippery identity, particularly the co-location of potential educational and entertainment applications in one technology, made the home computer a fertile terrain through which our case study families negotiated their values and beliefs – in particular, their views about childhood.

While computers may have been brought into the home for a variety of reasons, there was a universal expectation amongst parents that the home computer should be used to support particular constructions of childhood. Namely, as a time for learning:

> The reason why I brought it, one of the reasons I bought it was for these two really so they could grow up with computers. Everything's going that way anyway, so the sooner they can get along with it

really. I know that obviously there's computers at school but there's only a limited time, whereas they can come here and mess about.

(Stephanie's father, Saxingham)

And a time for preparing for the adult world of work:

... Computers are really important things in their generation. It's going to be a skill that you're going to have to have ...

(Jamilla's mother, Pandy)

... So I think it's because the more they learn the more experience they have. Offices, everything is just computers ...

(Faezal's father, Pandy)

... There isn't going to be that many jobs where you can't have some time spent in front of the computer screen ...

(Samantha's mother, Pen-y-Bryn)

In contrast, most of the children first encountered computer technology through games environments. In many cases, before purchasing a home computer, they had owned games consoles, and in most of the households Playstations, Nintendos and Game Boys were prevalent alongside the computer. Arguably, as we shall see in later chapters, games play is a central feature of many peer group cultures; indeed, as Downes (1998) has argued, the computer, for younger people, could be seen as a 'playable' machine. Within this context, childhood is produced as a time for play.

This potential clash of cultures between entertainment uses and educational uses is not simply a clash of different views of the computer but of differing views about how children's time should most profitably be spent. Negotiations surrounding computer use, then, were not only negotiations about *access to the computer* but about how children should spend their time in the family home.

... we try to stick to only two hours on the computer each in any one day ... Generally speaking that's probably about enough. In terms of playing games. If they want to then go on and do some homework, then that's fine, but as far as playing games on the computer is concerned, then two hours is the maximum we let them go on.

(Helen's mother, Deanbridge)

In certain families, this timetabling of what the children saw as their leisure time led to conflict, with children actively attempting to subvert these rules, and reinstate the place of digital play within their day-to-day activities. In other households, however, the children actively supported their parents' construction of childhood as a time for learning and preparing for the future world of work. This was evidenced in a relatively unproblematic assumption in most families that homework should always take priority over other activities on the computer.

Int: Right, and if one person wanted to use the computer for games and one person wanted to use it for homework, who gets to go on it?
All: Homework

(Heather, family interview, Deanbridge)

In these cases, the prioritisation of homework uses on the computer was also supported in the management of the computer hardware, as games software was sometimes de-installed by parents, while encyclopaedias and office software were left intact and parents and wider family members bought educational software for their children.

In contrast, in other families, the enthusiasm of children for games playing led to a revision of what individual parents interpreted as 'educational' uses of the computer.

I think another important skill is being able to figure things out relatively quickly as well, you know. Even with games and things, you know, the fact that they can look at it and they can figure out they press this button here and they'd adjust something there depending which game it is they're working at then helps improve their performance of them using the game. Because I think it's a skill that not everybody has, I mean I can look at a computer and I can look at a program and it only takes me five or 10 minutes to figure out what it is.

(Nick and James' father, Saxingham)

Int: So you don't mind if they use it for games?
Mother: They learn things, they learn.
Int: When they're playing games.
Mother: Yes. And they know how to use a computer, which is very good.

(Jamilla's mother, Pandy)

In these families, the construction of childhood as a time for learning and preparation for the adult world were not challenged by games play, as games were reinterpreted as valid educational activities for a digital age. Interestingly, these were either households where parents were active and enthusiastic games players themselves or where parents had little or no interactions with computers.

Towards the end of the project, we noticed a gradual movement away from the easy delineation of computer games as only something that children did, as a growing number of parents themselves became interested in games. In families where this happened we saw computer games play becoming a site for parents to negotiate new roles for themselves, roles that were not always without tension:

Huw's mum: Sometimes when I come home from working an afternoon shift for me to unwind, rather than sit down and have a cup of coffee and watch TV, I will sit down and play on the computer, and it annoys Sam sometimes.

Huw's step-dad: Yes, that does annoy me sometimes. Sometimes till like 1 o'clock in the morning. And it's like 'We never see each other because we're both working' and it's bumf, straight home, on that seat there, on the computer and it's 'Hello! I'm here!'

(Huw, family interview, Pen-y-Bryn)

Negotiations surrounding access to and use of the computer need, then, to be seen within a wider picture of ongoing negotiations within families about how children could and should spend their time at home. Consequently, even for those children for whom there was no competition to use the computer, we need to recognise that their access to the computer was in fact negotiated within family definitions of appropriate allocation of time.

Negotiating childhood 'space'

Negotiations over children's access to and use of computers within the home were also shaped by life outside the walls of the family. Indeed, parents' views of their children's ability safely to occupy and explore spaces outside the home were heavily implicated in the roles assigned to the computer within the family.

All of the families, for example, exercised rules about their children's access to public space – when they were allowed outside, who with, using what sort of transport, for how long and so on. In Faezal's family, they had purchased the computer explicitly to keep the children inside where the parents could see them, and where they would use the computer for approved activities within the home, rather than out on the streets:

> I thought it was a good thing, you know, they'd enjoy it. Rather than they go into an arcade or something, going out, messing about, money involved. I don't like these kind of stuff. It's always the best thing in the home. Because he's got a brother to play with, a sister as well. So they get all involved.
>
> (Faezal's father, Pandy)

While Faezal lived in the centre of a large city, Heather's family had moved from a city to a small village. Her whole family emphasised that this had enabled the children to have a much more relaxed attitude to spending time outside. It was not only geography, however, that informed the degree to which children were able to have access to outdoors space but, unsurprisingly, age, perceived maturity and, notably, the time of year, with the children spending much more time indoors during the dark winter months.[6]

The introduction of the Internet-connected computer into the home, however, provides a challenge to parents wishing to maintain the home and the family as a private space protected from the threats of the outside world. As Lupton (1995) has argued:

> [T]he main anxiety here is in the insidious nature of contact with others through the Internet. The home is now no longer a place of safety and refuge for children, the computer no longer simply an educational tool or source of entertainment but is the possible site of children's corruption. 'Outside' danger is brought 'inside', into the very heart of the home, via the Internet.
>
> (Lupton, 1995, p110)

The boundaries of domestic space are made permeable in the introduction of the Internet into the home; not only can the world introduce itself into the living room but, with email and chat rooms, children are able to roam the world from the apparent security of their home computer. Management of access to the computer, then, becomes not simply a question of management of children's *time* but of their *spatiality*: their freedom to explore the digital landscape.

> A friend of ours, her father had a stroke back in October and she was on the Internet looking for any information about strokes. You

know you just … you can imagine the things that came up. In the end she had to start putting technical terms in to actually narrow it down to what the search was finding because she was amazed. She said 'My God, you know …' They have a computer at home, they have three little girls and they all have access to the computer and she said, 'I shudder to think, you know, if one of the girls had got on there and started looking up about their grampy's stroke and come across it' so … (LAUGHTER) yes, we supervise the Internet.

(Nick and James' mother, Saxingham)

Massey (2002) has argued that 'control of spatiality is one of the defining features of youth itself' (p127). In other words, the process of defining certain spaces as suitable or unsuitable for children is a key mechanism by which families and society define what they mean by 'childhood'. That access to the Internet was primarily defined according to age and perceived maturity, marks it out as an important site through which childhood is defined and negotiated by families today.

In our wider questionnaire surveys, it was clear that age remained the key criterion that families used for determining whether children should be allowed into the Internet landscape. As a rule, families with younger children were less likely to even have the Internet at home and primary-aged children were more likely than secondary-aged children to report that they needed to ask parents for permission before going online, or needed parents to access the Web for them.

Where children in our case study families were perceived as insufficiently mature to access the Internet, parents attempted to control access through a variety of mechanisms. Some simply decided not to enable Internet connections, others were Internet connected but told their children that they were not. More technologically expert parents set up password protection systems. In other cases, parents ensured that access to the Internet could only take place when parents were aware of it, as children were required to link up cables and unplug the telephone.

The increasing technological literacy and personal maturity of some young people, however, placed pressure on parents' rudimentary means of policing access to the Internet. In response to this, unsupervised access was often granted on an understanding achieved between parents and children, which relied on an internalised moral code, or on more subtle forms of surveillance, for its effectiveness. In these cases, it was not the Internet that parents had to come to trust, but the child themselves:

Mother: Yeah I do trust him but then everybody trusts their kids don't they? I mean if when we were out one night I came back and

Heather said, 'Oh Scott's been on the Internet looking at this that and the other,' I would be most shocked and disappointed in him, wouldn't you?

Dad: Yeah.

Mother: And very very surprised, cos he's very sensible.

Int: So did you explain all that to him before you got him on there or did you just … I mean you know your son, so …

Mother: Scott has got a conscience which is to the extreme really. I mean he can't do anything that he shouldn't without having to come and confess.

Int: Really?

Mother: Yeah. And if it's anything bad he'll get really upset about it. So if he's got the choice to make to do something bad or not do it he will always choose to not do it because of the knock-on effects it would have with us, isn't it?

(Heather's mother and father, parents' interview, Deanbridge)

David: Well I do chat, but not very much. Because you get people on there with rather explicit language and alternative methods of …

Int: Who polices that? You or your mother, or both?

David: Well I know when people are getting silly. So I stop it. But if Mum comes in and she sees you …

Int: She sees you on the screen (LAUGHTER).

David: She'll stop it too.

(David, aged 12, Deanbridge)

In bringing a Internet-connected computer into the home, families are intentionally weakening the boundaries of the home. They are actively attempting to connect with a wider world of educational, informational and entertainment resources. At the same time, having weakened these boundaries, they are required to improvise, to explore different strategies for managing their children's navigation of this space, at once attempting to ensure that their children can benefit from this resource, and at the same time attempting to limit its intrusion and their children's exploration. The Internet, like life in the outside world, however, evidently cannot be edited with any degree of certainty. Unsurprisingly, then, it was through discussion and negotiation with their children that the majority of parents in our case study families attempted to negotiate the significance of this weakening of the family boundaries with the outside world. Negotiation of unsupervised access to the Internet then, may today hold the same sort of status for defining the different ages of childhood as negotiation of unsupervised access to the world outside the front door held for earlier generations.

Conclusion

Overall, what our case studies of these 16 households show is that 'the computer' does not have a *fixed* or *universal* identity within different families. Rather, the computer may be the last in a long line of artefacts around and through which childhood, adolescent and adult identities within families have been negotiated. The various decisions individual families took to locate computers in specific sites, the ways in which access was negotiated, and the activities for which children were encouraged or discouraged from using the computer, all represented particular and changing views of what it means to be 'successfully young' in the digital age. Some of these mechanisms are deadly serious, resulting in drawn out conflicts between siblings or parents and children, some playful and exploratory, a form of digital graffiti, arguably enabling different family members to come together to explore the computer (as we shall discuss in Chapter 10).

We may, however, be observing computer technology only beginning to find its place within family life. As we discussed in the previous chapter, for example, today's parents bring into the home concerns about the educational role of computers, possibly as a result of their own 'late arrival' to the digital landscape. Similarly, we see parents today only recently discovering computer games as an acceptable form of leisure activity. The delineation of generations around competing definitions of the computer as a production tool or entertainment device may well be short lived.

Similarly, today, we see families attempting to manage an equitable distribution of access to the computer as a shared resource within the home. If we enter, as the telecommunications agencies promise, an age where domestic computing systems are centralised, where handheld personal digital assistants (PDAs) are ubiquitous, where mobile phones provide Internet access, these questions of access and management may radically change. Not least as families will no longer be able to mediate access via the spatial arrangements in their homes. Notwithstanding this, the ways in which particular individuals are able to claim ownership of computer technology through expertise and gatekeeping is likely to remain – whatever the technology.

Today, what is clear is that 'having a computer at home' should not, in and of itself, be taken to equate with 'having access' to a computer, as children are required to negotiate with parents and siblings not only time on the computer, but the activities they wish to participate in on the computer. At the same time, we should be wary, even as computers proliferate, of assuming that the increasing prevalence of computers in the home is leading to the development of secluded children, isolated from family and the outside world in their bedrooms.

What is likely to remain a significant challenge for families, both today and in the future, however, is the ongoing production of childhood around questions of access to digital and virtual spaces. The potential that Internet technology affords for two-way conversation with strangers via email and chat rooms, or to access pornography online, is likely only to increase as broadband, for example, comes into homes. The increasing tendency to attempt to manage this through the designation of sites as 'child-friendly' or through setting up walled gardens, is likely to meet the same problems as attempting to designate 'real world' spaces for children alone. The Web, like the world outside it, brings with it both opportunities and threats for young people. We have the choice of increasingly restricting children's access, as we do in the physical world, to designated areas in which we can supervise them, or we could attempt to support them to develop the skills to negotiate that space as safely as possible. It is here, perhaps, rather than in the development of ever more complex Net nannying systems, or the production of government sanctioned 'safe' Websites, that parents and children would most benefit from support.

Part III

Young people's computer use in the home

Chapter 5

The digital landscape
Games and information navigation

As we outlined in the previous chapter, the home computer today needs to be seen not as 'one' technology, but many. It can function as a communications device, an entertainment medium, an information resource and a production tool. It can be used for homework, for games play, for correspondence, for publication and it can locate the user at the centre of a vast network of information resources, people, images and experiences. In recent years there has been much theoretical interest in how these different interactions may be changing the nature of childhood and, even, of our understanding of 'reality'.

Some commentators have argued, for example, that the very speed of communication afforded by digital technologies means that we now live in 'speed space', an environment in which the speed of new information technologies distorts the ways in which we view and interact with the world, affecting social relations and psychological processing.[1] Others, observing the increasing prevalence of games play, argue that the younger generation of frequent games players now occupy 'twitch time', a term reflecting the reportedly increased ability to quickly process and respond to massive and rapidly changing information resources.[2] Moreover, many commentators argue that it is not only in respect of accessing and processing information that new technologies have impacted on our relations with the world: the very nature of our interactions with the cultural landscape is said to be changing as interactive media locate the user as central to and in control of the cultural experience – shifting us away from the supposedly 'passive' role of viewers, to the 'active' role of players and makers. 'Interactivity' is the buzz word of these emerging relations with new media technologies, offering the possibility that it is the *user* rather than the maker who controls and determines the experience within these environments.[3] These new resources in the heart of the domestic environment, then, are seen as responsible for transforming children's relations with space, with time, with information and with narrative.

Many of these arguments, however, are more the product of 'grand and utopian narratives' than the result of detailed empirical research. A contrasting perspective from the studies of older technologies such as television argues that we might need to be sceptical about such grand theorising and instead listen intently to how young people themselves describe their interactions with these new resources. This research suggests that only in this way will we understand the significance of new technologies in the lived experiences of the 'digital generation'.[4]

The central aim of this and the next chapter, then, is to begin to map out the different uses that young people make of these powerful new technologies in their homes. We will examine how young people interact with the information landscapes that these technologies open up, with the tools that, in theory, enable production and play, and with the processing power that sees worlds conjured up on screen, deleted and restored at the click of a mouse. In this first chapter, we will begin with a brief overview of the range of activities children are using computers for in the home, then go on to discuss in more detail their uses of the computer for games and information navigation, the two uses of the home computer subject to the most contentious debate within educational and public arenas. The second chapter will go on to explore children's other uses of the computer and to ask, in conclusion, how this wide range of activities may be changing notions of literacy and expertise.

Diverse computer uses

If we look at our case study children's individual activities, we see a picture of wide diversity. Table 5.1 summarises all the computer-based activities our case study children reported during a half-term week in May 1999. They were asked to log what they did on a computer each morning, afternoon and evening during that week.

This simple record serves to highlight what a range of different 'types' of computer user there are – from the 'monocultural' (for this week at least) children reporting only a single type of computer use, to the polymaths (for this week at least) reporting a wide range of different activities; from the seeming non-users to those, such as David, Jamilla and Helen, who used a computer in over half of their mornings, afternoons and evenings that week. Indeed, we can say that out of all these children only two reported identical use of a computer that week, and these were the twins Emma and Rebecca. Moreover, we need to recognise that this is *just one week* and that, three weeks later, the children may have and

Table 5.1 Case study log of one week's activities on the computer

Child	Total number of time segments (morning/afternoon/ evening) in which computer was used at home	Activities reported that week (some overlap within segments)	Child age
Alistair	5	2 × programming (HTML) 3 × games	9
David	16	2 × email 3 × computer management 3 × DTP 1 × Web download 2 × databases 1 × edutainment 5 × Web browsing 1 × writing	12
Emma	1	1 × games	10
Faezal	10	6 × games 2 × image manipulation 2 × computer management	12
Heather	6	3 × games 1 × image manipulation 2 × info seeking (CD)	12
Helen	15	13 × games 2 × DTP	9
Huw	8	4 × games 2 × image manipulation 2 × Web browsing 1 × writing	12
James	4	4 × games	10
Jamilla	13	4 × info seeking (CD) 6 × games 1 × image manipulation 1 × writing 1 × computer management	12
Karen	0	0	9
Maria	5	3 × writing 1 × image manipulation 1 × designing artefacts	13
Nick	3	3 × games	10

(continued …)

Table 5.1 (continued)

Child	Total number of time segments (morning/afternoon/ evening) in which computer was used at home	Activities reported that week (some overlap within segments)	Child age
Paul	4	3 × games 1 × designing/making	12
Rebecca	1	1 × games	10
Samantha	6	2 × writing 2 × info seek 2 × games	12
Simon	9	9 × games	9
Stephanie	1	1 × writing	9
Tim	8	8 × games	9

often did report very different activities. Arguing, as many of the grand theories do, that there is a single way in which technologies are changing *all* young people's interactions with the world, then, may be problematic. If we take an overview of the activities the children reported over the full duration of the study, however, we see a picture emerging that is familiar from our wider surveys (discussed in Chapter 2), in which games play, information navigation, writing and making images are all prevalent (see Table 5.2).

These two tables serve to provide both an overview of children's activities on the computer at home, and an insight into how diverse these experiences may be amongst any given group of young people. The remainder of this chapter will focus in some detail on the question of young people's games play and information navigation. In the next chapter, we will go on to explore some of the characteristics of children's interactions with computers across a whole range of different activities including writing, publishing, making, programming and designing.

Games play

Given that games play, both amongst our case study children and in the wider statistical surveys, should now be considered a pervasive feature of childhood today, it is with a discussion of games that we will begin.

Table 5.2 Summary of case study uses of the computer

Activities	Number of case study children reporting
Games (any mainstream, non-educational)	All
Wordprocessing	All
CD-ROM browsing and retrieval	11
Desktop publishing (making magazines, laying out written texts)	10
Image manipulation (altering or making drawings and photographs)	10
Designing artefacts (making cards, invitations etc., using computer design packages)	7
Computer personalisation (altering screen savers, changing settings)	7
Web browsing (looking for/browsing but not downloading information from the Web)	6
Edutainment (using educational software)	6
Computer file management (managing the computer system, organising files and memory and installing/deleting software	5
Email/chat rooms	4
Programming (any, including using HTML to program Websites)	3
Web producing (making Websites)	3
Spreadsheets	2
Web retrieving (downloading software/information from the Web)	2

As we highlighted in the previous chapter, computer games are the subject of much debate both between parents and children and in the wider public sphere, with games now subject to the same classificatory and legal principles as films. It is around games, as well, that the theoretical debates on the changing relations with media are coalescing – games are seen as a new form of media, enabling true 'interactivity' for the first time, as the user is said to control and determine narrative in a way impossible in traditional linear media such as television, books or films. In the educational arena, too, there is an interest in computer games, ranging from concerns that children are playing games instead of participating in more authorised pursuits (like doing homework) to an increasing desire to understand what it is about games that enables young people to seemingly play them for hours on end by choice, while they become bored with other more 'educational' activities. What then, are the characteristics of children's interactions with games at home?

Challenge

The one phrase that continually cropped up when talking to children about their games play, regardless of game genre or child age and interest, was '*you've got to …*'. Regardless of the format of the game, this trope was repeated:

> You're in a police helicopter in this and you've got to go on missions. It tells you all about it on the briefing.
> (Helen's brother, Deanbridge, unspecified game)

> It's Theme Park, you've got to build your own theme parks and you can go on the rides and things and you've got to hire and sack staff.
> (David's sister, Deanbridge, Theme Hospital)

> You've got to walk on this without falling in it.
> (Emma, Pandy, Croc)

> It's really good because you've got to go through the caves, you've got to shoot, you've got to kill evil baddies and stuff.
> (Rebecca, Pandy, Tomb Raider)

Simply by tracking the occurrence of this phrase, it is evident that young people are experiencing a wide range of challenges – they have to '*get up another level*; *go back up and keep on collecting*; *build citadels*; *try and kill them*; *walk*; *go through the caves*; *get all your minions*' and so on … through racing cars and planes, adding and subtracting, placing circles in bubbles, shooting arrows at a dart board, building civilisations. Within the game the player is positioned as the only person responsible for achieving these objectives and overcoming these challenges; they are not simply 'observing' the action, but personally responsible for determining the outcome.

The role of challenge in engaging and motivating games players is already well recognised and has been identified as an experience of a 'flow' state characterised by:

1   correspondence between level of challenge and the players ability;
2   isolation of activity from other stimuli;
3   clear criteria for performance;
4   feedback;
5   range of challenges.

(Csikszentmihalyi, cited in Malone, 1980, p14)

That children enjoy the experience of this 'flow' state is clear in their selection of games. We saw them reject games that were simply too complex, and equally get bored with those that were too simple, or which had already been completed. We saw them respond to game feedback on a second-by-second basis. We saw them check their performance against previous scores, against other players' efforts, and against digital opponents.

And yet, if it is the 'flow' of experience that creates motivation and engagement with games, then we need to ask whether games offer the degree of 'true' user control, true 'interactivity', many commentators suggest, since, necessarily, this experience is hugely *structured*. Games designers, for example, often map out games to include peaks and troughs of challenge, to gradually increase the level of obstacles and excitement that a player must face. If anything, as Turkle (1984) and Provenzo (1991) have argued, the process of playing a game may be a process of learning how to work *within* the structures and rules offered in that environment, rather than determining and controlling that environment for one's own imaginative and emotional ends. The new opportunities for autonomy and control that this medium offers young people may well, indeed, only be opportunities to experience an *illusion* of control and responsibility within a tightly constrained set of rules.

Fantasy and reality

Nevertheless, as Malone (1980) has argued, that this control may only be illusory may be significant in explaining games players' fascination with these types of interactions. In some circumstances, for example, it is the occupation of an ambiguous space in which semiotic links to reality are merged with actions without real world consequences that seems to be enjoyed, as in the ever popular Grand Theft Auto games:

Girl: You change from real life.
Girl: Yeah, go round shooting everyone. (LAUGHTER)
Girl: It's like if you (INAUDIBLE) the police car's after you and you jump out get a flame thrower and start burning their cars up.
Int: So it's kind of like things you're not allowed to do.
Girls: Yeah.
Int: Is that one of the reasons you like it?
Girls: Yeah.
Girl: It's not real, it's a computer game.
Girl: Just a game. Enjoyment.

(Samantha and friends, aged 13, Pen-y-Bryn,
talking about Grand Theft Auto)

The frequently reported activity of intentionally opposing the ostensible aims of the game (killing the patients in Theme Hospital, refusing to take over any worlds in Risk) seems also to fall within this category of activity, where otherwise 'taboo' actions can safely be explored and even enjoyed:

Int: Who likes 'Catz'?
Girl: Yeah me.
Girl: I killed the cats.
Int: You killed them? Did you kill them intentionally?
Girl: One I thought it would do it good if I killed it then I found out it was fun killing them.
Girl: (LAUGHTER)
Girl: It's the way they fell over when they died.
Heather: (LAUGHTER)
            (Heather and friends, aged 12, Deanbridge, talking about Catz)

In the same way that it is possible for Marxists to play Monopoly and enjoy it, so too it seems these children are able to 'bracket off' the implications of the representations in these games. Arguably, when listening to children's descriptions of their roles in the games play world, we might want to suggest that these games environments offer them the opportunity to explore and model different experiences, to project themselves and their aspirations *onto* a fantasy world, to examine what it would be like *if* they were able to take responsibility for cities, empires, soldiers, creatures. Perhaps part of the appeal of games play to young people (as we shall go on to discuss in more detail in Chapter 9) is the opportunity to imaginatively inhabit alternative realities in which they were able to test out what it was like to 'take control'.

Developing a games literacy

It has also been argued that this sort of games play is instrumental in developing new cognitive abilities amongst young people.[5] Looking at the requirements of these games environments, and at the prevalence of games play amongst this age group, we might want to begin to argue that the characteristic practices in games environments are leading to a new form of 'games literacy', a literacy which we might define as 'the competencies required to operate successfully within the games environment'. On a pragmatic basis, it is clear that there must be *some* forms of games literacy if we consider how difficult it is for a non-games player to even begin to function effectively within a new games environment.

On a fairly basic level, most of the games require *fast* information processing and, in many cases, high levels of hand-eye co-ordination – these, however, are simply amplifications of existing skills. More striking is the requirement to interact with information arriving simultaneously on the screen in a variety of formats. The average strategy game, for example, requires the user to make sense of at least three different information sources – the 'first person' view of the ground, the 'top level' two-dimensional (2D) map of the environment, and a range of monitors of the health and wealth of the organism being controlled. The player needs to know not only that these sources of information exist, but how, when and why they might want to focus on each particular one:

James: Well you can actually look right from above. The only way you can look right from above is if you change from 3D to 2D like that.

Int: Why do you want to watch it in 2D instead? Like from overhead yeah?

James: Not only that, cos some of the time all of a sudden this player will pop up all out of the blue, you don't know where he's come from, and he's just there suddenly.

Int: But if you'd have been watching it in 2D you'd have been able to see him coming, is that right?

Nick: Yeah because you could see the whole scene. The problem is you can't see whether he hacked him or not. You can't see his fouls.

(Nick and James, aged 10, Saxingham, talking about
Championship Manager)

Moreover, it almost goes without saying that the player needs to be able to interpret visual information rapidly – from graphs to complex three dimensional environments. A reliance for feedback on written text would, in most cases, ensure that the player lost the game in the first five minutes. The experience of handling large and indeterminate amounts of information presented graphically, numerically and in text was a central feature of many games:

Nick: There are two sections to this, there's the business and the coaching. We need to make money. It tells you about the status, the things you want to do with the players.

James: you've got your cashflow, you've got your season totals, your income.

(Nick and James, aged 10, Saxingham, talking about
Championship Manager)

Managing large amounts of information was therefore central to this particular game but the same was true of many other computer games whether they were strategy games or 'virtual pets'; in each case it was the management of complex information flows that provided a key challenge within the game. And as a consequence, as Faezal (12) said of the army strategy games he loved, 'It speeds up my mind. I really like it. I like my mind working as hard'.

Arguably, then, part of games literacy involves managing the speed and volume of information. As Eilola (1998) has argued:

> To cope with environments such as these offered by simulation games, users learn to juggle multiple, dynamic vectors of information without attempting to understand them fully. Instead, they play out multiple hypotheses about connections among numerous symbolic forces.
>
> (Eilola, 1998, pp94–195)

When we look at other activities on the computer, whether looking things up on Encarta or making Websites, or deciding how to design a text, learning how to live with large and indeterminate amounts of information that could be instantaneously accessed became a routine feature of the children's lives when they engaged with the computer.

Interestingly, in terms of competencies that might form part of an emerging definition of games literacy, we might also want to recognise the important role played by collaboration. By this we do not mean the games designed for two or more players; rather, the seemingly intuitive reaching out to other sources of support – people, manuals, online cheats – that characterises very effective games players. James and Nick, for example, when confronted with Championship Manager, decided that it was too hard to play on their own, and always played together, one leaning over the other's shoulder giving advice and then taking turns. In 'looser' networks, however, we see that the culture of games play, the sharing of cheats, the scouring of magazines and the Internet for resources, the 'resourceful seeking' for help is part of becoming games literate, it is part of the process of learning to play the game:[6]

I asked my friend to do something on my Nintendo and he told me, he came up, my mother let him come and then I got this cheat.

(Simon, aged 9, Pen-y-Bryn)

Yeah sometimes I invite Hannah round and say 'Right, I've got a new cheat, let's see if it works or not.' I've got through the whole of Tomb Raider by cheating.

(Helen, aged 9, Deanbridge)

To be a great games player then, as well as the cognitive abilities to navigate, interpret and rapidly comprehend information presented in a range of different media and in parallel, requires more social abilities – the ability to interact with and engage others in developing strategies to overcome problems, to identify individuals with relevant information and to combine these different 'human resources' in developing innovative solutions to games challenges.

Navigating information resources

Information and 'education'

The ability to access large amounts of information at the click of a mouse has been the feature of home computing technology most often represented as socially transformative. In the education arena, in particular, access to information resources has been the most rapidly adopted use of technology and the most heavily promoted by government:

Because information can be distributed virtually free over the Internet, the Grid will open up learning to the individual and take it beyond the confines of institutional walls ... In this way the Grid will make available to all learners the riches of the world's intellectual, cultural and scientific heritage.

(DfEE 1997: p5)

At the start of the ScreenPlay study, the construction of the computer as a site for consumption of information was embedded in the discourses of the majority of families that we studied. All of the case study children reported using the computer to look up information for a range of purposes, predominantly for schoolwork and revision activities but increasingly, amongst the older age range, for leisure activities. In 12 of the 16 families, 'access to information', whether on CD-ROM or the Internet, was a key factor in purchasing or upgrading home computers.

> But they keep saying computers is no good without Internet because you don't get into information a lot. I said 'Well, we'll buy information.' We'll go and buy a disk. [...].
>
> (Faezal's father, Pandy)

This view of computers and the Internet as a 'candy store' of information, waiting to be consumed by the computer user, informed a range of different strategies employed by the young people in this study. When searching for information for school projects, for example, many seemed to employ a specific 'shopping list principle', clearly identifying the 'nuggets' of information that they needed in order to complete the assigned task, as is the case with the following example from Jamilla, completing her homework on Martin Luther King 'to order':

Jamilla: I go to the outline and see what's in there. If it's got the education, early life, and what happened and what did he do.
Int: Okay. So basically, you're very specific about what you're looking for. You know you want Martin Luther King, you don't care what else is either side of it.
Jamilla: No just about him, not about anything else.

> (Jamilla,aged 12, Pandy, using Encarta)

This production of information to order was also reflected in the processes that some children employed on translating their information from the digital realm to the print-based versions required for marking by teachers:

> I can print it out, put into one project, neatly presented and ...
>
> (Huw, aged 12, Pen-y-Bryn)

> I print it out, then copy that in my own words. I use the computer but I do write it back up in my music book. I print out the information and write it up in my book.
>
> (Samantha, aged 12, Pen-y-Bryn)

This emphasis on retrieval and presentation in a 'finished' print form, however, also engendered a series of interesting strategies on the part of one young person who, confronted with a complex information resource and needing to present work as 'her own', generated a range of techniques effectively to 'disguise' her sources:

Samantha:	[...] So you highlight it, you copy, minimise Encarta [...] paste [...] Then just change all the fonts so it doesn't look like ... doesn't look like I've just printed it off the Encarta or something. So I just highlight it all again, delete all that ...
Int:	Delete the footnotes, yes.
Samantha:	Then just delete things like that.
Int:	Things like 'See Bronze'. Then you put 'What is brass?' as a header, and start off with 'An alloy of copper and zinc ...' as opposed to 'Brass (alloy), alloy of copper and zinc.'

(Samantha, aged 12, Pen-y-Bryn)

The construction of the computer as a resource for accessing information for educational purposes seemed to present a challenge to the young people in this study. On the one hand, the use of the computer as a powerful information resource and educational tool was encouraged at home; on the other, using this resource is often seen as 'cheating' in a school setting and children were often required to conceal the origins of the information they presented.

Information as exploration

Importantly, these processes of concealment hide some of the more challenging and innovative aspects of children's use of digital resources. The following quotation, for example, highlights a range of innovative strategies employed by Nick to *interpret* and *connect* different information sources to produce a coherent story.

[...]I'll say Walrus [...] So you type it in, click and you get it [...] I particularly like the picture and also I like the noise. [...] and what I did was I listened to the noise very carefully and I described the noise in it [...] I said it was some kind of grunting noise, it sounds like a large belch [...] We actually saw a seal on our holiday [...] He didn't make a noise. He was just lying on the rock getting all the sun [...] The thing about this is it doesn't actually give you about what the walrus's food is. What I do is instead I go to Find after that [...] so I look in Seals and I presume that's what sort of food they [Walrus] eat.

(Nick, aged 10, Saxingham)

Nick, in this example, was supported by a range of characteristics of the encyclopaedia environment – he was encouraged to make links between different animals with similar characteristics through hypertext links and alphabetical search categories, he was encouraged to recollect his holiday experiences through videos of the animals, which encouraged him to think about seals and then to link the information on seals with the walrus he was actually seeking information about. In translating this into work for school, however, he was not encouraged to reflect upon these processes, but simply to present the finished 'content'.

In contrast, it seemed that the greatest appeal to these children in using these environments was in multiple and overlapping *mechanisms* by which the user was able to navigate through and collate information. Their emphasis lay less on the *content* to be 'consumed', than on the *processes* by which that content was identified and interpreted. Indeed, the expectation that information on most subjects would be quickly and easily available led to a subtle shift in emphasis away from content towards an appreciation of the ways in which different media afforded different strategies for selection, navigation and testing of content against the values and needs of the child – indeed, afforded different approaches for exploring and learning about particular issues.

Moreover, this emphasis was also supported by the search mechanisms embedded in the design of the digital encyclopaedia, which provided new ways of linking and thinking about the information they were using. In particular, through observing their computer use, it was clear that the multi-media capacity of the encyclopaedia afforded these young people the potential to create links through auditory and visual as well as linguistic information. In the course of the study, for example, we saw children using a wide range of search techniques, including:

- Language-based searches of alphabetical lists
- Catalogues of sounds and pictures
- Hypertext connections between different content
- Historical timelines to narrow and focus searches
- Key word searches
- Geographical searches (using maps to locate information).

Often, many of these tools would be employed in conjunction with each other to narrow down or widen search areas in order to solve information-seeking problems. Importantly, however, the key factor in determining which searches were used was the individual's sense of what constituted 'sufficient' information for their purposes. This meant that even when a wide range of search options were available, if the information was readily accessible through the most commonly used mechanism (language-based searches of alphabetical lists) then the additional strategies were unlikely to be employed. It was only when either 'content' proved difficult to extract *or* when the information that they were seeking was not clearly defined in advance, that the children diversified to wider techniques.

While we may want to celebrate the new strategies of information navigation open to young people in digital encyclopaedia environments, we also need to document the extent to which, particularly in online environments, these strategies may be rendered unnecessarily complex by design and infrastructure difficulties. A short transcript of a video of one case study child's attempts to access resources on the Web demonstrates this point well. Originally, Paul (aged 12, Saxingham) was attempting to look up some information for school:

Minutes	On-screen information	Description of actions
0.00	Screen opens of Website directory 'Websites grouped by subject'.	Websites are grouped according to category (e.g. travel, reference, games, etc.). Paul scrolls down the screen to have a look. Clicks on 'reference'.
0.01–0.06	*8 error messages, 6 minutes and two reconnections to the Web later, Paul gives up on trying to access 'reference' section of the site and clicks on the Pokemon link.*	
0.07	Pokemon World Website opens.	Paul moves mouse around screen to 'read' the different contents of the Web page. Paul selects 'TV listings' button.
0.08	Message appears 'Coming soon'.	Paul looks at the almost blank screen for a while, then clicks on another button, 'Encyclopaedia'.
0.09	Pokemon encyclopaedia button comes up.	
0.10	Error message comes up on screen: 'error in Java script'.	Paul clicks on the 'TV listings' hotlink embedded in the text.
0.12	'Coming soon' screen.	

In 12 minutes Paul has failed to either access the original resources he was hoping to find (under reference) or to download the resources he decided to look for after his initial failure. The online candy shop for information may be available, but in some cases and for some systems, particularly with this slow domestic connection, it simply doesn't want to open for business.

Transforming 'information'

The simple construction of the computer as a 'window' on a world of information, however, is also rendered problematic when we consider the ways in which the digital environment potentially alters the very status of the information children are attempting to access. Embedded in the digital resources children are using to look for information, for example, are a range of different representational systems. Children are increasingly required to interpret information in text, in images and, increasingly in models and simulations. These 'modes' of communication, as Kress and van Leeuwen (1996) have argued, do not simply represent the same information in different ways, or serve only to illustrate text, but, through their different modalities, alter the *meanings* of the information presented and the readers' relations with that information.

Later in the same Internet session described above, for example, Paul went to one of his favourite and most reliable sites – the NASA Earth Moon Viewer. The following is a transcript of his demonstration of this site to one of the authors:

James: This is the earth [...] This is a proper picture – that's all the lights on in America at night. [...] This is the very edge, that's dusk, someone's on that line right now, that's Mexico. [...] This is as far as it will zoom in, but it's quite close. [...] You see the hemisphere – that's what it's about, it actually shows it properly as a sphere. (Picture 5.1)

[James uses mouse to rotate image of world.]

James: It's a very small world, I'm making it spin. [...] Look at those clouds in Africa ... is that clouds?

[Uses mouse to focus on different points. Scrolls down screen. Shifts to sun view.]

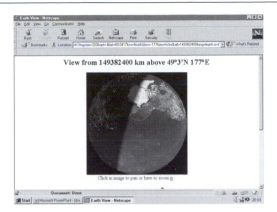

Picture 5.1 NASA Earth Moon Viewer, image 1

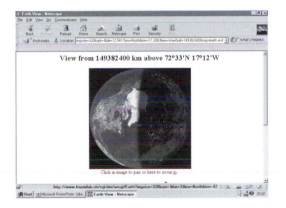

Picture 5.2 NASA Earth Moon Viewer, image 2

James: We're going to see it on the daylight side now, we're looking from the sun. […] It's all done at an angle see, if we tilted it the opposite way round that would be all white see. (Picture 5.2)

[Clicks on another viewing option 'view from satellite'.]

James: Which satellite do you want to go on?

[Opens up menu of satellites – shows how many satellites there are by the point on the menu list.]

James: These are all the Australia satellites, these are all the ones over Brazil.
Int: How do you know that?
James: Because it's got the names.

> (James, aged 10, Saxingham, demonstrating
> NASA Earth Moon Viewer)

Because the simulation was designed to represent the earth at the exact time at which the user accessed it, there was some ambiguity evidenced in Paul's language as to whether what he was seeing was a 'real' view from a satellite or a simulation. The nature of the reality of the object with which he was interacting was ambiguous – the images represented were, indeed, what you would see on earth from that vantage point at that particular point in time (assuming earth had no clouds). And Paul's assertion, 'This is the very edge, that's dusk, someone's on that line right now, that's Mexico', is in all probability correct, although the impression given by the simulation that if you were only able to zoom in closely enough you would see that person, i.e. that this is a 'real' view from space, was evidently untenable. The simulation, however, has an ontological ambiguity that allows Paul to treat it as both 'real' and representational, a powerful combination that underlines his statement, 'It's a very small world, I'm making it spin.'

These transformations in the ontological status of knowledge problematise the notion that digital resources can simply be seen as a commodification of information, that all we are doing when we are accessing an encyclopaedia or setting up Internet access is 'buying information'; rather, these resources may fundamentally change the nature of interaction with knowledge.[7]

New information literacies?

From our studies of these children's use of information resources we would agree with commentators such as Eilola (1998) that children's information literacy is now shifting away from a modernist information processing perspective, and with Kress (1998), that we are increasingly seeing a shift towards 'multi-modal' literacies, in which information is consumed through a variety of different modalities of sound, text, image, animation, etc. We would also, however, want to raise a series of concerns regarding young people's 'critical' and 'cultural' literacies in operation within these information resources. As Snyder (2001) and others have argued, being 'literate' in the digital age needs to be seen as more than becoming proficient in the mechanisms for information seeking. Rather, they suggest that literacy operates on three dimensions – 'operational', 'cultural' and 'critical'.[8] 'Operational' refers to understanding how to 'work' the computer and language requirements; 'cultural' refers to realising that the 'ability to operate language and technology systems is always in the service of participating in "authentic" forms of social practice and meaning' and 'critical' refers to the ability to 'critique [resources], to read and use them against the grain, to appropriate and even re-design them, as well as to be able to actively envisage and contribute to transforming social practices'.[9] As Selwyn (2002) contends, being digitally literate entails not only understanding 'how to use' computers for information purposes but, crucially, understanding the development and use of information and communications technologies within a social context.[10]

If we consider how these children were using computers in the home, it is clear that these latter aspects of the 'new literacies' are in many cases yet to be developed in home computer use. The young people in our case studies, for example, often seemed unclear about how and why information was produced for the Web or in digital encyclopaedias. In some cases, for example, the computer 'itself' was seen as the source of knowledge:

> Well it [the computer] is sort of got an artificial brain sort of thing, but it can feed information onto it. It's like a memory, like a really big memory that it can store loads of stuff on it.
>
> (Stephanie, aged 9, Saxingham)

Whereas other children simply assumed that benevolent individuals were responsible for uploading information onto the Web.

> Because like teachers know a lot of things but most of the time computers know a lot more, nearly everything about that subject, because they … like they can either log onto things and find out about them or people can read loads and loads of books and type it onto computers and stuff.
>
> (Friend of Emma and Rebecca, aged 9, Pandy)

Overall there was either a lack of interest in or lack of knowledge about how 'information' was produced for and within digital environments. These resources were often seen as originating not from people, organisations and businesses with particular cultural inclinations or objectives, but as a universal repository that simply existed 'out there'. Further, very few children, with notable exceptions that we shall discuss in the next chapter, viewed the Web as a resource to which they themselves could contribute, raising questions about their degree of participation in 'cultural' literacy practices. Rather, the digital landscape of information, unlike the digital landscape of games, tended to be seen as an environment through which they passed, leaving little trace of themselves.

Conclusion

Games environments and information resources are among the most popular uses of the home computer. Our study of these children suggests that these environments both provide digital landscapes within which young people are developing new ways of accessing, exploring and interpreting information and, at the same time, are influenced by children's day-to-day contexts of school and home.

We can see, for example, that the realities of slow domestic Internet connections continue to play a role in shaping the quality and nature of exploration within the world of the Web. We can also see how children's perception of 'appropriate' activities for schoolwork impact on their actions in the digital environment. Knowing, for example, that in current educational systems, one is supposed to produce 'original' work, at times leads to strategies of concealment rather than critical acknowledgement of information resources. Similarly, the persisting reluctance of schools to accept digital materials leads to the practice of 'translating' digital information into printed or handwritten documents. Digital and physical landscapes also intersect around computer games, as games expertise and understanding is developed not only through playing games, but in playground, classroom and living room discussions between children. More importantly, we would suggest that the dominant discursive production of 'computer literacy' in the UK curriculum as the vocational application of computer 'skills' would seem to leave young people ill-prepared to engage with the social and cultural influences that shape the terrain of the digital landscape.

The low levels of children producing their own Websites (as we shall discuss in the next chapter), and the general lack of understanding about how these information resources are produced within social, economic and cultural worlds, raises questions, then, about how far these children could really be considered 'information literate'. They may be fast at processing relevant information, expecting to live in an information rich environment, and able to manipulate and transform information to meet specific objectives, but are, it seemed to us, generally ill-equipped with the social and cultural understanding about *how* and *why* information resources are produced or the ability to produce them for themselves in the online world. The implications of this for young people whose interests and concerns may not be represented within the 'global' digital environment will be discussed later in Chapter 9.

At the same time, however, these resources are offering young people new ways of viewing the world around them. Within the new information landscape, children are increasingly coming to expect that a wealth of information resources are available to them and that they themselves, through the digital technologies in the home, should be able to find, manipulate and translate these resources. Rather than having to negotiate access to knowledge through books, through libraries, or through other socially sanctioned resources (such as schools), our case study children were growing up with the expectation that 'finding things out' was an activity for which they were readily qualified through the use of the home computer. The use of the computer for games or information purposes can also be seen to encourage young people to expect that 'information' or 'content' has not one but many different representations. In the games environment, as we have discussed, landscapes are represented through maps, through first person perspectives, through graphs and tables. In digital information resources, the same information is conveyed through moving image, through text, through audio-files and through simulation. The child is invited to select different perspectives, different ways of viewing these worlds, and to move smoothly between them. Knowledge, content and information, are being rendered ontologically ambivalent through these multiple representations.

The implications of these experiences for children's identities are discussed in more detail in Chapter 9. In the next chapter, however, we will move on from games and information resources to explore the other activities, such as writing, design, publishing, making, Web design and programming that children participate in on their home computers and to ask, in conclusion, how the full range of uses of the home computer may be changing notions of literacy and expertise.

Chapter 6

Writing, designing and making

In the last chapter we discussed how young people were using computers in the home to play games and navigate digital information resources. We argued that interaction with these environments required young people to develop a diverse set of 'games' and 'information' literacies. In this chapter, we shall build on this by examining our case study children's use of the computer for a range of other activities, including: writing, designing, making artefacts, drawing, programming, and designing Web pages. We shall ask: what sorts of interactions characterised children's use of the computer for these activities? What sorts of literacies are required of children when working in these environments?

In recent years there has been substantial interest in what has become known as the New Literacy Studies[1] movement. Research in this field, importantly, cautions us against the temptation to look for a generalised set of characteristics definable as 'the new computer literacy'.[2] Instead, these researchers argue that 'literacies are multiple rather than singular, and take divergent forms depending on the contexts which sustain them'.[3]

Context is seen to be important in shaping literacy practices because different contexts make available different tools and resources, and these resources, in turn, are seen to shape how different groups and individuals make meaning. Here we refer to work by, among others, the New London Group (1996, p65), who argue that we are 'both inheritors of patterns and conventions of meaning and at the same time active designers of meaning'. This latter perspective suggests that, when for example we use information and communication technologies (ICTs), we draw upon the available representational resources in the communities we live in and in the technologies that we use, to create culturally specific literacy practices. At the same time, through our literacy practices, they argue, we are reshaping the representational resources available within particular contexts. At a time of rapid change in technology and the representational resources available to children, this approach seems particularly relevant. It enables us to move beyond studying children's computer use in the home through a perspective in which we 'evaluate' their work against some fixed, external criteria of 'good practice'.[4] Instead, we are able to explore how children's digital literacies emerge in interrelation between the tools they use, the socio-cultural contexts they live in and the interests of the individual child.

This is not to say, however, that these research perspectives themselves are 'value neutral'; indeed, researchers within these fields repeatedly argue that literacy, in all its forms, is highly politicised. As we outlined at the end of the previous chapter, these researchers argue that literacy practices incorporate the possibility of participating in the shaping of 'social futures'. In other words, they suggest that to be 'truly' literate means both understanding that the resources we use to make meaning are shaped by social and cultural practices and, reciprocally, that we can reshape these practices through our meaning making.

In order to understand children's use of the computer at home for activities such as writing, designing and making, we therefore want to pay attention to how children make use of the resources available within the computer environments, to examine how different literacies are emerging in interaction with the specific local contexts of children's own lives and to ask how children are engaging with the social and cultural practices that shape the tools and representations they are using.

Diverse computer uses

As we have indicated in the last chapter, no two of our case study children used the computer in exactly the same way, nor used the computer for the same purposes at all times. In fact it seemed to us that children's computer use was usually an extension of already existing interests in their lives. So, for example, Nick and James were passionate about reading; at the same time, they spent a large amount of time on the computer writing and illustrating their own stories. Alistair was fascinated by electronics both on and off the screen; he used the computer to design a workbook on electronics and on computers, and was our only programmer, having taught himself Visual Basic at home. Emma and Rebecca were passionate about their pet kittens, newly purchased during the project. At the same time, in a strange instance of physical and digital symmetry, they used the computer to play the digital pet game, Dogz. Jamilla was interested in textiles and fashion and used the computer to find out information about make-up and beauty.

When we look beyond games or looking up information, therefore, we can see that different children used the computer for very different purposes and that, to an important degree, what they chose to use the computer for was influenced by existing interests. In terms of understanding the different 'literacies' children were developing through this process, it is important to emphasise that these different computer uses afforded different sorts of interactions with the computer through specific software environments. There was an evident difference, for example, in the use of the computer to program solutions to maths problems set for homework (as Alistair did) and the use of the computer and digital camera to create a family photograph album online (as Huw did), or again, in the use of the computer to make a manual on child nutrition (as Heather did). Given that these were fundamentally different activities, the literacies that these children developed through their interactions with the computer were themselves different; they necessarily varied from child to child according to the particular purposes for which they chose to use the computer.

Different tools, different resources

What, then, are the features of these different uses of the computer in the home? What sorts of literacies do they require? In the following section, we will discuss the characteristics of children's use of the computer for writing, programming, emailing, Web designing, playing edutainment software, designing artefacts and for drawing and manipulating images. However, while we will discuss these as discrete categories, we will go on to argue that, in reality, children's use of the computer, driven as it is by particular interests, is rarely constrained to only one sort of activity.

Writing

As we have already discussed in Chapter 2, writing was a widely prevalent activity amongst our larger survey populations, with almost as many children (68 per cent of home computer owners) reporting using a computer to write as using a computer to play games.[5] Similarly, *all* of our case study children used the computer to write at one time or other.

However, 'writing' on a computer is not simply one activity, but many. As with other uses of the computer, writing takes on a range of different characteristics depending upon the child's purposes at the time and the tools that they are using. Writing on the computer for our case study children included, for example, sending emails, writing diaries, jotting down notes, typing song lyrics, producing reports for school, and designing and writing magazines and Web pages. Writing took place within a similarly wide range of different software environments – from the 'pared down' capabilities of Word Pad or email environments, in which the child had very little choice about how their writing was presented, to environments such as Publisher, or Front Page, in which children were working within complex templates, able to manipulate not simply the font, colours and layout, but the mechanisms for *reading* the texts, through the inclusion of hyperlinks when the text was translated to Web pages.

Writing on the computer in all of these environments does, however, have a common characteristic, namely, that computer text is *impermanent*: it can be easily deleted and altered. Many commentators[6] have argued that this is a key feature in enabling young people to write differently on a computer than with pen and paper, as it enables them to overcome motor difficulties, to develop more complex and sophisticated writing strategies, and to develop a flexible approach to writing which combines thinking, writing and product in one 'recursive and evolving text'.[7] Indeed, we did see, amongst our case studies, several notable examples of how using the computer actively supported some young people to 'become writers' through obviating the need for time-consuming revisions and corrections (see Chapter 10). Huw, for example, used the computer to overcome difficulties in writing by hand:

> I cannot stand writing. I cannot stand my writing. I can't change it and I cannot stand it. So I use a computer a lot in school to get quality out of my writing. It's just my writing. Don't like it.
>
> (Huw, aged 12, Pen-y-Bryn)

Similarly James enjoyed being freed from the constraints of pen and ink, and also able to change and reflect upon his writing with the support of tools, such as Spell Checker, within the word-processing software:

Int:　　And why do you do it on the computer instead of in a book?

James:　Well for a start my handwriting isn't very good and secondly if I make a mistake in spelling on this, you know, I won't know if I wrote on a piece of paper, but if I do it on this I know if I've made it wrong and I know how to change it. I know what I have to do to change it too.

> (James, aged 10, Saxingham)

Commentators have also argued that writing in digital environments today can be characterised as multi-modal, encouraging writers to communicate not only through text but through image, colour and form. Snyder (1994 p185) argues that this choice of modalities 'makes each writer a graphic designer as well as a composer of words', while Kress (1998) describes this as a (re)turn to the visual in which 'the "look of the page" is now not a matter only for a specialised group of producers of texts; it is a general concern and the means of page design are readily there' (p56).

This shift towards multi-modality in 'writing' was widely in evidence amongst our case study children. Indeed, the majority of the children in the study viewed the computer as a site for experimentation with different forms of representation. Almost all of the children, for example, made explicit choices about representational features, colours, fonts, images and layout of school homework assignments. Samantha, for example, was writing a piece about Asia and chose a near illegible font that she felt was similar to Chinese writing. Helen was writing a piece on forests and chose to write the full text in green.

Similarly, Nick (Fig 6.1) was completing a piece of homework on volcanoes and used the WordArt facility to transform the simple word 'Magma' into a representation that conveyed, through reds and oranges and a flowing form, the characteristics of magma he felt to be most important – heat and movement. Through these choices, Helen, Nick and Samantha were exploiting the capabilities of the software environment to convey *meaning* rather than simply 'improving the look' of their texts. As Kress and van Leeuwen (1996, p6) have argued:

> … we see representation as a process in which the makers of signs … seek to make a representation of some object or entity, whether physical or semiotic, and in which their interest in the object, at the point of making the representation, is a complex one, arising out of

Figure 6.1 Nick's representation of the word 'magma' for a homework assignment

the cultural, social and psychological history of the sign-maker, and focussed by the specific context in which the sign is produced. Interest guides the selection of what is seen as the criterial aspects of the object, and this criterial aspect is then regarded as adequately or sufficiently representative of the object in the given context.

These choices should be seen, then, as part of an ongoing dialogue between the child as writer and the wider socio-cultural context of representation. That Helen chose 'green' or Samantha chose *Lucida Handwriting,* is not a process of random selection. Rather, it is the development of a literacy practice in which the child draws on the wider socio-cultural resources available to them, in interaction with the new affordances of the computer environment, to convey meaning through both visual and lexical modes.

In understanding emerging literacy practices with the computer, then, we need to move away from an assumption that children's experimentation with different visual forms is simply an attempt to 'improve presentation'; rather, it can function as a new medium through which children communicate their understanding of the 'criterial aspects' of the subject matter.

Localised writing practices

Through our research, we also came to recognise that the computer can support a wide range of different approaches to writing; as Moss (2001) states, literacies can be 'multiple rather than singular, [taking] divergent forms depending on the contexts which sustain them' (p146).

James, for example, lived in a highly 'literate' household in which both parents had degrees and where the children were actively encouraged to read and write their own stories. When he decided to write a story on the computer, it was for a competition taking place locally and his criteria for production of the story were developed through his sense of what a 'published' book should look like. He organised the story into chapters, found pictures for illustrating the front page of each chapter, and carefully reproduced 'official' formatting within his text.

Int: Okay. So how did you decide to like put all the inverted commas in and your exclamation marks. Why did you put some bits in italic? Cos you've put that bit in italics there, haven't you?

James: Well some of the time I just, you know, know whether I'm meant to do that or not. But some of the time it's because I've read it in a book and I've learnt the sort of expressions you use and in school as well I've learnt the expressions. We have to write these things, but they don't tell you where to write in italics, but reading the books I've got you can see where to write it.

(James, aged 10, Saxingham)

From his explicit attempt to produce a story that was in the style of the books he was reading, and from the conventions he has been taught in school and through reading, James operated within a tightly defined framework, drawn mainly from printed materials, which shaped his definitions of appropriate representations in both lexis and 'look' for his story.

In a different way, Paul's writing developed in *conjunction* with the computer. A child fascinated with fantasy and computer games, Paul decided to write a series of stories based on his favourite game Soul Blade. To begin with, he copied the text directly from the pamphlet accompanying the game, then gradually branched out to develop his own narrative. In doing so, however, he worked *with* the computer to determine his style and grammatical choices:

Cos what you can do on here is … there's grammar up there and it says 'What type of story are you writing?' and you read down and it says 'Fiction', so it gives you like reading scores and tells you how to get people more interested in the book.

(Paul, aged 12, Saxingham)

Also, halfway through writing up his story, his computer was upgraded. Where he had begun his story writing in the only available font – courier – he now changed the fonts to more accurately convey the 'atmosphere' of the story he was writing.

Paul: Yeah. I changed it about two days ago. I didn't like the other font, it was boring.
Int: Why did you choose this one?
Paul: Um, it looked more in the past … More old fashioned … Because it's based in the olden days.

(Paul, aged 12, Saxingham)

Paul did not finish his story. As with many of his other creative projects – his model aeroplane, his wall mural – he left it half-completed. Arguably, in writing these stories, Paul was playing with the 'nature' of writing, testing out different fonts, different styles of writing, different grammatical rules. Rather than developing a literacy in which 'product' and 'process' become inextricably combined, as Balestri (1988) suggests, Paul was using the computer as a site in which to play with writing free from the constraints of having to achieve completion, in which he could use the flexibility of the resource to explore different aspects of writing – from 'story', to grammar, to representation.

Stephanie shaped the resources of the software environment very differently in her writing. As we shall discuss in the next chapter, Stephanie very rarely used her multi-media home computer, preferring to spend time on other outdoors activities; the computer was viewed with some distrust by family members who were concerned that this expensive tool might easily break. One of Stephanie's few uses of the computer was for writing letters to friends. What was clear was that her writing practices were shaped heavily by her mother and her school's view of 'good writing':

Int:	Now when you write letters on here do you do it on your own or do you do it with your mum?
Stephanie:	I do it on my own then my mum comes and then does the spelling. And normally she deletes it all.
Int:	Does she? Why?
Stephanie:	Because it's bits of each thing. [...] I'm used to writing like that in school.
Int:	So your mum keeps an eye on you ... is it your mum who says the way you write, you've got to change it, or is it the computer?
Stephanie:	It's my mum.
Int:	Okay. But is it different writing on the computer from writing by hand?
Stephanie:	Not really no.
Int:	Okay.
Stephanie:	Um, well the writing's the same ... then you can put (IN-AUDIBLE) like you can make the lines go down and stuff, and you can put them across if you wanted to, like that ...

(Stephanie, aged 9, Saxingham)

Stephanie was aware that using the computer could, in principle, support different writing practices, enabling the reorganisation of text, for example. The family context within which she was operating, however, actively promoted 'literacy' as purely language based, and viewed experimentation with different resources within the computer system as risky rather than playful. Stephanie, as a result, and despite having a powerful multi-media computer at her disposal, never experimented with the representational options in the software, nor revised her own work, and indeed, approached the computer for writing with some degree of trepidation.

In all of these cases, the children's writing practices were shaped by the resources available within the computer and their intentions in writing. Importantly, however, their writing practices were also shaped by the wider literacy practices within the home and conventions of writing within the wider culture. These factors combine to suggest that the potential for computer technologies to require a new set of literacy practices, such as developing increasingly visual forms of representation, or 'blending' different stages of writing, while evidently emerging, needs to be understood within the context of the specific and particular literacy practices and technological resources present in different home settings.

Design and image manipulation

While less prevalent than writing, the use of the computer for designing or for making images through drawing and photography was nevertheless a very popular use of the computer, both amongst our case study children and in our wider surveys. In our most recent survey[8] 55 per cent of children with home computers reported regularly (at least once a month) using a computer to draw or manipulate photographs, and 45 per cent reported regular use of the computer to make and design things. In our case studies 10 of the children used the computer to play with images (photographs or drawings) and 7 used the computer to make or design things.

These high levels of use should not be surprising given that today the home computer is often marketed as a site for domestic 'creative' production.[9] New tools to support this practice, such as digital cameras and scanners, and animation and film-making packages, are increasingly available for the domestic market. The prevalence of these technologies in the home is, moreover, leading to the suggestion in popular and academic debate that the traditional boundaries between 'professional' and 'amateur' are being eroded. Again, Kress (1998) and others argue that these new resources in the domestic environment are enabling young people to develop truly 'multi-modal' productions, incorporating images, sound, movement and text.

> The landscape of communication … is … irrefutably a multi-semiotic one; and the visual mode in particular has already taken on a central position in this landscape. Other modes are becoming more

significant ... Sound ... whether in the form of 'soundtrack', 'music', or 'background noise', is one of these; and as the body is coming to be used as a medium of communication, so aspects of bodily motion are increasingly used as modes of representation and communication.

(Kress, 1998, p58)

Amongst our case study children, however, the predominant use of the computer was for creating still images, or for designing objects that could be printed and used outside the computer. While three of the children had animation packages, they rarely if ever used them. The only use, amongst these children, of the computer for music was for playing CDs (something that was very much in evidence with our teenage girls). While several of the children had scanners, many did not; similarly many were not able to get access to the Internet to source other pictorial resources and only two of the children in the study had digital stills cameras that could be connected to their home computer. As a rule, then, our case study children were reliant upon the pictorial resources (such as clipart) available within the computer or on CD-ROM, or upon their own production of images through drawing packages. At this point, however, we might want to suggest that this situation is likely to change in future as the technologies available to support the incorporation of a wider range of modalities are becoming much less expensive and, probably more importantly, increasingly easy to use. At the time of our study, however, these tools were still the preserve of a few early and affluent adopters and indeed, our more recent survey[10] suggests that there are still only small numbers of children using the computer in this way.

Even setting aside the use of 'rich' multi-media, however, in the children's 'visual' practices on the computer, as in their writing practices, we saw a great deal of diversity. The children used the computer to design things, to doodle pictures, to create illustrations for stories; to redesign existing images, to manipulate photographs, and to reconfigure photographs for other uses. These interactions also ranged from children following simple instructions within highly structured environments, to subverting the rules of these environments to create novel visual representations, to working in drawing and image manipulation environments to create 'new' images.

Designing

In many environments, children were using templates and highly structured software package 'wizards' to produce visual representations. Paul, Nick, James and Samantha, for example, all used the Printmaster software to produce paper artefacts. In this software they worked through a series of drop-down menus giving category options, such as 'hats', or 'invitations' or 'front covers' and made choices about what types of images would be slotted into the pre-determined locations on artefacts, which they then printed out as objects to give to friends and family. Samantha's description of the production of a front cover for a homework project for school illustrates the processes involved in this type of activity.

Samantha: I always go in through a template.
Int: Okay, why's that?
Samantha: I don't know. It's easier.
Int: So you've got a Mega ClipArt 7000 for Windows. So that's got loads of different pictures and things in has it?
Samantha: Yeah […] You just delete that one and press insert, no minimise it first then go into ClipArt, from there then open the screen, then just pick the picture you want and copy it, open the file back up and paste it to where you want it.
                                      (Samantha, aged 12, Pen-y-Bryn)

In these environments, the resources available to the child are heavily structured by the computer package they are working within. Often, these packages reproduce a highly commercialised aesthetic of production – with computer generated images placed according to pre-determined guidelines on artefacts you would expect to buy in 'party packs' – such as hats, banners, invitations and so on. Arguably, we could critique these activities (as have many other commentators), saying that the way in which children interact with these environments is less an example of children imaginatively exploring and redesigning the visual environment, than of children being 'programmed' to function within a pre-specified set of rules.[11]

This, however, would be to ignore, on the one hand, the purpose of these activities and, on the other, the degree to which even these small choices can be considered part of the process of communicative action. As a rule, for example, the children themselves did not describe these activities as 'creative' – yes, they took great pleasure from them, they valued the experience of producing a product that could happily sit alongside professionally produced objects in stores, they enjoyed giving these products to friends and family, but they did not themselves hold them up as examples of their best or most 'creative work'. For us to critique them from this perspective would be to ignore the context and purposes for which children engaged in these activities. Interestingly,

Samantha and the other children were aware of the ease with which products such as this could be produced and found it amusing that such a quick and easy way of producing a front cover for homework, for example, could gain such good grades in school.

We might also return to Kress and Van Leeuwen's (1996) assertion that even these small scale choices (of different illustrations for party hats for example) are part of the process of making meaning, of selection from a variety of resources to communicate key aspects of the children's understanding. Paul's selection, for example, of Vikings (as opposed to, say, bubbles) as an image on the party hat and banner for his dad, went some way to communicating, not what he thought the 'hat' should be, but his understanding of his dad's identity.

> Yeah and I chose the Viking person for Dad. [...] It's the way he is, like one of those rugged men. [...] He doesn't like computers. He likes the whole survival, great outdoors and stuff.
>
> (Paul, aged 12, Saxingham)

The design of the hat, in this instance, brought into the representational resources of the household the image of the father as a Viking and enabled Paul, in his quiet way, to tease his father through a new representation.

It is the extent to which these images, available in pre-packaged tools such as Printmaster, or in resources such as Mega ClipArt, represent uniform rather than diverse aesthetics, that might cause most concern for commentators interested in the development of children's visual literacy on the computer. While the *range* of resources on offer may present a wide variety of choices in terms of content, there is little diversity in the aesthetic of representation on offer.

Redesign on the computer

In contrast to these highly structured forms of production, we did at times see different sorts of interactions that served potentially to frustrate a pre-given 'aesthetic'. As anyone familiar with academic or business conferences will be aware, Powerpoint is often a tool for ensuring uniform banality across all sorts of presentations. One of the children in our study, however, took the relatively strict rules of this environment and refashioned the resources available within it to meet her own needs. Kerry, Simon's younger sister, was writing a story about aliens. In order to illustrate the story, she chose a corporate slide design from Powerpoint (black, with a fireball) and translated this into an alien landscape. She took clipart images from her encyclopaedia, of rockets, stars and moons, and inserted these onto the generic slide design, drawing over them with shiny green lines to indicate lights and aliens. Through this process she transformed what was designed as a corporate image to convey business efficiency and modernity, into a fantastical representation of a world of aliens, space ships and comets.

Similarly, when Nick, for example, was producing a piece of science homework that he wanted to illustrate with a picture of a chameleon in a tree, he turned first to his bank of clipart. Despite the hundreds of images available, he couldn't find a picture that accurately represented what he wanted to convey. Instead, he spent a substantial amount of time combining two existing pieces of clipart to create the result he wanted.

Nick: These [pointing to images on the screen] are all ones that I used for the thing for school […] It was a science project we were doing about animals. We had set these animals that we had to write about and I got some pictures from clipart because I find they're quite good, quite useful. […] I was doing a chameleon. I stuck that one on top of that one and then they looked like leaves so it was quite good. […]

Int: Okay. And why did you choose those particular pictures then?

Nick: Well that one because it's very detailed and I quite liked that one. And this one because I really liked that idea. […]

(Nick, aged 10, Saxingham)

It seemed to us that as children became used to the idea that there were massive image banks available for them to use, so they increasingly saw these as flexible and malleable resources to be redesigned to create the *particular* meanings they wanted. Just as in the last chapter we saw some children combining information from a range of different sources to produce their own narratives, so too might we increasingly see children combining and manipulating 'pre-existing' images to create their own visual representations. In the process, they are not 'simply' downloading images, but redesigning these resources.

Image manipulation

The digital redesign of pre-existing images was most in evidence when children were working with photographs. In some cases, it was the comedy provided by juxtaposing different images that was, in itself, the reason for manipulating photographs. Simon's father, for example, had recently bought a digital camera and he and Simon spent many hours mutilating photographs of family members to comic effect – adding new hairstyles, elongating noses, and so on. The pleasure in this interaction was in the new malleability of images and of photographic 'reality'.

Huw used his digital camera and the image manipulation software within his computer in a different way and to great effect to complete his school Art homework. In this case, he was less 'playing with reality' than playing with visual imagery. First, he took a photograph of his room, he then loaded this into the computer. Using Photoshop, he reconfigured the picture by increasing the contrast, then turned the image into a line-drawing of his bedroom. Having done this, he then 'touched up' the lines that were incomplete or wavy, leaving him with a very polished black and white sketch of his bedroom – he submitted this for homework and received a high mark in Art for the first time ever. Interestingly, just as the children who used Encarta often felt that they needed to disguise their information sources when using these tools for schoolwork, so Huw felt that this use of the computer for homework was 'cheating'.

Int: Do you do art at school?
Huw: Yeah but I'm rubbish at it.
Int: You're rubbish at it.
Huw: Yeah, sorry. I can do art on the computer, that's easy. But when it comes to anything else like drawing, no. I haven't got the patience.
Int: So you don't feel embarrassed about being creative on the computer.
Huw: On the computer yeah. Yeah quite creative. I cheat at many other things as well.

Was Huw being creative? Was he cheating in his Art homework? We would suggest that the digital environments provided by the computer for drawing, for image manipulation and for design encourage the user to appropriate visual images, formats and layouts from a range of different sources. The user is encouraged to treat pre-existing photographs or drawings as the raw material for their own production. In this context, the images all achieve a degree of equivalence – whether using a repro-duction photograph of Van Gogh's sunflowers, a piece of clipart, or a photograph taken two days before – these images all become resources that can be copied, pasted, manipulated and redesigned within the digital environment. This is one of the key features of a digital landscape of rich information resources (whether textual or digital) and suggests that we might need to revisit our notions of what is and what is not 'cheating'. As Beavis (1998, p243) has argued:

> As literacy is redefined by the protean capacities of electronic verbal and visual text generation, questions are raised about virtually all our current concepts of text: of authorship and authority; of ownership, intellectual property, creativity, originality and identity; of reading and writing, production and reception, making and consuming; of access and power.

Arguably, we need to move beyond a notion of 'cheating' as anything not involving producing a representation 'from scratch' using pen and paper, towards a more elaborated description of the features of visual literacy that we might want to encourage. As Snyder has argued: 'being literate in the context of these technologies is to do with understanding how the different modalities are combined in complex ways to create meaning' (Snyder, 2001, p119). Understanding how the combination of different textual resources can be used to develop individual voices may then be an important feature of a new definition of 'literacy' today.

What was not in evidence amongst these young people, however, was any understanding of how, for example, tools such as Powerpoint or Photoshop, designed as they are for specific cultural practices and within specific cultural and commercial traditions, shape what it is or is not possible to make with these tools. Similarly, these young people had no framework within which to evaluate or critique the representations that these tools offer of the world around them. In sum, these representations and packages were used by these young people as 'neutral' tools, either badly or well designed to fit their needs.

In the home, arguably, young people are primarily experimenting, exploring and testing out different types of interactions and representations. One would hope, however, that in school settings, these critical perspectives might be made available to children as useful resources, in order to enable them to reflect upon how the representations that surround them every day in an increasingly visual world shape and are shaped by particular social and cultural practices.

Exotic uses of the computer

As we have already mentioned, almost all of our case study children used the computer to write, to play games and to look up information, and large numbers were using the computer to design and play with visual images. In contrast, there was a range of activities on the computer that might be termed 'exotic',[12] in that very few of the children used the computer for these purposes. These included: using spreadsheets (2 children), programming on the computer (3 children), Web design (3 children), using edutainment software (5 children), sending emails and talking in chat rooms (4 children). Our surveys similarly highlighted these as unusual activities amongst the wider survey samples.

We could make the case that there is a range of technological and cultural factors that might contribute to the low frequencies of these activities. In the case of using spreadsheets and programming, foexample, we might argue that numeracy, as compared with language-based literacy, is rarely privileged within the home environment. Or again, as some commentators[13] have argued, that the shift towards a Windows-based computing environment actively discourages users from going 'beneath the surface' to explore the programming languages that shape the software.

In respect of the low uses of edutainment software, which although used by five of the children in the study, was, even then, used only infrequently by almost all of them, we might argue that children were actively attempting to protect their 'leisure time' from formal schooled activities. On the other hand, we might argue that the software environments offered in edutainment packages can rarely compete with more sophisticated and challenging mainstream games. As Steven, Helen's brother, put it:

> I had educational software for ages. When I was old enough to realise that there were better games out there I pestered my mum to get those better games. And she would say, 'You're not going to play on these games until you've had half an hour on this game.'
>
> (Steven, aged 13, Deanbridge)

In the case of Web design and email and chat room use, we can clearly see that the availability of Internet connections in the home and the cost of Internet usage played a role in determining which children would be able even to access the Internet. Similarly, email use requires that children are part of a culture in which there is, to put it simply, someone to write to. At the time of this study there were few children with sufficient friends also using email to encourage wide take up of this activity at home, particularly as mobile phone usage and text messaging were also booming activities at the time. Arguably, this has changed over the last two or more years, suggesting much higher uses of email in the home by children today. The low levels of Web design might also be attributed to wider societal and educational factors. In schools, according to our most recent survey, Web design remains the least prevalent use of computers, with over 80 per cent of children reporting *never* having used a computer for this activity.[14] At the same time, the Web is actively promoted in educational and marketing discourses as a site for shopping, and for getting access to information; the reciprocal discourse that promotes the Web as a site for children's own production and communication activities tends to be restricted only to sectors of the educational community promoting 'creative' or equitable uses of information and communications technologies.[15] As the interface for Web design becomes more user friendly, however, it is possible that, both in schools and at home, these practices might increase.

Diverse practices

Even within these 'exotic' uses of the computers, however, we can see clear differences between the children in this study. In respect of programming, for example, Huw and David were using the computer to design Web pages and, as a result, had to learn to use certain basic features of HTML in order to develop their sites. As David said:

> It takes maybe 15/20 minutes, I only do the coding if it crashes in the program. Because when you do the program it's just a case of putting Typing and it pops up.
>
> (David, aged 12, Deanbridge)

As a rule, however, this programming was incidental to their main activity of designing and communicating through text and images online. It was a question of learning specific 'bits' of programming needed at the time.

In contrast, Alistair was interested in programming *in its own right*. When we first met him, he was 9 years old, and had taught himself to program Q Basic and Visual Basic on his computer at home. Interestingly, he lived in a household in which there was a heavy emphasis on learning foreign languages and his father, who lived separately, was very interested in electronics. It also seemed important that Alistair was the child using the oldest computer in our sample; he only had access to an old daisy-wheel printer at home, and none of the CD-ROM, multi-media capabilities that many of the other children took for granted. Alistair, while he did play games and produce homework, could be described first and foremost as a programmer. He approached programming by setting himself a series of challenges to complete – in some cases this was as simple as designing a program to complete his Maths homework (a process which may have encouraged more complex mathematical understanding than the homework itself); in others, he wanted to see how he might program the computer to design beautiful images on the screen. In these environments, Alistair was interacting with a very different interface from those of other children in our study; he was operating within linear and hierarchical structures that required an understanding of sequence and a detailed engagement with the symbolic numeric languages of the program.

> This is a timer, it's activated, well it depends on the properties. This is the property window, this is the form of the window, the command button which says X, which doesn't actually do anything. The timer can be set to an interval and when you include the subroutine Timer then it will activate every … I think that's milliseconds. So every millisecond it draws a circle around a location on the screen.
>
> (Alistair, aged 9, Deanbridge)

Similarly, in respect of email use we see diverse practices emerging: where Helen and Simon were encouraged by their parents to send emails to their grandparents and wider family (and as a result quickly became bored), David and Huw used email as an integral part of their developing networks of technological support and within their peer groups. And again, in respect of edutainment software – while Karen enjoyed testing her knowledge of Maths and French against the computer, Maria explored language learning within an encyclopaedia alongside cultural narratives of different countries, while Simon saw learning about dinosaurs as both another game (in the Dinosaur Hunter software) and as an ongoing expansion of his interests in history.

As with other uses of the computer, then, in these more exotic activities, the children's interests and intentions were shaping the ways in which and purposes for which they decided to adopt, interpret and use the software environments.

Conclusion

Beyond category boxes

In this and the last chapter we have discussed children's use of the computer at home as though there were discrete boundaries between different activities. We have discussed, for example, writing, information seeking and Web design as though these were not linked as part of the same process; we have discussed games as though this were a discrete category from the processes involved in edutainment or from programming. In practice, however, such divisions did not exist in this way. Indeed, during the course of the study, we came to feel that it was almost meaningless to ask simply how children interact with, for example, the word-processing environment, or the digital encyclopaedia environments. This was for three reasons. First, because, as we have discussed, many of these different resources now encourage increasingly multi-modal forms of interpretation and communication, making a nonsense of talking about 'writing', 'reading' and 'design' as distinct processes. Second, because characteristics of interaction in these environments often overlap. For example, three-dimensional design in computer aided design (CAD), has many similarities with three-dimensional games play in Theme Hospital; synthesising different resources was a characteristic both of researching and designing on the computer. Finally, because in the process of an activity many of the children tended to adopt a multiple 'window' strategy in their computer use, in which they toggled from one software package to another to combine the resources of different environments. The completion of a homework report, for example, may be written in one environment, information sought from another, then the images manipulated in a third, before being incorporated into the written text, and finally transformed within a desktop publishing environment. To attempt to discuss children's activities within discrete category boxes, then, seems increasingly inappropriate.

Arguably, these overlapping practices developed because children's use of the computer was driven by a particular activity or interest, rather than by a desire to develop particular 'skills'. It was clear, for example, that young people were almost never 'using a piece of software'; rather they were involved in a particular activity, such as games play, or writing a story, or designing a garden, or doing their homework. We never heard the children talk about doing 'word-processing' or 'desktop publishing' or 'making spreadsheets'. Indeed, if we reflect upon our own, adult, computer use, this would seem sensible. When at work, we are rarely 'using the wordprocessor' or 'spreadsheet'; we are writing reports, doing the accounts, figuring out design problems or writing up 'to do' lists. The common assumption that children's activities can indeed be separated out into distinct domains may be a result of the perception of children as 'becoming' rather than 'being'; as being in preparation for a world of work for which they may need distinct 'skills sets', rather than already being engaged in meaningful activities. Through studying children's use of the computer at home and their daily practices and interests we became aware that these sorts of separations into distinct domains are increasingly problematic.

It was in observing David's use of the computer that these overlapping practices embedded within authentic and meaningful activity was most apparent. David produced a magazine at home, published four times a year. In this process, we saw the boundaries between image and text, between different software environments and between 'original source' and reconfigured new resource, being blurred. David, in the course of producing this magazine, drew on a range of different software packages – FrontPage Express, Publisher, Outlook, Explorer, Word, Encarta. His information resources for advice on how to produce his magazine included the Web, online chat rooms, friends (via email and in person), telephone help desks, manuals borrowed from school, advice from his father (who lived 150 miles away), from staff in the school and from computer magazines.

David's magazine included 20–30 pages of text and images and actively drew from the cultural 'templates' of existing publishing formats, reflecting the overall structure of front pages, contents pages, letters pages and quizzes, combined with features and lists that are the staple of many teenage magazines. Similarly, he formatted the whole magazine broadly in accordance with dominant publishing styles, using columns, headers, and even classified advertisement sections; he also incorporated some features of Web publishing, such as banner advertisements on the bottom of pages. The text he included in the magazine itself was drawn from similarly diverse sources. He commissioned much of it from friends, wrote some himself, talked a teacher into contributing articles, and required his sister and wider family to contribute. These sat alongside documents downloaded from the Web – from government documents, from chat rooms, from pop music Websites. His images were a similar combination of self-produced photographs, clipart and Web-sourced or magazine-sourced pictures. These, however, were not simply included in their original format, but were often redesigned, manipulated or combined to fit the context. On completion of his magazine every three months, he also used newsgroups and chat rooms to advertise it back out to the Web communities he spent most time in.

Within these myriad practices David achieved a form of 'bricolage',[16] shaping and juxtaposing pre-existing resources to create a unique representation of his views of important issues in life – from getting through school exams, to pop stars, to government legislation on new technologies. Arguably, in the process of making this magazine he was beginning to participate in the practice of 'shaping social futures' and, at the same time, shaping and carving out his own identity. While we recognise that David was the highest user of computers in our study, this extreme case points out the difficulties of separating out children's activities into discrete 'category boxes'; instead it requires that we pay close attention to how these practices develop in conjunction with children's daily lives and interests. It is therefore to this aspect of children's computer use at home we will now turn in the next three chapters, away from the detailed interactions with the screen and the family, and towards the experiences of these children as individuals, developing their own personal identities in the digital age.

Part IV

Digital cultures

Chapter 7

Computers, consumption and identity

Across the world, children have entered a passionate and enduring love affair with the computer. What they do with computers is as varied as their activities. The greatest amount of time is devoted to playing games, with the result that names like Nintendo have become household words. They use computers to write, to draw, to communicate, to obtain information. Some use computers as a means to establish social ties, while others use them to isolate themselves. In many cases their zeal has such force that it brings the word addiction to the minds of concerned parents.

(Papert, 1993: p.ix)

In this and the next two chapters we want to explore what it means for young people to be growing up in a world where computers are routinely part of their everyday lives; what it means to have a 'digital childhood'. As we argued in the opening chapter, in recent years many commentators[1] have argued that computer mediated technologies are changing childhood; that they are establishing entirely new subjectivities and identities for young people. But is this really so? Does the very existence of the computer in the home mean that young people are somehow different from children a generation ago? Our aim in these three chapters is to explore this issue, mapping the ways in which childhood is and is not changing; the way it is lived by the young people we worked with, in a world where access to computer-based technologies is now almost ubiquitous. In this chapter we focus particularly on the issue of computers and identity, exploring what computers came to mean in the lives of the young people we researched. In the next chapter we look at the influence of gender and class on children's computer use and in the final chapter of this section we examine the evidence for the impact of factors such as globalisation and commercialisation on childhood.

Consumption and identity

> As the child learns to shop it also learns to be a particular sort of child.
> (Kenway and Bullen, 2001, p35)

One useful way of understanding what the computer means in children's lives is to see computer use as a form of 'consumption'. Children using a computer in the home, for example, may be participating in consumption in a variety of ways – both directly, through purchasing, or encouraging their parents to purchase, hardware, software and the peripherals that surround contemporary computer use (magazines, toys, etc.); and indirectly, in their 'consumption' and 'reproduction' of the meanings that the computer, as a medium for information and representations, offers.

As Kenway and Bullen (2001) note, there are two rather different ways of considering the impact of consumption on children. Some authors represent consumer culture as an implacable force which has shaped history, society and individual identities over the past two centuries, in which mass-produced representations of the world shape the ways in which we come to know it.[2] On the other hand, a rather different point of view suggests that we as consumers take these representations and meanings and *remake* them to meet our own needs and interests; in other words we engage in our own day-to-day acts of production.[3] These different approaches offer very different views of children as consumers – as passive or creative.

For us, seeing children's computer use as a form of consumption is helpful because of the potential relationship between consumption and the production of children's identities. According to Giddens (1991), a central feature of contemporary life can be seen to be the self-conscious concern with the development and expression of our own identities, what he calls 'life politics'. All of us, he argues, are to greater and lesser degrees concerned with a form of 'self-assembly'; taking control of the shape of our own lives by negotiating a particular self-identity. In a world of consumer products, such as computers, Giddens argues that the act of consumption itself contributes many of the resources through which we fashion our personal and public identities.

In a similar vein, Lury (1996) argues that contemporary Euro-American societies are characterised by the strongly rooted belief that 'to have is to be'. She argues that people increasingly define themselves and others in terms of the things they possess and use. As a result, 'possessions have come to serve as key symbols for personal qualities, attachments and interests' (p7). Consumption from this point of view therefore is not just about economics. In contemporary society, people, she argues, are increasingly coming to think of themselves, to construct their identities, at least in part through the objects they buy and use in their everyday lives.

According to this line of argument, consumer goods, such as computers, can come to play this role because they are themselves 'drenched with meanings'; as such, they can potentially act as 'totems' in the modern world, communicating distinct social identities and symbolising participation within or differences from other social groups.[4] The computer, as we have seen in earlier chapters, can symbolise many different things: its owners' participation in the 'modern world', concern for children's welfare, access to the future, a mundane object for daily living. And yet, this process is not straightforward – the 'meanings' attached to an object (for example, a computer or particular game) are not static; they change over time. Today's 'cutting edge' computer game can move, sometimes in a very short period of time, to be seen as redundant and then later revived as 'retro'. Moreover, mass consumption offers up the possibility of combining a range of different items in the creation of our identities, creating meaning through the juxtaposition of different products in a process that has been called 'bricolage'.[5] The computer may be attached to one set of meanings, and yet its juxtaposition with different items, different acts of consumption, can serve to produce distinct identities for their individual user.

What is the significance of these arguments for understanding children's computer use? We have found them useful in that they allow us to ask what role, if any, the computer plays in the identities being constructed by young people today. As we will see, in contrast to arguments put forward by some commentators,[6] we found that the meanings attributed to computer ownership and use by young people are by no means fixed; the plasticity of computer-based technologies supports the development of a wide range of different identities. It can mean very different things to different children: for some it is central, for others it is entirely irrelevant; for some it can, for example, support the development of a particular form of femininity while for others its meanings are essentially male. Below we focus on four of our case study children who illustrate something of the diversity of meanings information and communications technologies (ICTs) may have in young people's lives. We then, in subsequent chapters, go on to consider the range of cultural and other resources that allowed them to exploit these meanings in the particular ways they did.

Nerds, boffs and other enthusiasts

Int: Do any of you ever get [called] computer nerds?
Joe: No.
Huw: Me!
Joe: I just get called a boff, a boff child.
Huw: Computer boffs, that's the word we've got.

(Interview with Huw and friends, aged 13, Pen-y-Bryn)

For some of our young people, it became clear that the computer was central to their identity; they literally 'lived through' the computer. The computer was so important for Huw, David, Alistair, Karen and Faezal, for example, that each of them was jokingly called a 'computer nerd' or 'boff' by their friends during our group interviews. Each of them was highly technologically literate and each spent a large part of their free time logged onto the computer. Interestingly, being called a 'computer nerd' or a 'boff' was not an identity that these young people were always unhappy with. As we will see, their expertise provided them with an important space in and through which they were able to explore and express themselves.

David was a case in point. David was selected as a case study because, as we discussed in the previous chapter, of all of the 855 children across eight schools who completed our questionnaire, he emerged as the individual using the computer the most at the age of 12. Being proficient at the computer was central to his identity; it was something that he constantly worked at and was proud to display at school and to us as researchers.

David was born into a technological household in that his father, who worked in computers, had already had several home computers by the time David was born. David's parents separated when he was quite young and the family had no computer at all for a while. However, while still at primary school in Deanbridge, David started using an old second-hand computer his mother had acquired from a neighbour. As she explained, 'He was so enthusiastic. He used it as a tool … he preferred to write on the computer rather than write with a pen and paper.'

By the time he was 12, David was occupying a place in the family as ICT expert. When they came to buy a new computer shortly before we met the family, it was David who took the lead in deciding what to buy.

> I subscribe to a PC magazine, so I looked through there and found all the ones with specifications I liked and then we looked for the best price.

(David, aged 12, Deanbridge)

During the 18 months we got to know David, he was spending several hours every evening and a large part of his weekends working on the computer. The main focus for his work was the production of a teenage magazine called *CO2*. As we discussed in Chapter 6, this magazine was published four times a year with a readership of around 30 family and school friends; the magazine was usually 20–30 sides of A4 paper with commissioned articles, jokes and commentary from David himself as editor. *CO2* gave David a focus, and, more importantly, a legitimacy for his computer work. If he was working on it, he was allowed to spend hours every week downloading images, laying out text, editing commissioned articles and writing articles himself.

As with other technologically able children we met, school was a key context for the display of David's expertise.

Int: Right. What do they think of you at school? Are you the mad professor?

David: I'm not quite the mad professor, I'm sort of the person that everyone knows gets all the questions right. So it's the person that everyone asks with 5 minutes left of lunchtime, 'Could you do my homework for me?'

(David, aged 12, Deanbridge)

He frequently found himself called on by teachers and other pupils to sort out computer problems, and as an ongoing task, he had also volunteered to put into hypertext mark-up language (HTML) format every back edition of the school magazine.

> What I'm doing here is putting in the back numbers of the school magazine. I'm laying them all out using Publisher but I've got the same text, I'm typing it all in. We've got up to 56 volumes and I've got back to 51 …
>
> (David, aged 12, Deanbridge)

As a result of this work and his general expertise, David had been given special privileges at school; he took computer classes with pupils two years older than himself (taking an 'AS Level' rather than 'GCSE Level' course) and had been given access to the Internet.

> Most kids aren't allowed access to their email without school supervision even though they've got it. That's up until Year 9, but I've been given it because I've also got access to the Internet … It's only me.
>
> (David, aged 12, Deanbridge)

As a young teenager, David was relatively retiring. Although sociable, he seemed to have few close friends and (despite encouragement from his mother) was not particularly good or even interested in sports or other outdoor activities. In this regard he was not dissimilar from some of the other computer enthusiasts that we met such as Karen or Alistair. All three of them, through their particular approach to the 'consumption' of technology, had developed public and personal identities as computer experts, yet none of them seemed particularly well integrated to a strong group of friends at school.

It seemed to us that the attraction of developing this sort of identity for these children came from their appropriation of the symbolic power of the computer itself. Through his expertise, David gained the unusual privilege of moving easily between the world of childhood and adults. In his home he was the undisputed expert and both his mother and his younger sister looked to him to sort out their computing problems and to help develop their own expertise; taking the lead in this aspect of family life was something that David particularly enjoyed doing. Perhaps more unusually, given the traditional hierarchies of schooling, David's knowledge was respected by his teachers too. He was much more technically competent than most of them and the recognition of his abilities was reflected in the special privileges he had been granted. His peers too found that they often needed his expertise to sort out problems in the classroom or to give advice on their home computers.

In all aspects of his life, therefore – home, school and peer group – David, through computing, was able to achieve a far greater authority and respect than would otherwise have been possible for him. Unlike most other popular cultural forms available to teenagers, the social significance of the computer makes it a universally powerful symbolic tool to command. For David, it seems, the benefits of developing himself as an expert far outweighed the disadvantages of occasionally being teased as a computer nerd.

The computer as bricolage

Constructing an Anglo-Asian identity

All of the young people we chose to work with as case studies were moderate or high users of ICT at home – all of them were more than competent. However, just because they were competent with the technology did not mean that they necessarily consumed it in a way that implied it was central to their identities. Several of our young people were highly technologically literate but saw the computer as relatively marginal to their lives; it was something that they used selectively, either as a straightforward tool or in a way that fitted in with a particular 'story' they were developing for and about themselves. For these young people, the computer was just one of a range of cultural resources available to them in building their identities. In other words they were engaged in what de Certeau (1988), following Levi-Strauss (1966), calls 'bricolage': taking what lay to hand (in this case the computer) and selectively reinter-preting or reassigning its symbolic meanings for their own purposes. Jamilla illustrated this approach to using technology particularly well.

Jamilla was 12 when we first met her and living in Pandy. She was a member of a Muslim family with a British-born Asian mother and a father who was born in Pakistan. She was the second of five children with an older sister, aged 14, one younger brother of nine and two younger sisters of seven and five. Her mother was raised in Glasgow, though English was still her second language. Perhaps significantly in terms of her aspirations for her children's education, her mother told us that she considered that her own education was incomplete in that when she was 15, her parents had taken her out of school to return to Pakistan. She was now a full-time housewife and spent most of her time looking after her substantial family. Jamilla's father was a taxi driver working nights. He too was strongly committed to the family and his children's education but because of his working hours his time with the family was often limited.

Jamilla's interests and hobbies made her typical of many teenage girls. She was interested in boy bands, romance and shopping for clothes and makeup. Her choice of TV programmes reflected these interests: Top of the Pops, CD UK, Alive and Kicking, EastEnders. And while her brothers read computer magazines, she read *Bliss*, *Sugar* and *Smash Hits*.

Jamilla was a member of a group of girls with a very strong friendship; they walked to school together, talked for hours on the phone, visited each others' homes and sometimes went out together in the evenings and weekends. From her description, it seems that much of her days, both in school and out, were spent with these friends talking about the same things – boys, pop music, TV and shopping.

In addition to this, however, her family's religious and cultural back-ground informed her day-to-day life equally as strongly as her participation in dominant teenage cultures. For example, much of her social life was based in her home or in the homes of her friends who were also Muslim and whom her parents knew; she was seldom allowed out at night and when she and her friends went into the city centre for shopping, Jamilla's mother took them there herself in the car even though it was less than a mile away.

What came through our discussions with Jamilla was her interest in developing a lifestyle for herself that could accommodate both the demands of her particular cultural background and her interest in contemporary teenage life. She seemed particularly keen, for example, to use clothes and other items in a way that would allow her to cross the boundaries between the two cultures she inhabited.

Jamilla: Um, if it's at a wedding we wear saris because you know like everyone's wearing them. But if it's like … if I go to the park or something I'd usually wear like trousers and all that, jeans or something …

Int: Where did you get your clothes you're wearing now?

Jamilla: Um this, they sell it separately. It's just material and you have to buy how many yards and then we went on holiday to Pakistan last year and I got this sewn there. I bought the material from here but I sewed it over there.

(Jamilla, aged 12, Pandy)

Like many girls of her age, she had recently had her nose pierced but wore a gold sleeper which she had bought in Pakistan; the bangles she wore, though purchased in Pakistan, were also available in local shops. She was also experimenting with henna on her hands as a product that was both traditional and highly fashionable in Britain:

Int: That's lovely. How did you learn how to do that then?

Jamilla: My mum just done them. You know. It takes a lot of hard work … So like she did it like really delicate designs and all that.

(Jamilla, aged 12, Pandy)

Jamilla therefore actively constructed herself as a modern Anglo-Asian teenager. Like the young women Dwyer (1998) and Gillespie (1995) have described, she was constructing a 'new ethnicity' for herself as a modern Anglo-Asian teenager. She was confident and competent both in the dominant popular culture of her age group and in her particular religious and cultural world.[7] Moreover, her parents, and particularly her mother, seemed happy to support her in her strategy for accommodating her two worlds. But where did the computer fit into this particular identity?

Both of Jamilla's parents were strongly supportive of their children developing expertise on the computer – for conventional reasons (because 'everything's computer now') and because they saw it as fitting in well with their lives as Muslims. This is Jamilla's mother describing the decision to purchase the computer:

> At last I thought, why not? Why not? It's for the small ones as well, they use it as well. It's a good pastime, because I'm so busy I don't have time to take them out … we don't have much social life, you see, because we're strict Muslims as well.
>
> (Jamilla's mother, Pandy)

Jamilla herself was competent with the computer. She could access a wide range of software and regularly used the computer for homework and was proud of the fact that it allowed her to hand in very well-presented work. As she explained about a book cover she had illustrated with clipart 'It looks more effective.' She was also proud of the fact that, at school, she could help friends who were less competent than herself. At home she used the computer for both work and entertainment. However, she was very clear about what sort of activities she did and did not like; she particularly did not like conventional computer games – something that her younger brother was obsessed with.

> No I don't bother with stuff like that. I'm not interested in things like that. Blokestone, Aliens of Gold. With lots of big blokes running around with guns … I'm just not into it because it's like shooting and stuff and it's boring.
>
> (Jamilla, aged 12, Pandy)

However, a CD that was concerned with beauty advice was an entirely different matter. In this extract, the interviewer and Jamilla were sitting at her computer in the front room downstairs:

Int: The Elle Beauty Guide. All right. Let's have a look at that.

Computer: This is what we do for Elle, try out lipsticks, test new creams, smell new perfumes, even powder our noses. Every day we ask ourselves the same questions as you do … 'Why is my skin changing?' 'Which is the best anti-wrinkle cream?' … To find the answers to all these questions we went to the pros, the scientists, the people in the laboratory …

Int: So things on applying foundation, a glamorous mouth. A glamorous mouth. Okay. Oh so we've got a little video clip have we? So it shows you what to do. Oh, so it shows you

> how to fill it in … Right so how often do you go on this
> then?
>
> *Jamilla:*   At first when we first got it I went on it quite a lot, and then
> my friends wanted to go on it.
>
> *Int:*   So did your girlfriends come over and you had a look at it
> did you? You did it all together.
>
> *Jamilla:*   Yeah.
>
> (Jamilla, aged 12, Pandy)

After school, Jamilla and her friends regularly attended the computer club as this gave them the chance to get onto the Internet. But again this was accessed in a way that was relevant to their particular identities and interests.

> *Int:*   So you're going on the Internet then, is it mainly to shop or is
> it for any other things? You were saying about the music you
> can buy.
>
> *Jamilla:*   No, because me and her, we're the same culture but they're
> different, so we learn about some Arabic words … And we
> hear their music … Or traditional clothes.
>
> (Jamilla, aged 12, Pandy)

Jamilla was certainly competent on the computer, more so than many of her peers. She was able to play a wide range of games, to work with photographs and was particularly good at using the computer for writing and for looking things up on digital encyclopedias. And as we have indicated, she was proud of her abilities. However, using the computer was in no way central to the identity she was constructing for herself; her central focus was elsewhere. Rather than building an identity *through* the computer as David did, for Jamilla, the computer was simply one cultural resource amongst many that she employed in the construction of herself as a 'modern Anglo-Asian teenager'. She seemed well aware of the computer's symbolic power within school and amongst her peers. In school she used it to present herself as both competent and modern and she believed that the skills she had developed would serve her well in her future life at work which was 'all computers now'. But as we have seen, at the ages of 12, 13 and 14, Jamilla's primary concerns were rather different and she was able to 'consume' the computer in a way that supported the distinctive bi-cultural identity she was developing for herself.

The computer as 'natural'

Play and childhood in a digital home

In both of the cases we have discussed so far, young people were deliberately using the computer as part of the development of their own identities. For David, it was central; to an important degree, he seemed to 'live through' the computer. For Jamilla it was less significant but remained a valuable resource in constructing her identity.

However, the computer was not always consumed in such a deliberate way. For some of our case study children, and particularly the younger ones, it seemed less marked as a cultural resource; something that fitted 'naturally' into their lives alongside other forms of entertainment and other tools for school and for play. Helen, who was 9 when we first met her, was particularly interesting from this point of view in that she lived in a strongly technological family.

Helen's parents were both professionally involved with computers. Her mother was the technician at the local secondary school in Deanbridge but she also taught computer literacy to adults and had recently begun to run classes for teachers in her school as well. She thought of herself mainly as a 'computer user' rather than a technical person.

> I mean there's two different kinds of people. Everybody drives a car but doesn't necessarily know how it works. (LAUGHTER) Although I know more technical stuff, I consider myself as a user rather than a technical person, whereas you [Dad] are definitely a technical person, you know how computers work.
>
> (Helen's mother, Deanbridge)

In fact, she was much more than a user; she had learned to program in Pascal and, as we saw on several occasions during our visits, was a highly proficient troubleshooter. Her expertise was, however, different from Helen's father who was involved in the technical side of computers. Largely self-taught, her father had now got a job 'where his hobby has become his career'. As Helen wryly commented, 'If he didn't have computers his life wouldn't be worth living.'

Helen also had an older brother, Steven (aged 12), with whom she was highly competitive and constantly fighting. Steven was an avid games player and spent much of his free time playing networked games – so much so that his parents had recently begun to be concerned about it. All in all, it was therefore a highly computer literate household. As Helen explained 'Yeah. Well if Steven didn't exist (oh please!) then we would have a computer anyway because my mum and dad are just bonkers about them.'

The house itself was saturated with ICTs. As Helen's mother put it: 'This house is growing computers at the rate of knots at the moment.' At the start of the project there were two upstairs, one with a printer that was networked to another computer in the dining room, which 'is supposed to be the children's computer, but Mum uses it as well'. Mum also had a laptop. Though the big computer upstairs was primarily for Dad, it was also used by other members of the family on occasions, for printing and as a TV. There were many other technologies too: cable TV, mobile phones, pagers, 'And we've got lots of music things all around. I think in every single room apart from … the toilet and the bathroom.' By the conclusion of the project, the family had at least six computers in the home.

To an important degree, therefore, life for Helen at home meant living and talking computers. Even though she did not always understand everything that was being discussed, 'computer talk' was often the medium through which the family interacted with each other.

> I sit at the dinner table when they're talking about the things they did at work and I think 'Oooh, what on earth are they talking about?' I listen to them, I try to understand it, but then the very next day I forget it all. If I'm told what a motherboard is one day, the next day Mum asks me what a motherboard is and I haven't a clue.
>
> (Helen, aged 9, Deanbridge)

However, in reality, a great deal did actually 'rub off' on Helen. She may have been the least competent in her own family, but compared with boys and girls of her age she was highly computer literate. She routinely used Publisher for her homework and used the Internet. At the time of our visits, she had also started designing a Web page for herself, gaining inspiration from the Web page her mother was currently developing for her school.

Games were particularly important for Helen. Interestingly, she enjoyed both 'shoot 'em up' games as well as strategy games. However, her two current favourites were Age of Empires and Creatures – a game which involved looking after 'virtual' creatures:

Int: And how would you describe Creatures then if you had to describe it?

Helen: It's sweet, because you get to teach all these creatures how to do things … That's Lauren, she gave birth to Bengy … They can talk to you and you can talk to them. You can teach them things. When they're very old they can learn how to control things like the computer which Lauren can't do at the moment. But when she gets to about 2 hours she probably could.

(Helen, aged 9, Deanbridge)

What sort of girl was Helen and how then did this computer use fit into her life more generally? A highly social girl with a strong group of friends, she described herself as the 'giggly', 'funny' type; it was certainly noticeable how much she entered into all sorts of activities with the same sense of fun and enthusiasm.

Int: Okay. So what are the main things you do with your time outside school?
Helen: I play on the computer, I listen to music, I read, I go outside in the summer and if it's not the summer I'll watch the telly.

(Helen, aged 9, Deanbridge)

Her mother confirmed that she was an avid book reader, *Danny the Champion of the World* and *The Suitcase Kid* were current favourites. 'At night … I have to keep peeking up here and making sure that she's actually switched the light off and gone to sleep.' She also played the violin and the mandolin and had recently sung in a large concert. As she explained: '[I like music] I can bob about to. I cannot sit still to music that I like. And with my violin I like playing songs that I know.'

As in her computer world, a significant proportion of the activities she engaged with were commercially available forms of consumption. She loved shopping and had high expectations about being able to own the latest toys. The current fad was for Beanie Babies:

You know. It's just a sudden craze. You know like yo-yos. Everybody got suddenly into them and had to have a yo-yo. And now everybody's got suddenly into Beanie Babies and has to have a Beanie Baby. That one was bought in Florida for me.

(Helen, aged 9, Deanbridge)

However, not everything was commercially produced. In summer, she loved being out of doors and, as with other children, this was seen as standing in marked opposition to the world of computers.

Int: If you had to make a choice between going outside ... if you had to give up one thing – going outside, telly or computer, what would you give up?

Helen: Oh, uh, hard. Computer. Sad to say it but yes. Going outside I love. Just now I climbed a tree with my friends and we walked about, we followed someone.

(Helen, aged 9, Deanbridge)

Computers then were very much part of Helen's life, a part of the consumer world she lived in, but no more nor less important than many other childhood activities. As she said when asked if she and her friends talked much about computers at school: 'Yes ... but we complain about the teachers much much more than we talk about computers!'[8]

The computer as 'other'

> They're all right, but you've got to have a life other than computers really.
>
> (13-year-old boy, 'low user' interview, Saxingham)

Our final example is from children for whom the computer was either irrelevant or was seen in opposition to the sort of identity they were developing for themselves. A number of the young people we met as part of studying children specifically selected as part of our 'low and ambivalent users' group fell into this category, but, interestingly, so too did Stephanie, one of our case study children.

Stephanie was nine when we first met her. She lived in the countryside a few miles outside Saxingham with her father, mother and one older sister aged 13. Her father was an agricultural worker and they lived in a farm cottage next to the dairy sheds where he worked; her mother had recently returned to work as a receptionist in the local dentists.

Stephanie was selected as a case study because she identified herself on our questionnaire as a 'moderate' user. However, when we met the family six months later, her parents immediately insisted that no one in the family used the computer very much:

> I'll say now from the start, we hardly use it. We're more outdoor people really aren't we?
>
> (Stephanie's mother, Saxingham)

The family had bought the computer for Christmas three years previously but it had not been working consistently since they had had it. Initially it had taken several weeks to get it set up and recently, after they moved house, it was not set up again for five months. At the time we met the family, the colour printer was no long working (because Mum had fiddled with the 'dip switch') and there was a problem with the sound.

The financial investment necessary to buy the computer in the first place was considerable and, initially, Stephanie's mother had not been keen.

Father: Julie thought they were too young to mess about with it to start with didn't you? You were afraid they were going to muck it up or whatever.

Mother: Yeah I was. They did something with it once and I had to ring up the helpline to reboot it and he talked me through how to do it again and they done something again and I've got to reboot it again. I don't know how to do it. I should ring up and find out how to do it again.

(Stephanie's father and mother, Saxingham)

Three years on, Stephanie's mother was still concerned about the children's breaking the computer and as a result Stephanie and her sister were only allowed to use it under supervision. Their range of activities was quite limited. Stephanie had a few games she liked playing – she particularly liked the Lion King which came as a demo with the computer – and she occasionally wrote letters. She also used one or two educational games designed to help her with spelling, science and maths and would sometimes play these with her father. However, the computer did seem to go wrong quite frequently and Stephanie had not learned how to manage its idiosyncrasies: 'Yeah I fiddle around and then I get fed up and I turn it off and go off in a temper.'

Despite identifying herself as a moderate user on our questionnaire, it was clear that the computer was only of marginal importance in Stephanie's life. Her interests were elsewhere. She was very keen on sport:

I play quite a few games … I'm on the hockey team, I've played rounders, I play cricket during school … I do quite a lot …

(Stephanie, aged 9, Saxingham)

But Stephanie's real passion was the farm and working with animals.

I come home. On Monday, Clare … my mum, or mum's friend, she picks me up and I normally play with Tilly for about an hour or two

..., I walk the dog, the spaniels, then I go over to the farm over there where Tilly's nan and granddad live. And Tilly's always over there. We play on the tractors and stuff ... little toy ones.

(Stephanie, aged 9, Saxingham)

She also regularly helped her father with the cows – milking, cleaning out the stalls – and had even carried out an artificial insemination and helped with a caesarean. When she left school her ambition was to be a vet.

Country life – looking after the cows, going to shows, going beating during the shooting season – all of these activities were seen as in opposition to the computer. For Stephanie, the computer was identified as an indoor activity and as a form of entertainment. Like the television which she liked, the computer was something to be engaged with for relaxation purposes only; she did not see it as helping her engage with the most important things in her life.

Interestingly, many of these views were shared by young people in our 'low and ambivalent users' group. The construction of the computer as an indoor activity was a common one. It was therefore seen by some of these young people as being in opposition to sports and to other outdoor activities.

Int: Does it make any difference to you not having a computer?
Girl: Well, it doesn't make any difference to me because I go riding every night after school anyway and friends come round anyway, and I've got quite a lot of friends, so it doesn't make any difference to me, no.

(Girl, aged 11, Saxingham)

Boy: I use it every now and again, as I said I'd rather be out with my friends playing football or out on my bike, more active like that than ...

(Boy, aged 13, Pen-y-Bryn)

Conclusion

Computers therefore came to mean very different things in the lives of the young people we met in our research. As an object, the home computer, at present at least, is a very powerful and complex cultural symbol; it is, to use Featherstone's (1991) term, 'drenched' with a wide range of different meanings – by manufacturers, by society, by families and by young people themselves. By 'consuming' the computer in particular ways our case study children were therefore able to use it in the construction of very different identities. Of course, David, Jamilla, Helen and Stephanie in no way represent all of the different ways in which the home computer can be used. Each of our case study children had their own particular identity that they were forging; each of them therefore consumed the computer in different ways. What these four case studies do indicate however is something of the *range* of different meanings computers can have for young people: from central to irrelevant, from strongly marked 'resource' to 'natural'.

Yet we also have to recognise that the meanings assigned to any domestic technology change over time. Today the home computer may well be a powerful cultural symbol that everyone has to respond to in some way – either negatively or positively. But as ownership and use becomes ubiquitous, it is unlikely to retain this powerful position. It may therefore be that Helen is the best predictor of the future. As we have seen, for Helen, the computer was no different from other domestic technologies like the telephone, television, or the motor car; it was simply a normal part of her everyday life. What Helen highlights is that the historical period where owning and using a computer at home is central to many young people's identities may well be a short-lived one.

Chapter 8

Computers, gender and class

In the last chapter we saw how the computer could have very different meanings for young people in their day-to-day lives; we argued that the plasticity and complexity of the computer as a symbolic object in contemporary society means that it can be 'consumed' in an almost infinitely variable number of ways; it can be used to support a whole variety of different sorts of identity.

But given that it can have such variable meanings, what is it that influences young people in their particular interpretations? How is it that the domestic computer appears 'natural' to some and alien to others. How is it that for some children it is seen as no more than a sophisticated games machine, while for others it becomes an object for supporting creative production or a technology to be mastered as an end in itself?

One way of considering such questions is to examine the influence of two key factors in the 'structuration' of young people's lives – gender and class. Giddens (1984) developed the concept of 'structuration' to draw attention to the fact that features of social life such as gender and class, which are often referred to by sociologists as 'social structures', are not in fact external objects that have a life of their own. Rather, social structures are, at one and the same time, powerful sets of rules and sets of resources that we draw upon in our day-to-day lives. And it is by drawing on them, either wittingly or unwittingly, that we reproduce their significance in our lives and those of others.

To an extent then one might say that all of us are 'produced' by social structures such as gender and class, as they provide us with key resources in the identities we create for ourselves; they give us definitions of what we ought to do, be and feel. But when we use them as a resource, we are also reproducing them by acting them out and giving them a social reality.

In this chapter we want to explore how issues of gender and class entered into our young people's interpretations of information and communication technologies (ICTs); how these social structures helped to provide the rules and resources they used in assigning meaning to computers in their lives. In this sense, then, we want to ask how gender and class were in part 'lived' and reproduced through computer use. As we will see, both of these factors were extremely powerful in influencing children's interpretations; they were also highly complex and multifaceted.

Gender and ICT

Int: So where do you all ... like you help each other out but where do you all get your information from? Do you get it ... like in school who do you get information from?

Girl: Maybe from school from the networks you know here and sometimes from the boys, when they're talking like 'Oh what did you say? How do you do that?' and they're saying 'wa wa wa wa wa' and we're like 'wa wa wa wa wa'.

Int: So they're talking about stuff and you go ...

Girl: Yeah we're eavesdropping. (LAUGHTER)

Int: But why do you not join in the conversations?

Girl: Well because it's all the boys (INAUDIBLE) conversation.

(Interview with Maria and friends, aged 14, Saxingham)

The history of the how computers have become incorporated into social life is a history rich with complexity. This is because, as Murdock *et al.* (1992) have pointed out, there is 'continual cultural struggle over the meaning of the machine and its appropriate uses'(p146). Central to these 'struggles' are those based around gender.[1] Computers enter already gendered worlds and in this section of the chapter we want to look at those gendered worlds and the ways in which they come to influence the meanings computers have for young people. What we have come to recognise through our research is that the 'gendering' of computer practices operates at a variety of different levels. In public discourse amongst young people themselves, computer use, and particularly games playing, is often presented in strongly gendered terms. However, day-to-day reality is often more complex. As computers are becoming a more routine part of family, work and school life, gendered practices are, we found, becoming more complex and more differentiated.

Gender differences in access and use

The first question we need to ask is whether, overall, boys and girls access and use the computer differently and if so in what ways. And as we saw in Chapter 2, there is evidence from our own and other large scale surveys that they do indeed use them differently. What recent surveys reveal[2] is that although there is little difference between boys and girls in terms of presence of computers in their homes, boys are more likely than girls to own their own computers (50 per cent boys compared with 37 per cent girls) and higher numbers of boys than girls use the computer at home on at least a weekly basis (82 per cent compared with 74 per cent). Similarly there are some differences in terms of actual use of the computer for different activities, notably in games play, with 33 per cent of boys as opposed to 13 per cent of girls reporting daily games playing. While fewer girls report *never* using the computer for writing, for using charts/graphs, for making/designing, and for using educational software (>7 per cent), as a rule, boys are more frequent users of the computer across the full range of activities.[3]

The idea that girls and boys access and use computers differently was frequently articulated by our case study children and their friends. For example, Huw and his friends saw differences in terms of interest:

Int:　So do you find, by the way, that the girls are using it as much as the boys? Or not so much?

Boy:　I think boys are using them more.

Boy:　Boys are using them more now.

Int:　And are the girls going to be disadvantaged do you think?

Boy:　No girls are not that type of person you see.

Boy:　They're different. They just do their homework … these days as far as I know, my sister, she just does her homework. They're not into like looking with interest, they just want to go on it like, something you just get to type with. Don't think they're really interested in computers.

　　　　　(Interview with Huw and friends, aged 13, Pen-y-Bryn)

This difference in interest was confirmed by some of our girls too. For example, Heather and her friends thought there were differences too but they were to do with ways of engaging with the computer rather than actual interest.

Girl:　Boys don't have enough patience.

Girl:　No, if it was like a game, sort of games where you've got to like work it out with your brain, the boys like my brother, he'll go 'Oh I can't do this, stuff it, I don't want it'[…]

Girl:　If it's a shooting game, where you go bang, bang, bang, bang (INAUDIBLE).

Girl: Whereas with me it's like I last longer trying to get through it, and I'll find it more interesting.

Girl: My brother's just like really impatient. He likes all the like war games and shooting games and stuff.

(Interview with Heather and friends, aged 13, Deanbridge)

Several commentators have argued that another key difference between boys and girls is the social interaction that goes on around computers. McNamee (1998) and Tobin (1998), among others, have argued that young men construct friendships around specific activities which 'mediate' their social interactions; in other words, computer games and computer technology function as a means by which young men are 'allowed' to speak to each other. The exchange of cheats, games and computer expertise, it is argued, functions as a currency by which friendship is constructed, and which thereby prioritises these activities as masculine pursuits. Young women, on the other hand, it is argued, construct friendship as a subject for discussion and as an end in itself; the computer is therefore less important in 'doing' friendship (McNamee, 1998). Certainly our evidence supported the idea that, on the whole, computers were far more important for boys than girls in their social lives. Indeed as Holloway and Valentine (2003) noted, they were a key dimension of boys' socialising. As one of Samantha's friends put it: 'All they [boys] talk about is computers and games [...] we'd talk about more girlie stuff.'

Another key difference was that boys often saw the computer as an opportunity for the competitive display of their expertise. Indeed on many occasions girls complained about this aspect of boys' computer cultures which they found aggressive and undermining.

Int: Why wouldn't you ask them [for help]?

Girl: It's embarrassing.

Girl: Yeah they would probably think 'Oh, what ...'

Girl: They would boast, 'Oh I've got past that level, haven't you?' [...] 'I am superior.'

Int: Whereas you will tell each other will you?

Girls: Yeah.

Girl: For nothing.

(Interview with Helen and friends, aged 10, Deanbridge)

As other commentators have noted,[4] if not properly managed, this competitive behaviour can become unpleasant for girls, potentially silencing or excluding them from computer use. In a number of our families where there were boys and girls, parents found that they had to manage access if their sons were not going to dominate the computer (see chapter 4 for a discussion of this in more detail). A more extreme example happened in this school computer club which did not seem well managed in this regard.

Int: But is it mainly boys or girls at lunch time in the computer club?
Girl: Boys.
Girl: I'd say more boys.
Girl: Yeah they all like rushing. [...] And they push and shove you.
Girl: You know when the door, okay, and the teacher can't actually get in there and open the door. When they do like they're all like ... they're killing the teacher to get to the computer.
Girl: Yeah they trample over him, like.

(Group interview with Jamilla and friends, aged 13, Pandy)

Computer games and gender rivalries

Many of our discussions with children about gender differences centred on games and indeed it was in relation to games that the most marked gender differences were articulated. Again and again boys and girls would suggest that there were gender differences in the frequency and types of games play they enjoyed. In most cases, boys claimed they were better at games than girls. As Huw said,

> Boys are better at playing games on computers than girls, I have to say. I'm not sexist but it is true [...] Girls like socialising a lot I think and, not being sexist again, but make-up and stuff like that.
>
> (Huw, aged 12, Pen-y-Bryn)

And many boys showed a preference for particular sorts of games – what some girls referred to disparagingly as 'shoot 'em up' games.[5] Paul, Faezal, Tim, Simon, Jamilla's brother and Helen's brother, for example, all played on these sorts of games incessantly.

Int: Are there any games you play like this that you really like that aren't fighting.
Paul: No.
Int: They're all fighting games.
Paul: Yeah. All my favourites are fighting games.
Int: Go on, tell us why then?

Paul: I don't know. I don't like racing. And I don't really like football sports [...] And that's all that's left [...] I'm quite happy with these types of game. My favourite game's got to be Tekken.

(Paul, aged 12, Saxonbridge)

As one of Simon's friends graphically put it:

Girls like the softy pinky things, but we like blowing each other up and punching each other and killing each other and stabbing each other.

(Interview with Simon and friends, aged 10, Pen-y-Bryn)

Quite a number of our girls, on the other hand, expressed considerable hostility to violent games. We described in the last chapter how Jamilla really disliked her bother's 'shoot 'em up' games. Theresa and Karen had similar views, as did these friends of Heather's:

Girl: I play on more feminine games, not where you shoot each other and stuff.

Girl: I like where you've got like this little purse and you have to collect all these things and kill all these little baddies [...] I just like little adventure games. They're more comical and more funny and like, characteristic [...]

Girl: I like ones where you have to think a bit more. Because like often my brother can't (INAUDIBLE) bang, right, hitting thing, but shoot something, and I just think 'How boring.' I like ones where you have to like (INAUDIBLE) certain jumps to get onto certain bits.

Girl: Tomb Raider, like that.

Girl: And collect things like ... you have to collect ones, and you know like you have to go back, you have to go and then get extra gems or whatever. When you have to actually think about what you're doing.

(Interview with Heather and friends, aged 13, Deanbridge)

Public discussion about boys' and girls' abilities on the computer and particularly their abilities on computer games was therefore often highly gendered. Why was this the case?

Part of the explanation lies in the fact that games are often marketed in highly gendered terms. As Cassell and Jenkins (1998) have argued, while some computer and console games such as Sonic the Hedgehog, and Super Mario have always been marketed at both boys and girls, the majority are designed by and conceived for men and boys. More recently, they argue, a 'girls games' movement has emerged within the games industry as a result of 'an unusual and highly unstable alliance between feminist activists (who want to change the 'gendering' of digital technology) and industry leaders (who want to create a girl's market for their games)'.[6] This has resulted in the development of a range of different sorts of games – Barbie Fashion Designer, and Creatures, designed to appeal to girls or, in the case of Tomb Raider or The Sims, to both boys and girls.

Such marketing perhaps works because children live in such strongly gendered worlds – at home, at school and amongst their friends. Throughout our interviews, boys and girls showed that they were highly skilled at playing 'gender games': poking fun at the opposite sex or expressing outrage when teachers or others in authority appeared sexist. The computer, perhaps because of its symbolic importance in contemporary life, seemed to be a particularly rich resource for this sort of display; it provided a vehicle through which gender rivalries could be 'lived'.

Many of our group interviews themselves provided opportunities for this sort of banter. On numerous occasions an otherwise serious discussion would turn into an opportunity for making fun of the opposite sex.[7]

Girl: And I think that the boys just like when they go on the computer they think 'Oh yes, I can go on (INAUDIBLE) now, I can go on racing games' but girls would listen to the teachers and just look up information.

Girl: Yes, girls are sensible.

Girl: Yes, boys are crazy.

Girl: Boys are crazy.

Girl: Boys are insaniacs!

(Interview with Karen and friends, aged 10, Pen-y-Bryn)

School life for the 10–14-year-old is to an important degree lived in terms of gender rivalries and divisions;[8] the same is true in families too.[9] Relationships between brothers and sisters were often characterised by a mixture of rivalry and support and computer use entered into those complex relationships. As we discussed in Chapter 4, Helen had a particularly stormy relationship with her brother but she still turned to him to learn things.

Helen: And I was having a go at that and I couldn't get past this particular bit and I called Steven …

Steven: I did it in 30 seconds.
Helen: He did it in 30 seconds.
Int: Right. So if Steven shows you something …
Steven: He normally does it.
Int: He normally does it and then you carry on.
Helen: And then I carry on. Or he normally does it. He pushes me off and he goes the rest of the game. He does that a lot of the time.
(Helen, aged 9, and brother Steven, aged 12, Deanbridge)

Many other sibling relationships were similar, though perhaps less intense. Maria would get irritated by her younger brothers who always wanted to come into her bedroom to play games on the computer; however, she was still willing to support them in learning how to use the computer for other things. Jamilla derided her young brother's obsession with computer games but, like Helen, she would turn to him for technical advice when she needed it. David was on occasions rude about the fact that his younger sister was less competent than he was on the computer but he was also willing to help her learn. In many of these relationships, gender rivalries were an important dimension. Part of the reason David's sister was no good and needed help was 'because she was a girl'; Jamilla's brother was obviously obsessed at games 'because he was a boy'. Just as at school, sibling relationships were at least in part 'lived' in these stereotypical gendered terms.

Computers, gender and identity

The symbolic meanings attached to computers, we came to recognise, function on a number of different levels. In public discourse about computers, games playing, which itself is strongly gender marked, is particularly important. Perhaps because of this, the computer as a whole can at times be seen in gendered terms; it can be constructed as more of a boys' than a girls' medium. This 'public gendering' of the computer was often supported by the sexist behaviour and attitudes of boys both at home and at school.[10] Yet in reality, the relationship between gender and computer use was much more complex than this.

For example, some girls, like this friend of Jamilla's, privately admitted liking 'boys' games' – especially violent ones:

Girl: I play Streetfighter down my cousin's house and I just like if I beat anyone I just love it (LAUGHTER) […] I just like the fighting ones […] I like it when they say the little words. They say 'Aha!' I like that one […] And I like the moves as well, you know, when

> they roll on the floor, and when they have like bleeding eye or something [...] It's funny cos there's blood. You've killed them. [...]

Int: But you won't play them in school?

Girl: No. Because in school they'll probably think 'Oh my God, look at her, she's playing like boys' games.'
>   (Interview with Jamilla and friends, aged 13, Pandy)

And many of the boys, after a moment's thought, recognised that some girls could be just as good as them – even at games. For example, Paul had to admit that his friend's mother was excellent:

> Um, well I'm not actually agreeing with Matt because the last time I actually took my Playstation round to his house his mum thrashed us like 20 times without us beating her.
>   (Paul, aged 12, Saxonbridge)

Moreover, when we come to look at the full range of computer uses, as we did in Chapters 5 and 6, we can see that whatever the public discourse, our case study boys and girls typically used computers for a very similar range of activities – writing, looking things up, image manipulation as well as playing games. Apart from games, we found little evidence to support the view[11] that particular activities – email and chat roooms – are becoming 'coded' as things which girls do, while others – designing and browsing Web pages – are becoming 'coded' as boys' activities. Differences, if they do exist, are more subtle than that. For example, both Paul and Maria wrote stories, but they wrote very different types of stories which were gendered in important ways (Paul wrote science fiction while Maria wrote poetry and imaginative stories). Both Jamilla and David looked things up on the Web; but while David worked alone and was interested in finding sites to download images and information for his publishing project, Jamilla was more interested in sharing activities with her girlfriends – shopping, learning about Islamic language, culture and fashion.

Because of its richness and complexity as a cultural object, the computer, we came to recognise, can support a plurality of gendered identities. Playing violent and aggressive games is, therefore, not the only way of 'living' masculinity on the screen. Indeed, two of our highest computer users, David and Alistair, rarely played games, yet their approach to the computer was, we felt, closely related to their construction of their particular masculinities. Both of them were highly technically competent – though in very different domains – Alistair in programming and David in publishing. It was through their technical control of the medium that they were able to assume distinctive positions within their families and amongst their peer groups as 'experts'. David in particular was able to achieve considerable male authority in his family in relation to technology; that authority was clearly very important to him and seemed to give him powerful encouragement in the pursuit of his hobby.

Computers can support different femininities too. We have already seen how some girls liked games, even violent ones. Others, such as Karen and her friend Rhian, were just as serious about computer use as any of the boys; indeed they were teased as 'computer nerds' by their friends despite the fact that they were girls:

> They don't look like computer nerds, but they are computer nerds because in Rhian's house the computer is always on except for at night time when everyone's asleep and the same in Karen's and she always plays the Nintendo and stuff.
>
> (Karen's friend, aged 10, Pen-y-Bryn)

Although she rejected the idea of being called a 'nerd', Karen did see herself as a highly competent computer user – she was 'that sort of girl'.

Finally we have to recognise that although many of our boys did indeed engage in sexist behaviour and attitudes which at times challenged girls' participation, girls' responses were not straightforward; the computer was not necessarily central to their particular gendered identity. As Samantha explained:

> It's not the most important thing to me. It's there and I'm glad it's there because I can use it, it's good, but everything doesn't revolve around the computer or anything. I've got a social life like.
>
> (Samantha, aged 12, Pen-y-Bryn)

The computer, and its different uses, we concluded, was intimately bound up with individual children's gender projects. As pre- and young adolescents, the need to explore and develop their own form of masculinity or femininity was a powerful force in their lives. And while some boys, particularly the younger ones, did live their masculinity through the stereotyped world of violent games play, for the majority of our young people, their use of the computer in their gender projects was more complex than this.

Gender, computers and family life

We gain some insight into the particular ways in which young people can use the computer in the construction of their gendered identities by looking at our case study children in relation to their families. For example, both Jamilla and Faezal lived in families with strongly marked, explicit divisions between men and women. Jamilla and her sister had to do quite a lot of housework, especially cleaning, whereas her brother did not have to do anything in the house. Divisions between men and women, though sometimes resented, were 'only natural' to Jamilla; a view reflected in her construction of technology:

Jamilla: I'm the one who spends the most time on the phone in this house.

Int: How come why's that?

Jamilla: Because […] Musti [her brother] he's a boy and no-one's going to phone him […] Because he's a boy and you know boys don't talk on the phone much do they?

(Jamilla, aged 12, Pandy)

And as we saw in the last chapter, Jamilla's view of the computer was also strongly gender marked. Boys played 'shoot 'em up games' whereas she and her friends used the computer for socialising, for learning about make-up, clothes and doing their homework. The computer was one cultural resource amongst many through which she constructed her particular femininity – as a modern Anglo-Asian teenage girl. Faezal was similar; he too lived in a strongly gender-divided world. He described his mother spending most of her time in the kitchen while his father, when he was not working, watched TV. Faezal thought it was perfectly natural that his mother took no interest in the computer; her world was mainly a domestic one. It is therefore perhaps not surprising that Faezal was taken aback when, during the course of one of our interviews, he came to recognise that some women – the school secretaries – were in fact highly computer literate.

Other families that we met were also gender marked but in less explicit ways. Nevertheless these values often seemed to be reflected in young people's attitudes to the computer. For example, Helen's was a very tech-nological family with both parents working in computers. In the home there was a degree of equality with her father and the children taking on domestic responsibilities while her mother completed her Open University degree. That was now over and things, according to Helen's mother, 'were slipping'. Interestingly, despite the fact that both parents were highly technologically competent, gender divisions still emerged in the way in which they described their competences. Helen's mother saw herself as a 'user' while her father was the real 'techie', knowledgeable about how computers actually worked. Despite their apparent equality in terms of expertise, both parents acknowledged important differences between themselves; differences that reflected relatively traditional gender divisions. Similar divisions emerged between Helen and her brother. Both of them were highly computer literate for their ages but used the computer quite differently. Steven was obsessed by networked games, so much so that his parents had started to worry about it. Helen, as we have seen, was more diverse in her use and, despite her competence, was anything but obsessive. The computer was just one of the many commercially available products available to her in her home.

In each of these cases then, how the computer fitted into their lives bore a close relationship to gender divisions in the home. For Faezal, serious computer use by women was unexpected; for Helen, it was natural but so too was the expectation that boys and girls would use it differently. None of these interpretations are of course determined by family cultures; young people still have a choice in how they interpret such practices. Nevertheless it is clear that family life provides powerful messages to children about what are and what are not appropriate ways of behaving.

In conclusion, we can say that what our evidence demonstrates is that gender is a very powerful influence on how young people come to use ICTs in their lives. What we have documented is the process of structuration where gender, as a social structure, is both a constraint and a resource in the consumption of new technologies. The dominant meanings inscribed by manufacturers and society at large in computer products and computer practices are perfectly clear to young people; they are adept at reading their gendered significance. But how they interpret it, how they come to use such products and practices in the construction of their own, gendered identities, necessarily varies in more subtle ways. Here we see the influence of the family with its own powerful gendered practices, which also acts as a constraint and a resource for young people. As we will see in the next section of this chapter, the family is also central to understanding the role of social class in computer use as well.

The computer and social class

In the second half of this chapter we want to look at the impact on ICT use of another powerful factor in the structuration of young peoples' lives – social class. In doing so, we will be drawing broadly on the work of Bourdieu (1986, 1990). Like Marx, Bourdieu was concerned with ideas of class and conflict in society. However, he broke from classical Marxist ideas by suggesting that we need to understand class relations not simply by examining the economic sphere, but in a variety of different 'fields', including leisure, family patterns, consumption, work, artistic practices, and today, we might add, ICT. Bourdieu argued that, in any one of these fields, different groups or individuals are able to deploy at least three different sorts of resources – three different forms of 'capital'. These are economic capital (money, property, etc.); social capital (networks of family, friends, acquaintances, etc.) and cultural capital (cultural goods including artistic and educational knowledge). Bourdieu therefore suggests that because individuals and groups in society vary significantly in the amount and the type of economic, social and cultural capital they have, they vary in the different resources they bring to bear when engaging in any particular competitive field.

How might these ideas be used in understanding the role of social class in influencing the interpretations of ICTs made by our young people? If we see the world of ICT as yet another 'field' – and an increasingly important one in contemporary society – it becomes clear that each of the young people in our research lived in families and communities that were different in terms of social class. In Bourdieu's terms, they had different sets of economic, social and cultural resources with which to engage with the world. How they came to interpret the role of the computer in their lives is likely, we suggest, to have been strongly influenced by the different forms of economic, social and cultural capital made available to them by their particular families and their communities. Access to these different 'resources' therefore represents the way in which social class came to be 'lived' by them in relation to their use of computers.

In saying this, we do not want to suggest that such factors necessarily determined how these children interpreted the role of computers in their lives. Each of them had to make real choices (sometimes actively, sometimes without thinking) as to how they would engage with the computer. Nevertheless, what we saw were young people facing choices in family and community situations that were structured very differently. Our task in the second half of this chapter is therefore to illustrate this process by looking at the ways in which social class, realised through forms of economic, social and cultural capital, came to structure the choices our case study children faced.[12]

Consumption, the computer and economic capital

Economic issues surrounding the computer entered into the lives of our case study children in a variety of different ways. For example, what the vast majority of the families we studied had in common was that they all saw the computer as something that was very expensive to buy but educationally important; nearly all of our families talked about the computer as an educational investment for their children. However, it was also apparent that economic differences between families were important. For example, it was clear that the technical resources available to Helen, whom we described in the last chapter, were substantially greater than in almost any other family we met. It was not simply that her parents were relatively comfortably off. Like many families where technology is central to the parents' work, Helen benefited by having access to the technologies routinely brought into the home as part of their work. The 'natural' nature of Helen's response to computers seemed to us to at least in part be the product of her living in a world of such rich resources. Certainly it was a very different context from Stephanie's or Emma and Rebecca's homes where ongoing worries about the cost of the computer as an expensive physical object that could easily be broken seemed to inhibit full engagement with it.

In one sense, of course, our case study families were a biased sample in that all of them were selected because in one way or another they had been able to find the money to purchase a home computer in the first place. Not all families are that lucky. Findings from our original questionnaire clearly demonstrated that ownership of a home computer is significantly patterned along lines of socio-economic status. While, overall, 69 per cent of children in the sample (n = 855) reported having access to a computer in the home, the figure was 80 per cent for children from high income areas and 53 per cent for children from low income areas. Such patterning has been confirmed by more recent studies. Both the InterActive and Young People and ICT surveys have identified clear differences in levels of ownership of technologies according to socio-economic status. The Young People and ICT survey, for example, found that 91 per cent of households in social grade AB reported personal computer ownership compared with 78 per cent at grade C2 and 58 per cent at grade DE.[13] The InterActive survey used a different method of determining social class, but nevertheless reported similar findings, with 92 per cent of children from areas of high socio-economic status reporting computer ownership, compared with 76 per cent in the low socio-economic areas in the sample.[14] What these figures do not indicate are the potential differences in age and technical capacity of the computers within the different socio-economic groupings.

Given this patterning, it is perhaps unsurprising that we found that a disproportionate number of those children who identified themselves on our initial questionnaire as 'ambivalent or low users' of ICT came from lower income families. And many of the children we interviewed from this group had come to see the computer as a source of social exclusion.

> I think that computers are good and help you with school, but we are poor and cannot afford one. If I had one I could catch up with everyone, but it will never happen.
>
> (Boy, aged 13, Saxingham)

> It was horrible because everybody was saying 'Oh where did you get your information from?' and they were saying like 'The encyclopaedia on the computer.' And like me and my friend didn't have one so we had to look in books.
>
> (Girl, aged 14, Deanbridge)

Others in our low and ambivalent users group, like Stephanie and her family, saw the computer as an expensive object that could easily be broken. These two boys were both aged 11:

Peter: I think it's a bit dangerous because they cost so much and then if someone who didn't know anything about them just went on there they could damage it.

Int: Has anybody had a bad thing happen to them on a computer ever?

Darren: At my Nan's I was on my Nan's with a friend and my friend was shutting it down and he pressed the wrong button and shut the whole computer down, so the whole computer was blank and I can't play my games on my Nan's computer now.

(Boys, aged 11, Deanbridge)

But money was not only significant in relation to the initial purchasing of a computer. Virtually all of our case study families reported concerns about the ongoing investment needed in keeping hardware and software up to date, and in allowing access to the Internet. Some families also found it necessary to restrict access to printing, and particularly to the use of expensive colour printers which often came into the home 'bundled' as part of a computer package. Again, Helen was an exception in that she and her brother seemed to have relatively routine access to the Internet and whatever software they needed. Similarly, Nick and James came from a relatively affluent home in which the father, as computer consultant, was able to identify and bring home supplies for his family's computer use. Jamilla and Stephanie by contrast did not have access to the Internet and like many other families we met, cost was seen as a major issue.[15] Different again was David. In classic middle class style, he had had to save up for the new software that he needed in order to publish his teenage magazine and, although allowed access to the Internet, was made acutely aware of its cost:

Int: What do you think of first when I say the following words to
            you – 'Internet'?
Boy: Computers.
Boy: Research.
David: I think of the phone bill actually (LAUGHTER). Because that's
            what I get stick for when I get home and ask to go on the Internet
            'Oh but the phone bill was £120 last time.'

                                                    (David, aged 13, Deanbridge)

Each of our case study children therefore inhabited worlds that were structured differently in terms of the financial resources available to them through their families. Moreover, these economic factors seemed to us to be highly influential in how they came to construct computers in their lives. Some of the influences of money were direct (as in the case of whether or not children actually had a computer at home), and some were more complex, reflecting family values about consumption, the value of saving, or even, in the case of Simon, another of our case study children, the importance of 'do-it-yourself' in getting the best value for money (his father was constantly building computers and other technical equipment from different kits).

But as we indicated above, according to Bourdieu (1986; 1990), social class influences families and communities not only in terms of economic capital. Forms of social capital – contacts and networks – are equally important in structuring the opportunities available to individuals. As we will see below, through social networks, from work, from education, and from the community, some of our case study families were able to develop forms of technical knowledge and support while others were not.

Consumption, the computer and social capital

As we discussed in Chapter 3, parents' personal work and educational experiences were highly significant in developing their ICT expertise and those experiences were themselves largely patterned in terms of social class and gender. In general, the female parents' introduction to computers in the workplace was via office practices in which secretarial uses of the computer were foregrounded. Where female parents had professional careers, these were in teaching and medicine, where the computer has to date had only a minor impact on day-to-day practices. In contrast, the male parents in the study who first accessed technology through work were often involved in 'hard' engineering activities, either through the military or through working in aerospace, telecommunications or computer systems companies. Where the fathers in the study first came across technology in a more technologically neutral setting, such as a sales company, their managerial positions allowed them, in the early days, to delegate computer use to secretarial staff. Other fathers in our sample in working class occupations (taxi driver, farm worker, cook) had little or no experience of computers at work whatsoever.

As we also saw in Chapter 3, in a number of families, mothers' social networks and experiences outside the context of work were significant. Five of the mothers we met had taken up educational opportunities later in life, opportunities in which the computer played a central role: two did university degrees, one did an A Level, others gained professional qualifications – with the National Childbirth Trust, in IT literacy and in counselling. This further education, often at a distance, always involved coursework of some sort, which required these women to develop their computer expertise at home as a central means of gaining their qualifications. While in all these cases a computer was already available for use in the home as a result of husbands' interests or work experiences, the mother's use of the computer at home for educational or recreational purposes had a real impact in leading them to argue for better computing facilities, in pushing for upgrades or new computers in order to better facilitate these activities.

Because of their social capital – networks provided though work and other social and educational experiences – we found that some parents were well placed to develop forms of technological knowledge with which to support their children's computer use. So for example Helen's mother had recently completed an Open University degree and now both she and her husband were professionally involved with ICT; as a result, they had access to rich hardware and software resources, to formal and informal technical networks of colleagues and to various forms of professional development in relation to ICT. Her father, who worked as a systems engineer, brought substantial technical expertise into the home, networking computers around the home, repairing and upgrading machines; her mother, who worked in education, seemed more effective in actually teaching Helen how to use a wide range of software.

Stephanie's parents (a farm worker and a dental receptionist) were very different; not only did they have little or no technical knowledge, they seemed to have few work or community networks that were relevant to supporting the computer. (Their 'social capital' was based in a very different 'field', providing Stephanie entry into country life and animal husbandry.) Stephanie's aunt had helped with the computer on a couple of occasions but for most part the family had to rely on (expensive) online support when things went wrong. Again, in this regard, Stephanie seemed similar to many of the 'low or ambivalent' users we met. Amongst many of these children, it seemed their family networks were less able to provide either routine support or role models. Contacts that were available were often distant and difficult to call on. As one 11-year-old 'low user' explained:

> Well because we, first of all when we had it we had to call my aunty's boyfriend, we had to keep ringing him all the time because he worked in computers and we had to keep ringing him all the time when things were going wrong. If the printer wasn't working we had to keep ringing him and getting him to come down and set it up.
>
> (Boy, aged 11, Pandy)

David's mother, a hospital registrar, also had little technical knowledge with which to support his passion for the computer. However, she was able to employ a social capital of a different sort – a rich network of family and community contacts. A neighbour provided their initial second-hand computer and, to begin with at least, helped with trouble shooting. An older cousin who had founded the magazine *CO2* in the first place passed the editorship on to David because she was going to university; the local vet, whom the family knew socially, provided 'sponsorship' for *CO2* in the form of free photocopying, and family members from across the country and overseas were persuaded to subscribe to it and to give Christmas presents in the form of money so David could buy the software he needed. Apart from the neighbour, none of these networks provided technical support. What they did provide however was just as powerful – legitimacy and affirmation for David's publishing efforts.

Jamilla's parents were also unable to provide strong networks of ICT expertise; neither her father nor mother could use the computer and perhaps, as a result, their scanner, once it broke down, was not repaired for over a year. However, Jamilla, and particularly her younger brother, were part of a strong children's network through which technical knowledge was passed on – first to Jamilla herself and then to her own group of girlfriends.

Int: Now, how did you learn how to use the computer then? When you first got this one at home.

Jamilla: My [younger] brother knew quite a lot. He knew how to install things and we just went onto it and looked at things …

Int: And if there's a problem with the computer … would it be your brother that sorted it out then?

Jamilla: Yeah. Because he knows more about it than us. Because his friends had them before us and they tell each other stuff and if he wants to know something like he tells them, because they've had for a long time.

(Jamilla, aged 12, Pandy)

Although Jamilla's brother and his friends were primarily interested in 'shoot 'em-up' games – something Jamilla herself detested – she was able to learn from him and use his technical knowledge to support the forms of activity she and her friends liked. As two of her closest girlfriends explained in a group interview: 'Like we go to each others' houses, we all help each other.'

Several of our case study children had social networks that provided this sort of technical and social support. Faezal was particularly interesting in this regard in that his father encouraged all of his children to use the computer 24 hours a day: 'I keep saying, "This is what it's for so use it, wear it out."' He had high aspirations for his children's educational achievement and future careers and saw ICT as critical to their success. Yet, in reality, neither Faezal's father, a cook in a local restaurant, nor his mother had the social contacts or expertise with which to support their children's ICT knowledge.

Because I didn't know myself what it was, computers, you know. I used to think I wish I could do it, but I felt it was a so difficult thing to get into […] I said to myself, I wish I was that young and I could learn myself.

(Faezal's father, Pandy)

However, Faezal was part of a strong social network that met not just in school but also at his mosque every evening. Moreover, because he lived in the city centre, near the university, at the mosque he met a wide cross-section of Muslim boys. His best friend's father, for example, was studying for a PhD in computing. Each night Faezal and his friends would sit in silence for two hours, learning the Qur'an by heart and afterwards they would spend time talking about computers, and computer games, sharing technical knowledge as well as their fantasies of becoming computer games programmers.

> And my friend Rakesh, his name is, his father was saying because we were best friends, we'd do everything, we think the same. So he said 'Why don't you and Faezal become games designers?' and we decided, yeah, we said 'Yeah we want to become that.' So he's going to get some softwares, I'm going to go down his house to learn some things like that, down his house.
>
> (Faezal, aged 12, Pandy)

Given his family's lack of technical networks, Faezal's own social contacts were critical to his computer use. Through his shared social world, he and his friends were able to support each other's learning and to elaborate a 'magical' solution to their problem of how to carry on being avid games players while at the same time conforming to their parents' high educational and career expectations.

In summary, we can see that parents from different social class backgrounds had access to different forms of social capital: networks and technical knowledge achieved through work, education and other interests. This social capital was then extremely important in shaping the computer culture within their home. In each case, parents brought a different 'mix' of computer experience into the home and we might therefore, tentatively, categorise families into four types.

The first type were those families in which the parents had no computer experience either through work, through education or through using the computer in the home. In these cases, children's own networks were critical in developing their knowledge. Children, such as Stephanie or those in our 'low and ambivalent' users group, with neither family nor their own networks, seemed to face real difficulties in developing their expertise.

The second group, the largest within our study, were those families in which one or two parents had experience of computer use for primarily administrative or 'office' tasks. In these families parents were generally supportive but did not necessarily have strong expertise themselves. If they were to provide support, then like David's mother, they had to draw on other forms of social networking.

A third group comprised families, like Karen's, in which parents brought both administrative expertise and technical expertise to the home and in which both parents had experience of computer use. These families were characterised by regular computer use at home, by strong parental support of computer use as an activity and by ongoing support for children's use through day-to-day help with administrative use of the computer as well as an ability to manage the computer hardware to support these activities.

The final group comprised families, like Helen's, to which both parents brought computer experience and a range of technical and administrative skills, but in which the mothers in the household had also invested significant time in using the computer for their own educational activities. These families were characterised by a range of resources to support computer activity – both in terms of expertise and technical resources and substantial maternal interaction with children around the computer.

In relation to our discussion of social class, it is important to emphasise the degree to which these different groupings mapped onto the socio-economic backgrounds of the different families. Those families with the lowest family incomes were in the first group and those with the highest and with the greatest educational qualifications in the fourth group. Clearly there is a broad interrelationship between patterns of social class realised through economic capital and social class realised through social capital.

Consumption, the computer and cultural capital

As we have seen, social networks bring with them access to forms of technical and other expert knowledge. In practice, then, social capital is closely interrelated with Bourdieu's final form of capital – cultural capital. For Bourdieu, the concept of cultural capital does not refer to differences in cultural tastes (although that is how it is often measured), but to differences in cultural *resources* that we all acquire in the form of a *habitus*. Our *habitus,* according to Bourdieu, is our set of expectations and understandings that shape our sense of the 'rules of the game' with which we intuitively interpret the meaning of cultural activities – such as using the computer at home. These expectations and understandings therefore function on the practical level; they become our 'categories of perception and assessment' as well as being the 'organizing principles of action' (Bourdieu, 1990, p172).

Bourdieu goes on to explain how the notion of cultural capital can be used to explain the social patterns which he uncovers in a wide range of cultural preferences. As a result of their different cultural resources, Bourdieu suggests that different social groups develop quite different 'readings' of cultural activities in different social fields. Dominant groups will of course claim a natural legitimacy for their readings. These 'legitimate' readings are based on certain concepts and codes – certain ways of reading the significance of cultural activities. Those without these codes may stop at the surface meanings of things. They cannot move from the 'primary stratum of the meaning we can grasp on the basis of our ordinary experience' to the 'stratum of secondary meanings' that is the 'level of meaning of what is signified' (Bourdieu, 1986, p2).

This suggestion that some privileged groups in society, because of their cultural resources, may be able to 'read' a cultural field such as ICT in more sophisticated ways is an explicit link with the idea that there are 'deep' and 'surface' approaches in learning. The implication is that a 'deep' approach to learning is not merely a cognitive (or metacognitive) technique but an 'aesthetic', connected to much wider cultural predispositions. Naturally, this is not how those with the necessary codes see it – they have simply acquired concepts and codes 'by insensible familiarization within the family circle ... which implies forgetting the acquisition' (ibid, p3).

To what extent can these ideas be used to explore social class differences that emerged in the way the children in our case study families interpreted the meaning of ICTs in their lives? How was the computer 'read' in different families and how did that relate to how and what different groups of children came to learn through their home computer use? Certainly our families differed significantly in this regard. As we have indicated above, Faezal's father had only the most generalised understanding of the importance of technology in his children's educational future. Although the family provided high expectations of a general sort, Faezal and his brothers and sisters were dependent on the school and on their own social networks – from school, from the mosque – in order to 'operationalize' these expectations.

David, from a strongly middle class family, was very different. Although their technological expertise was also limited, what the family were able help him develop was a recognition of the potential of the computer to support his writing and editorial skills. His *CO2* magazine came to him through family networks and his mother encouraged and valued his use of the computer to publish it regularly. In other words, the 'reading' this family gave to the computer – what they saw as its 'deep structure' – was that it gave support for the development of quite traditional forms of literary expertise which they valued. This is why the computer was seen as educationally important for David. Expertise in the technology was not an end itself; rather it was a means to realise more traditional educational achievements.

Helen's family was different again. As we have already seen, both her father and her mother were able to establish within their family a *habitus* that was strongly technological in its focus. So much was the computer a part of family life that it became entirely natural for Helen. Learning how to develop her own Website, discussing 'motherboards' over dinner, standing on a chair in her parents' bedroom in order to turn on the 'server' when she wanted to use the Internet – all of these were entirely natural activities that Helen was able to learn to do without even thinking about them. What she also learned through her parents was that the computer had many purposes; it could function as a tool, as a place for play or as a technologically fascinating end in itself. And, as we have already seen, she also learned how such uses were potentially gendered. Where Helen differed from David however was that despite her family's technological expertise, there seemed little guidance on how that expertise might be used to support more conventional forms of learning. The deeper educational potential of the computer that David's family helped him to realise, for Helen remained only that – potential. Through her family, Helen was supported in becoming a real expert in managing the technology, but it seemed to us that she remained dependent on formal schooling in turning that potential into conventionally recognised educational achievement.

A very different example was Karen – another of our case study children. Karen's father, an ex-army technician, did not describe himself as a competent user of the computer. As he put it, 'I fiddle with it, as opposed to using it properly.' However, he was technologically highly proficient, constantly buying new machines and re-assembling old ones.

> Well there's a Sharp MZ88 which is in the loft and collecting dust. A BBC master which is in the kids' playroom which they play games on. I've got an IBM PS1 which is on the floor next door. I've got another 386 which arrived recently which I haven't done anything with, and a P150 which is the one that everyone uses.
>
> (Karen's father, Pen-y-Bryn)

He had bought his first home computer when he left the Army in the hope that it would help him getting a job by producing curriculum vitae which his wife used to type up. He now used computers regularly at work, but again was largely self-taught. For this reason he had recently enrolled on a computer course in the hope that he would learn how to use them properly and perhaps get a better job.

When we first met Karen at the age of 10, she was already highly proficient at using the computer and, as we have noted before, was seen in her family as something of an expert. Much of her time was spent playing with her extensive collection of educational games which her father acquired for her through his computer magazines. Her parents were proud of her abilities and they were confident that through the computer she was learning a great deal.

> There are other games like that where they're learning to spell, they're learning about animals, nature or whatever, rather than just the Playstation where it's beat them up and race round tracks and things like that […] So it's killing two birds with one stone […] they're playing games like the old Space Invaders where you shoot targets, but you're hitting things to learn. So … they are playing games but they're learning at the same time, rather than just playing the game for the sake of playing the game.
>
> (Karen's father, Pen-y-Bryn)

Karen therefore lived in a strongly technologically oriented world and she was indeed highly proficient on the computer. However, there was a sense in which her family had accepted the marketing messages of software manufacturers. Her father, in particular, seemed to hope that engaging with the computer would provide solutions to educational problems, teaching Karen new skills and knowledge and helping him find a new career. As we will discuss in Chapter 10, we ourselves were much more sceptical about what children actually learn from these sorts of 'edutainment', where the implicit teaching and learning strategies are often very limited. In contrast to David's family, Karen's parents did not in practice provide the same level of support for her learning – either explicitly or through role modelling. Though deeply committed to her education, they did not seem to have the same level of awareness of the 'deeper structure' of educational processes that a computer could be used to realise.

Karen's family also stood in marked contrast to that of Nick and James, two of our twins. Their father used computers in his work and their mother was a teacher; together these parents provided very powerful economic, social and technological support for their children's ICT learning. Like David's mother, these parents were both able to 'look beyond' the surface meaning of the computer to exploit its educational significance. For example, their mother encouraged them to use the computer to support their traditional reading and writing development by encouraging them to enter poetry competitions using the computer, and by validating their use of the computer for writing and by praising their stories. However, their father seemed to go further still, arguing that his sons' computer use was linked in with 'deep learning'; the sort of learning that was going to be of increasing significance in the modern world.

> It's a skill which I exploit in the job that I do. Because if somebody says, you know, 'I want to do this, this is the problem,' you know, I can pretty quickly figure out what it is that I can get my computer to do to make it happen for them. And I think that's an important skill as well. So even if they're just playing games and figuring things out for themselves I think the confidence to do it and then the sort of the ability to just play with things until they get it right is very important.
>
> (Nick and James' father, Saxonbridge)

Their father's vision was that digital technologies were not simply an efficient and attractive means of realising conventional education attainments. He seemed to be suggesting that digital technology may be altering what 'educational attainment' might mean in future. Such a vision, when combined with the family's strong economic and social resources, placed Nick and James in a privileged position. This is particularly so at a time when 'thinking skills' and 'creativity' are now increasingly recognised as important but when there is little agreement on how these might be taught, assessed or learned within the classroom. Arguably, these boys were learning 'thinking skills' and, more importantly, being encouraged to reflect on them as part of their day-to-day practices at home. As these are increasingly seen as essential attributes of 'successful' workers, the advantage of this perspective in the home environment is clear.[16]

Conclusion

What our study has shown therefore is that both gender and social class continue to be of fundamental significance in the structuration of young people's lives. For example, it is an extremely important corrective to contemporary utopian writing on the future of ICT to recognise that patterns of computer use and access are profoundly influenced by economic capital; the fact that the majority of our low and ambivalent users came from families in the lowest socio-economic group was a constant reminder of this fact.

However, the case study families we worked with in more detail were selected precisely because they *did* own a computer (even though their economic capital varied). What we became persuaded of by our data was the importance of a multifaceted approach to an understanding of how both social class and gender come to influence day-to-day practices such as computer use. Our families differed considerably in terms of their social and cultural capital and this in turn had a major impact on how their children came to value and work with the computer in their home. And as Bourdieu himself would have predicted, there was clearly a strong overlap between these different forms of capital. However, this was not uniformly so. Some families that were not particularly well off were able to compensate in supporting their children through their social networks. Others employed very traditional forms of cultural capital which allowed them to 'read' the educational significance of the computer in sophisticated ways. By recognising as we have done that, in contemporary society, ICT is an important and competitive 'field' and that families have very different resources with which to support their children's engagement with it, we, like Bourdieu, can start to see how social class is expressed and lived in day-to-day life.

We also became aware of how class, gender and other structural features such as ethnicity are closely intertwined. The forms of social and cultural capital families were able to deploy in support of their children's computer use were themselves highly gendered – fathers from their work bringing into the family particular sorts of technical expertise; mothers, from work and from education, bringing in different sorts of knowledge and skill. Such interrelationships, when combined with gendered cultures within the home, provided powerful but differentiated messages to boys and girls about what were and were not appropriate uses for computers both now and in their futures. It is not possible to understand the role that the computer came to play in the identity being constructed by, say, David without recognising that his identity was at one and the same time gendered and classed; his computer use supported the elaboration of a particular form of middle class masculinity. We cannot understand Jamilla's approach to the computer without recognising that her family culture was marked by an explicit recognition of religious and ethnic 'difference' from dominant British culture; her computer use supported the development of an identity that was both feminine and allowed the exploration of her own form of 'new ethnicity'.

Computers and ICTs in general are therefore a potent force in the construction of contemporary childhood identities. Even those children who have turned their back on them seem to recognise that the computer is a powerful cultural icon. *Not* engaging with them, either deliberately or by being excluded, is an important fact of life in itself.

However, as we have tried to show, there are many different meanings that computers can come to have in young people's lives. The suggestion that the computer is *the* dominant feature of contemporary childhood is not substantiated by our evidence; it is only true for a minority of children. What our research seems to show is that, as the computer becomes a more routine part of family life, it, like any other domestic technology, can be 'consumed' in a wide variety of different ways.

We also need to recognise that the identities young people develop, through their consumption of ICTs, may well not be permanent. Children and young adolescents inevitably 'play' with different identities as they grow up. Jamilla seemed to us to be 'playing' with a particular commercially available form of femininity and even David only played 'the computer expert' for a few years. By the age of 15 he had 'grown out of it' and become more interested in amateur dramatics; by 17 he was applying to university to study drama.

As they are growing up, children inevitably change and develop and their relationship to technology will change too. However, what we have tried to show through our discussion of gender and of different forms of family capital is that the interpretations of technology that individuals make are seldom entirely 'free'. In many cases the ways in which our case study children 'consumed' technologies were in important senses prefigured by the cultural and other resources they were able to draw from their families and communities. While ICTs represent a new and powerful force in society, the differences we saw operating between children from different economic, social and cultural backgrounds were in many ways only too familiar. As other research has consistently demonstrated, ICTs are just as likely to reinforce as to challenge existing social divisions in society. Our analysis of gendered practices and different forms of family capital perhaps gives some insight into how these divisions are reproduced.

Chapter 9

Digital childhood

> The pull between the local and the global, the reconfiguration of the consumer/user and changing power relations between teacher and taught are key parameters of the conditions in which young people are growing up.
>
> (Sefton-Green, 1998, p13)

As we saw in the last two chapters, children differ substantially in their engagement with information and communication technologies (ICT) – what they use it for, how much they use it and how important it is to them. For some of them, using the computer is almost a way of life, the primary medium through which they engage with the world and construct their identity. For others, it is of only moderate significance, and for yet others it is an irrelevance or even something to be rejected entirely in the construction of a very different life story. The significance of this observation for an understanding of the impact of computers on children's lives is that it challenges some of the more extreme commentators who have talked about a fundamental generational change with the emergence of a new form of childhood – the 'cyberkid'. At best, such a thesis, and the hopes and fears that go with it, can only be true for a minority of today's children because the meanings attributed to computers are immensely variable.

Nevertheless, and bearing in mind these important caveats, we can still ask if children's lives are being changed because of the very existence of computers in their day-to-day lives. We can ask if *potentially* the computer provides a new context, in and through which childhood is being lived, even if in varying degrees.

In this chapter we want to look at a range of different issues that commentators have suggested are indeed changing childhood. For example, what does it mean to suggest that ICTs are potentially changing the geography of childhood – where childhood is lived both virtually and physically,[1] that they are increasing the commercialisation of children's culture;[2] that they are changing power relationships between children and adults; that they are changing the temporal features of childhood and the interface between work and leisure?[3] What does it mean to suggest that the virtual reality of the screen provides a new powerful 'semiotic space'[4] in and through which children now play, work and live their lives?

In recent years, each of these issues has been the focus of much speculation – both positive and negative – in the press and in more academic writing. As Sefton-Green argues:

> Successive waves of moral panic continuously link the changing nature of young people's lives with an increase in the provision of media technology in the previously enclosed and protected domains of the family and the school. The concept of an 'audio-visual generation' (or what seems to be called at the moment 'cyberkids') seems to have become a shorthand way of labelling these hopes and fears.
>
> (Sefton-Green, 1998, p2)

Yet in reality little of the academic or more popular writing has been based on detailed research; much of it, both positive and negative, is the product of 'armchair theorising'. Our aim in this chapter, like that of Gillespie (1995) in relation to television, is to move beyond armchair theorising and explore how far and in what ways childhood in reality is changing.

Changing geographies of childhood?

> In the nineteenth century, children living along the frontier or on America's farms enjoyed free range over a space of ten square miles or more ... sociologists writing about the suburban America of my boyhood found that children enjoyed a play terrain of one to five blocks of spacious backyards and relatively safe subdivision streets. Today ... many of our children have access to one to five rooms inside their apartments.
>
> (Jenkins, 1998, pp265–6)

> ... from their fingertips [children today] can traverse the world. They have powerful tools for inquiry, analysis, self-expression, influence and play. They have unprecedented mobility. They are shrinking the planet in ways their parents could never imagine.
>
> (Tapscott, 1998, p3)

Much has been made in recent years[5] of the potentiality of ICTs to change the geography of childhood – altering where childhood is actually lived. However, as these two quotations above demonstrate, when we come to think about the geography of childhood, we can look at it from two very different points of view. We can think firstly about where our children are physically. And there is now a widespread assertion that all of us, including our children (and particularly boys)[6] are spending far more time at home than a generation ago. Jameson (1984), for example, estimates that we spend some 80 per cent of our leisure time at home. And one of the things that we do for entertainment at home is access ICTs.[7] As Donzelot (1980) says, the influx of leisure technologies into the home is an obvious physical manifestation of the 'withdrawal to interior space'.

The other side of the coin highlighted by the second quotation above is changes in virtual geography. As writers such as Castells (1989) have argued, at the same time as individuals and families are turning inwards to the home, leading to isolation and fragmentation of local communities, they are 'logging on' to new global communities. Digital technology is seen by many as a key feature in the growth of globalisation – what Giddens (1991) defines as 'the interlacing of social events and social relations "at a distance" with local contextualities' (p21).

Because of the globalising tendencies of digital culture, it has become a key site of anxiety about the changing nature of community and childhood.[8] In practice we found issues of globalisation closely intertwined with those of commercialisation. For the most part, if children's lives on the screen are more and more lived out with a global dimension, then the connections they are making are primarily mediated to them in commercial forms.[9]

The globalising tendencies of the computer were, we found, evidenced in a number of different ways, some of them familiar and some particular to the medium itself. For example, Huw used his computer to engage in email correspondence with a French penfriend. As is the case with email, his correspondence was more rapid and perhaps less polished than traditional penfriend letters but in principle it was a familiar enough activity. What made it distinctive though was that in contrast to many other 'leisure' activities on the computer, using the email in this way was not a strongly commercialised experience. By contrast, David's use of email lists and chat rooms was both new and, from his point of view, irritatingly commercialised. David seemed perfectly familiar and comfortable with the fact that he had no real idea who he was corresponding with. They were linked only because he had his name on an email list (which resulted in frustratingly large amounts of irrelevant promotional material) or, as in this case, by their interest in the popstar Billy.

Int: What sort of newsgroups are you involved with then?

David: Well Billy the popstar person. It's a discussion group, but it works out as being an advertising thing most of the time. But occasionally you do get good conversations. (POINTING TO THE SCREEN) This one's pretty good for conversations like, I don't know, find one that's recent … 'How to argue for Billy.' And then you read down and it's like: 'Argument: She's ugly.' 'No, your girlfriend, mother, wife, sister is ugly. Billy used to be a model and she's not ugly.' And then somebody replies to that saying … 'Oh God, you're actually teaching people how to make really poor arguments in Billy's defence. Do you have to teach people to be patronising. It's the least effective argument.' Yeah and this person called 'Cat' hates Billy.

Int: Oh right, I see, I see. Where does Cat live do you think?

David: I don't know, I can see if I can find out. (LOOKS ON SCREEN) Um, Global Internet. Doesn't say.

                                                (David, aged 12, Deanbridge)

David was very much aware that when he engaged with chat rooms and email lists he was participating in a medium that was both global and highly commercialised. What made it interesting and entertaining was that he was contacting people literally from across the world who had similar interests to him. As Holloway and Valentine (2003) have commented, such relationships are potentially rewarding because they have the characteristics of close face-to-face ties 'they are frequent, companionable, voluntary, reciprocal and support social and emotional needs' (p136). However, learning how to manage unwanted promotional material (including pornographic material) was a key strategy David had to develop if the process was not going to be a frustrating or embarrassing one. In order to do this, he set up email filters and maintained several different email addresses for different purposes – neither of which strategies was entirely satisfactory. Nevertheless, learning how to work his way through the commercialisation of the medium was part of the price he had to pay for using it.

   However, David and all the other children we met were much less aware of the commercialisation and globalisation of other aspects of their engagement with ICTs. For example, we have already seen how many of them used electronic encyclopaedias, particularly Encarta, as a routine part of homework. All of these 'infopaedias' are of course commercial, mainly American, products and many of them come 'free' when families buy new computers. The fact that children from across the globe now routinely turn to Encarta when looking up history, science or politics for their school projects is a new and powerful dimension of globalisation and some teachers we interviewed were certainly aware of the tensions involved in this process. However, amongst our children and their families there was little awareness or concern that the information they were accessing was highly partial. Samantha's experience of trying to look up Welsh Lovespoons on Encarta was interesting in this respect in that it potentially raised important issues about the partiality of knowledge available on Encarta and the invisibility of her own cultural identity and experiences.

> Um, I did try and look up Welsh Lovespoons for my technology homework but it wasn't on there [...] I typed in 'Culture' I think [...]You had to find out about Welsh culture and things like that, but it didn't come up [...] I tried under everything, crafts, art, sculpture. Even did try under Lovespoons because I couldn't find it anywhere else.
>
> (Samantha, aged 12, Pen-y-Bryn)

Samantha was frustrated by her experience but, without external intervention from parents or teachers, she was not able to make the connection between the lack of information on Welsh culture and the selectivity of Encarta – an American commercial product. When children like Samantha were completing their homework, most seemed to focus primarily on the importance of finding something (anything) that would answer the question and was in the right format. As we saw in Chapter 5, given that on most occasions they had access to a surplus of information, much of it tangential to their real interests, managing the medium was challenging. Few children or their families had the skills or the inclination to ask where the information itself was coming from. As we discussed in Chapter 5, the question of whether children were developing merely 'operational' rather than critical literacies is relevant at this point.[10]

Young people also seemed unaware and unconcerned about the fact that the overwhelming majority of the games they engaged with were American. For example, in this interview, Paul was describing a model town he was building with a kit he had printed out from a special program. He was vaguely aware that it was an American town he was building, but it was not particularly important to him (he virtually ignores the interviewer's question) and the 'product placement' from Pizzaland seemed entirely natural to him, simply adding 'authenticity' to the model he was making.

Paul: And there's loads of stuff, gas station, grocery store, hardware store, hotel, houses, ice cream shop, pet shop, Pizzaland ... police cars, police department, post office.

Int: Who makes this program? And where are they from, do you know?

Paul: No. There's roads, there's a school, post office trucks.

Int: What does the school bus look like? Ah, what country's that from?

Paul: I don't know. I think this might be like an American type thing.

Int: Yeah, definitely. Cos in America all the school buses are yellow, so ...

(Paul, aged 12, Saxingham)

A rather different manifestation of the processes of globalisation and commercialisation emerged in relation to entertainment and computer games. As we have already reported, 75 per cent of the children in our original survey stated that they had played computer games in the last week and all of them had played at some stage. Computer games playing is now therefore a normal part of everyday childhood, and through it, all children to some degree become familiar with key features of a childhood culture that is both global and commercial. However, it is important to recognise that this particular games culture is not confined to the medium of the computer. Many of our case study children moved easily between the computer and the games console when playing games; moreover, many of the games they played were related to films, to music, to videos and DVDs, and had 'spin off' products that they could buy, such as posters and models.

For example, in this interview, Tim, who loved playing Warhammer games, describes a poster in his bedroom and refers to heavy-metal music:

Tim: I think it's something like (INAUDIBLE) and it looks really cool, heavy metal and all that.

Int: What's cool about him? He's coming towards you, he's firing, he's got big teeth, big red eyes.

Tim: Looks like he can destroy the world and all ... Cos I like stuff like that. It's a bit like the Warhammer, so I like stuff like that.

(Tim, aged 9, Pandy)

In an important sense then, playing computer games is in no way unique; rather, gaming is embedded in a world of a highly commercial global entertainment that can be accessed through a wide range of popular media. Equally important is the fact that even when engaging with more traditional childhood activities – reading books, playing with dolls, supporting football teams – children were very often global consumers. Karen, for example, spoke with enthusiasm about the *Goosebumps* books she loved reading – children's horror stories published by the global corporation Scholastic Inc. And even Helen's more traditional books – *Danny the Champion of the World* and *The Suitcase Kid* – are themselves produced and marketed by global corporations with links to film, music and television industries. In reality, escaping global and commercial entertainment culture is, for most families, now almost impossible. The home computer may have eased access to a richer range of such products but, we would suggest, it has not in itself fundamentally changed childhood in this regard.

Our evidence clearly demonstrates that through the computer children do indeed participate in a world that is increasingly global, increasingly commercialised and increasingly American. As Holloway and Valentine (2003) say of children's 'online' activities: 'Contrary to popular representations of cyberspace as a placeless social space, somewhere that is both everywhere and nowhere, the children's on-line and off-line activities suggest that on-line places are often an Americanised place' (p152).

One interesting exception to this Americanised world of online activity was provided by Jamilla and her friends (from Bangladesh, Pakistan and North Africa) who described using the Internet to look up Asian clothes and fashion and to find out more about their common Islamic culture. The apparent Americanisation of the majority of British children's cyberspace may therefore be as much a reflection of their existing cultural affinities as a fundamental cause.

However, none of these features, we conclude, are the product of engaging with ICTs *per se*. Globalisation and commercialisation, we came to recognise, are intimately related but they are processes that already permeate many aspects of everyday childhood; using the computer is simply one more means of participating in this powerful process. And before we begin our lament of the passing of a lost (localised) innocence of childhood, we need to recognise that, as Massey (1998) reminds us, disentangling what is 'local' and what is 'global' is not straightforward; the 'global' is inside the 'local', and the 'local' affects the character of the 'global'. As she says in her discussion of youth cultures in rural Yucatan, Mexico:

> ... the room full of computer games was certainly a link between this small cluster of houses in eastern Mexico and something that might be characterised as 'global culture' ... And there are plenty of other links too – the T-shirts with slogans in English, the baseball

caps, the trainers, the endless litter of cola cans. And yet of course the 'youth culture' here is also quite different from that of say San Francisco, or a small American mid-west town or Redditch England or Tokyo. In each of these places the T-shirt and the computer games are mixed in with locally distinct cultures which have their own histories.

(Massey, 1998, p124)

To recognise the complexity of these interconnections is not to be naïve about the power of certain cultural forms – particularly the dominance of the American entertainment and computer industries. Nevertheless, we also need to recognise that despite the power of such cultural forms, young people do not 'live' in a global world; they 'live' in their own families, cities, towns and villages, each of which had its only local specificity. As Holloway and Valentine (2003) state:

> Children's … worlds of meaning are simultaneously global and local. They are global in terms of their interconnections with youth cultures in the wider world upon which they draw, but these global cultures are also interpreted through the lens of local social relations and as such are re-made in the process.
>
> (Holloway and Valentine, 2003, p130).

Flexible childhoods

In this section we want to examine a number of different traditional childhood 'roles' – the learner, the player, the consumer – asking in what ways engagement with ICTs may be contributing to their re-shaping or re-working in the home, in school and amongst peers. One of the important features of each of these roles is that traditionally they have been strongly marked by unequal power relations. Children as learners are traditionally seen as strongly separated from teachers; play, a children's activity, has been strongly demarcated from work; and because they do not have the skills to produce professional looking artefacts – games, books, pictures, music – children are frequently confined to being consumers rather than producers of the things that interest them (or at best producers of children's music, children's pictures, children's stories, etc.). In each of these areas, childhood has, to use Bernstein's (1977) terms, traditionally been strongly 'framed'; in ideal typical terms at least, there have been strong boundaries between parents and children, teachers and pupils.

Part of the popular conception of ICTs is that they disrupt many of these traditional demarcations. The apocryphal image of the teenage boy, able to hack into confidential files at the Pentagon, at a stroke challenges all of these divides. Most of us see him as more expert than we are and highly creative within an adult rather than a children's world. We also recognise the changing boundaries of play – indeed we are forced to ask if using the computer at this level and for these purposes is 'play' at all.

What did we learn about these potential changes to conventional childhood roles through our research? As we will see, although many of our young people did have experience of such changes, they were not as straightforward as the stereotype would suggest.

From learner to teacher?

> I don't feel threatened in any way by it but I'm humbled by the talent that they have. And their ability to not be frightened and try things out [...] I'm much more cautious. And the children will be non-cautious. Totally unphased by it all. They're not frightened at all. Sometimes perhaps I will limit what I do but it won't stop them. And you learn from it.
>
> (Secondary school teacher)

This quotation from one of our children's teachers reflects a popular view that when it comes to the computer, young people often know and can do much more than their teachers and parents. As Tapscott (1998) says, 'children are more comfortable, knowledgeable, and literate than their parents about an innovation central to society' (p2). And in certain respects there was plenty of evidence in our research that this was true for many if not all of our case study children. Alistair, who had taught himself to program computers, was a case in point; by the age of 11, he had so far outstripped his parents' knowledge that they found it impossible to help him:

Mum's partner: So I wish I could help more to say 'Here's something of substance to get your teeth into,' but I'm not really sure I can to be honest. I don't understand quite enough about it.

Mum: Yeah, it doesn't help, not understanding.

(Alistair's mother and her partner, Deanbridge)

David's mother was actually using his expertise to support her own learning:

> David has helped me a lot, teaches me how to do things [...] I rely
> on his knowledge [...] At first he couldn't understand why I could
> be so thick about why I couldn't see the obvious way to do things.
> But he's becoming much better at teaching me.
>
> (David's mother, Deanbridge)

Other children reported helping their parents more directly:

> I've helped my dad with things like the computer at the moment. In
> work he's designing a page on the Internet for his job, you know, for
> his boss. And I've helped him with stuff on that, doing Hyperlinks
> and things like that for the computer, and that's about it basically.
>
> (Joe, Huw's friend, Pen-y-Bryn)

And we heard of many instances of adults turning to children for
troubleshooting. Huw regularly helped his grandfather by giving advice
via email; Huw also had experience of helping his teachers:

> Year 9, Year 8 and Year 7 I was with a teacher called Miss Rees,
> she's a fantastic teacher, one of my best I would say. And she used
> computers with us and [me and Joe] we would do things like compress
> the hard drive, free some space, if anything went wrong she'd ask us
> to help her.
>
> (Huw, aged 12, Pen-y-Bryn)

Each of these different instances (child as 'expert', teacher, 'colleague',
troubleshooter) are important in giving children experience of a differently
constructed adult-child relationship. The idea of 'knowledgeable' children
is not of course unique to the computer, but the speed of technological
change means that for this generation, at least, knowing more than adults
is now a common experience in a way that would have been highly unusual
a generation ago. Even though only a minority of pupils may be looked
up to as real experts by their teachers and peers, most children will have
been witness to classroom and family scenes where traditional power
relations are suspended and children rather than adults are constructed
as experts.

Yet teaching and learning relationships were often more complex than
this in that the majority of our young people, not only the 'nerds' or
'boffs', had experience of being both a learner and a teacher. For example,
we have already described how Jamilla used her younger brother as a
source of technical knowledge which she then taught to her girlfriends at

school. Karen had a similarly multifaceted experience of teaching and learning. Initially her father introduced her to the computer, and she was then able to act as a teacher and source of support for her younger brothers. By the time we met Karen and her father, their 'pedagogical' relationships had changed and they often shared problems or worked together. At different times, being a learner, a teacher and an equal were experiences that were common for many of our children.

But before we get carried away with visions of a generational shift in adult-child relationships, it is important to recognise the limitations of what most children can achieve. While it is true that the children we met were often more technologically literate than some of the adults in their lives, when it came to more formal educational learning, that expertise was often seriously limited. Those limitations, as we discussed in Chapters 5 and 6, were most obviously apparent in relation to being able to critique and evaluate the relevance and socially constructed nature of the inform-ation tools they were regularly using. Children's technological skills were helping them readily access far more information than would have been available to children working at home a generation ago. They had the 'riches of the world' at their fingertips; they literally were able to go 'beyond the confines of institutional walls' (DfEE, 1997, p5). And yet those resources changed the nature of the problem, not how to 'find' but how to interpret, critique and manage that information. As the teacher we quoted above went on to explain:

> Cos very soon a child gets proficient at finding Websites and making links, but it's whether they then use the information. There's no more a skill than turning the pages of a book is it? There is a tendency to get, I think sometimes, so caught up in the technical side of it that the subject matter goes. So I wouldn't let them have access in that way. I mean obviously you can't stop them at home. That's up to them isn't it?
>
> (Secondary school teacher)

Managing the technology, developing the 'operational' literacy[11] to use the tools, therefore is a necessary but certainly not a sufficient skill in supporting more formal learning. And when it comes to what this teacher considered to be the real heart of learning – moving beyond information to knowledge and understanding – there was precious little evidence of changing pedagogical relationships. New technologies had perhaps altered what Bernstein (1997) called the 'framing' of knowledge (who could bring it into the classroom in the first place); they had done nothing, for this teacher at least, to alter what he called the 'classification' of knowledge, i.e. what does and does not count as legitimate knowledge in the first place.[12]

Today's generation of young learners do therefore have some experience of more flexible pedagogical roles than in the past and the significance of that experience may well be important in their future lives; what it is to be a learner and what it is to be a teacher is, for them, more open ended and more 'distributed' than in the past. However, it is important to remember that most teachers (as the one quoted above) and indeed most parents are able to maintain segmented relationships with children. When a child teaches its grandmother to use email or trouble-shoots for the teacher, it demonstrates that adult–child relationships can have a different dimension to them, but it does not, in itself, necessarily realise change in the relationship beyond that particular instance.

From work to play; from play to work

One of the consequences for many adults of introducing ICTs into the home is that they can serve to blur the boundary between home and work. Growing numbers of professionals now choose to work from home for at least part of the week and more use ICTs in order to support working at home in the evenings and weekends. For these adults, the strict demarcations of previous generations begin to disintegrate as home increasingly becomes a site for work as well as for its more traditional activities.[13] Amongst the children we met we also saw a blurring of boundaries between work and play. Interestingly, close observation showed that blurring to be complex as some activities associated with children's 'work' (homework, learning, etc.) took on the characteristics of play and some sorts of play developed identifiable features of children's work (involving learning, challenge and personal development).

Perhaps one of the reasons for this blurring of boundaries is that for children, play and work now have much in common. Some commentators have argued, for example, that children's early experience of the computer as a tool for games play leads to a view of the computer as a 'playable machine'.[14] As Simon's younger sister said when asked her favourite use of the computer, 'I like playing my First Encyclopedia.' The discourses and practices surrounding the computer 'tool' may then have helped to shape an expectation that 'work' and 'play' might be interlinked. Moreover, as we described in Chapter 5, there are certain commonalities between the games play and the 'work' experience for children in the home. For example, our fieldwork highlighted that whether children were playing games, looking things up on Encarta or engaging in other more complex activities, learning how to live with large and indeterminate amounts of information that could be instantaneously accessed became a routine feature of their lives. Management and navigation of information was, as Virilio (1991) has observed, central to the medium itself: equally motivating, equally challenging whether for work or for play.

Work as play

But boundaries between work and play were blurred in other ways too. For example, in Chapter 6 we discussed how Nick spent substantial time combining different clipart images to create a new picture of a chameleon in a tree for science homework. The fact that the teacher had said that, on this occasion, they should not use the computer to do anything more than find illustrations did not stop him putting substantial energy into exploring, and playing with representations in what was intended to be only a minor part of the assignment. It is clear that spending time finding and making the right illustrations was a rewarding activity in itself; indeed Nick probably spent more time doing this than the formal part of his homework. Work had become 'play' in this instance.

On almost every occasion that children described their use of the computer for homework it became apparent that actually using it took them more time than conventional methods. Sometimes they would spend hours on a particular task, often working on features that were formally tangential to the assignment itself, playing, as we discussed in Chapter 6, with new forms of literacy and representation.[15]

Play as work

When undertaken on the computer, work sometimes therefore had a play element. At the same time, many of their 'play' activities were often indistinguishable from 'work'. Perhaps the most obvious example of a commercial attempt to exploit this blurring is the development of 'edutainment' software packages where products are explicitly designed to be both 'fun' and educational. Several of our young people – Karen and Simon, for example – used these regularly, although others increasingly saw them as more 'work' than 'play' as a result of being *required* to use them (see Chapters 4 and 6).

As we discussed in Chapter 5, however, all of the children, when describing their mainstream games play, emphasised that it was the *challenge* of games that provided the motivation and interest to play.

They were not interested in 'easy' games, or in aimless exploration, rather they needed a task and obstacles to overcome to enjoy a game. The researchers at the Massachusetts Institute of Technology (MIT) in the 1980s described this, taking the words of one of the children they were studying, as 'hard fun'.[16] Arguably, the children in this, and other, studies enjoy *working at* playing games.

Blurring the boundaries

But many of our children themselves began blurring the boundaries between what might be recognised as work or experienced as play. We have already seen how David spent his time producing his *CO2* magazine which was highly professional in its standards of journalism as well as layout and design; Alistair spent time developing miniature mathematical programs; Maria wrote long and elaborate stories for her own amusement and Paul wrote science fiction stories that were an offshoot of his computer games.

Paul: (LAUGHTER) That's one of mine. Sci-fi story. That's as far as I got.

Int reads: 'Beyond belief. Once on a moon in the Delta galaxy outside the planet Totanus, a suncycle passes along the planet's surface and ploughs through a rockface, or so it seems. CUT.'

Int: So are you writing it as a screenplay?

Paul: No, what it is, it's meant to be … you think that this thing goes into a rock but what it is it's actually a team filming the thing going into the rock.

Int: So it opens up and that's what you can hear and then the first thing you hear is a voice saying 'Cut.'

Paul: Yeah.

Int: So it's actually a film crew.

(Paul, aged 12, Saxonbridge)

Many of the tasks the children set themselves 'just for fun' were indistinguishable from what they might have been asked to do by their teachers – plan a teenage magazine, write an autobiographical story, write in a science fiction genre. For some of our children, at least, the computer had started to dissolve the boundaries between schoolwork and play, play and schoolwork in a way that mirrored the changes being experienced by a growing number of adults in their working lives. As such, using the computer at home was perhaps an important vehicle for preparing these young people for more flexible patterns of working life that might confront them once they leave school. Other commentators have also argued that these experiences may be central in encouraging young people from a range of different backgrounds to expect and, perhaps, demand different approaches to 'work' in later life.[17]

Entering adult worlds

Int: So I'm wearing one of your hats which looks like something I might buy in WH Smiths or in a party shop. It's totally professional. What's it say on it?

Paul: It says Happy Birthday on it and it's got a big cake on it and balloons around it as well ... And also like [my Dad] does skittles so it's got like 10-pin bowling on the side and it says 'Strike. It's your birthday. Enjoy yourself.'

(Paul, aged 12, Saxingham)

Making things (music, drawings), collecting and learning about things (through books, encyclopaedias, TV) and writing things (stories, poems, diaries) – these activities are all part of what we traditionally consider to be a rich childhood. Children are hugely creative and often spend much of their 'play' time learning things of their own volition and producing a wide range of artefacts – pictures, music, 'collections', and of course paper hats. However, for the most part, the expectation is that when children make things or when they want to learn about something, they do so 'as children'. What they make is 'children's music'; what they draw are 'children's drawings'; what they choose to collect or become experts in are 'children's topics' – science fiction, dinosaurs – understood and appreciated at a level appropriate for their age. And as we have already noted, there is now a global industry (of publishers, software manufacturers, games manufacturers) surrounding our children, responding to and helping to shape these childhood interests.

And again, as we have noted, the children we met did indeed spend a considerable amount of their time engaging with this commercially available children's world – playing games, using forms of edutainment. However, this was not the whole story. We found that part of the appeal of the computer for many young people was that it also gave them access to what have traditionally been adult worlds, adult knowledge, adult activities, adult forms of production.

The software these young people were using, for example, enabled them to produce highly professional-looking products of a quality that in the past children would have found impossible to achieve. For example, Paul's party hats, Nick and James' story books or Samantha's front covers (as discussed in Chapter 6) could all be favourably compared with many commercial 'adult' products from a design perspective. Importantly, this software was often designed for adult and commercial contexts and as a result offered not only the opportunity to develop professional-looking products, but potentially access to adult 'ways of working'. Faezal, for example, because of the computer aided design (CAD) program that came with his computer, had developed an interest in interior and garden design – worlds he would have found it almost impossible to enter without the support of this tool. Through using this software, Faezal was able to generate designs and visualise these in a three-dimensional environment in a way that enabled him to act as the 'design consultant' for the household:

> You can design landscapes on the CAD [...] programs that help design. I like doing interior design ... I can design my own bedroom. I've got this CAD (INAUDIBLE) my back garden, my dad told me to ... it was all (INAUDIBLE) before, like all messed up, so my dad was saying he wants to change it, so he asked me for ideas so I gave it to him and he done it.
>
> (Faezel, aged 12, Pandy)

There is of course a debate as to how 'creative' children are when they are using such software, as we discussed in Chapter 6. However, whether the activity involved greater or lesser degrees of creativity or greater or lesser degrees of choice, was, for the children, not really the point. What motivated them, however complex or simple their input, was the production of something that they recognised as on a par with adult rather than children's production.

The connectivity of home computers also offered the potential to enter into adult worlds, this time through publication to a wider audience. Usually, young people have an audience of their parents or their teachers, where their work is proudly displayed on fridges or on classroom walls. The development of the Web offers, at least in principle, the opportunity for young people to be able to disseminate their work to a much wider audience, taking their work out of the 'children's domain' of home and school, and into a public arena.

Children entered adult worlds in other ways too, particularly through reading and looking up information. Samantha, whose father died of cancer, used the computer to learn much more about his particular disease and then shared that knowledge with her mother and sister; Maria, by using the software program Bodyworks, became fascinated with the internal workings of the human body and Jamilla and her friends gained access to the adult world of beauty, cosmetics and shopping.

And beneath the surface of our conversations with many children was an implicit recognition that through the computer they could gain access to an adult world of romance, sex and pornography. This was Jamilla and her friends:

Girl: Then we had letters saying that if we wanted to go on the Internet we had to sign there not to go onto, you know, those other sites […] If you go on, you know, on the other Web pages, they ban it. (LAUGHTER)

Int: Oh okay. So do other people do that then?

Girl: Um … Well when we went into the (LAUGHTER) when we went into the room, we saw this boy and Jenny goes 'Oh my God, look what he's doing over there,' and 'No, no he's not doing it' and then there's these two big printers, you print this page (INAUDIBLE) and the boy goes 'Oy, that's mine like that' and it was a poster like that, and she said 'Oh my God, look at that.'

Girl: It was of a naked woman.

(Jamilla and friends, aged 13, Pandy)

Again we would want to emphasise that in using the computer in these ways, children were not doing something that was in principle new. Children have always had opportunities to enter adult worlds in many different ways (through hobbies, through reading, through buying pornographic magazines that are available in every corner shop). However, it is the case that the computer, in putting an accessible new technology literally into their hands, does provide them with considerable numbers of opportunities to blur traditional boundaries between adulthood and childhood, through making artefacts of a similar quality to adults, through accessing previously 'adult information' or occupying previously 'adult spaces'.

In conclusion, it is clear that our research revealed many instances where children were, through the computer, experiencing new and more flexible roles. They were learning how to be teachers as well as learners, how to blend play with work and work with play and how to engage, at least to some degree, in worlds that were previously confined to adults. It is important to reiterate that from our small-scale qualitative study we are not in a position to make claims as to how frequent or even significant these experiences were. Nor do we claim that these experiences are only available to young people through the computer. What we can say, however, is that through their interaction with ICTs, nearly all of the young people in our sample did have some experience of different and more flexible childhood roles, particularly within the home.

ScreenPlay

Virtual play, virtual lives

> Little War – a game for boys from 12 to 150 and for that more intelligent sort of girl who likes boys' games and books.
>
> The beginning of the game of Little War, as we know it, became possible with the invention of the spring breech-loader gun. This priceless gift to boyhood appeared somewhere toward the end of the last century, a gun capable of hitting a toy soldier nine times out of ten at a distance of nine yards. It has completely superseded all the spiral-spring and other makes of gun hitherto used in playroom warfare.
>
> (HG Wells, 1913, p1)

This history of play has always been intimately bound up with technology; as toy technologies change and develop so too does the nature of play afforded by them. The yo-yo, the cap-gun, Barbie and Ken, transformers and GameBoy all involve technological developments, and like any other form of technology they afford the potentiality for new forms of interaction, new forms of play by children of all ages (from 12–150). In the final section of this chapter on digital childhoods we want to consider the ways in which ICTs offer young people new forms of play and new ways of being. What does it mean to play and indeed to 'live' on the screen?

Huizinga (1938), in his classic study of the nature and significance of play, says that play has a number of defining features: it is first and foremost a voluntary activity – it is free; it involves stepping out of ordinary and 'real' life for a period of time; it is played out within particular limits of time and place; and it has rules. 'All play has rules. They determine what 'holds' in the temporary world circumscribed by play.' (p67).

Through our research we became aware that children can play on, with and through the computer in a variety of different ways. Video games and other sorts of play software (from Sim City to Virtual Pets) are obvious examples but the children we worked with 'played' in many other ways too: they played on the Net, taking part in chat rooms, they played at redesigning their computers, putting new and ever more lurid screen savers on them, they played with written texts, experimenting with different layouts, colours, illustrations and, as we have seen above, they sometimes played with more adult software – CAD programs, for example.

What we saw through our research was that children do now spend substantial amounts of their time engaged in various forms of 'screen play'. For the majority of our young people it had not displaced more traditional pastimes – sports, reading, making things, collecting things – but it had certainly reduced the amount of time they could devote to them; in particular it seemed to reduce the amount of time they spent watching TV.[18] For all of the children we worked with, the computer screen, admittedly in different degrees, was a key medium in and through which they now played.

But just because such activities are 'play' does not mean that they are without significance. Again to quote Huizinga (1938, p65):

> Even in its simplest forms, play is more than a mere physiological phenomenon or a psychological reflex. It goes beyond the confines of purely physical and purely biological activity. It is a significant function – that is to say, there is some sense to it. In play there is something 'at play' which transcends the immediate needs of life and imparts meaning to the action. All play means something.

What then is the significance of 'screen play'? Turkle (1984) in *The Second Self* suggests that it has a number of different functions, depending on the age of the child: the computer, she argues, has a 'profound developmental vocation'. With younger children between three and eight, playing on the computer, she argues, provokes them to think about what is alive and what is not alive; it is, she says, a 'philosophical stage'. Our case study children were older than this, but as we will see below, they could still at times suspend disbelief and, through their play, get in touch with this earlier stage of development – a fascination with animation.

As children enter pre-adolescence, Turkle suggests that they turn from philosophising to competing. At this stage in their development, she argues, 'mastery' takes on a privileged role. 'It becomes the key to autonomy, to the growth of confidence in one's ability to move beyond parents to peers, to move into relationships of collaboration and competition' (Turkle, 1995, p274). Certainly we saw plenty of evidence amongst our younger aged children of this sort of engagement. Simon, Karen, Tim, Helen and Alistair all used their computers in this way; developing their expertise as competent and independent children was a key feature of their lives on the screen.

Finally, when adolescence begins with new sexual pressures and social demands, Turkle argues this mastery can provide respite, a 'safe haven' where children can be sheltered from what is sometimes a daunting and unpredictable world. However, as adolescents grow and develop, from this strong secure place, Turkle argues, 'they move out at their own pace to less secure terrain' (p274). Here David, Huw and Paul provide the best examples. When we met them as young adolescents, the computer did indeed seem to provide them with some kind of safe haven; it was at least in part a retreat from the world to a context where they were in control, where they were 'experts'. However, as, for example, David grew older, he developed new interests – amateur dramatics – which took him away from living on the screen and eventually provided him with a university career.

Certainly, therefore, we saw the computer fulfilling these developmental functions for some, though not all, of our young people. However, we would not support the view that the computer in any way caused these forms of development; adolescents have always sought refuge from the challenges of a newly sexualised world, pre-adolescents have always sought independence and autonomy through technical mastery within a domain of their own. As a popular and powerful medium, it is not surprising that the computer provides a vehicle for these well-established developmental functions but it does not mean that the computer is *responsible* for them.

However, we would not deny the significance of playing on the screen or that 'virtual play' and 'real life play' are different in important ways. Part of that difference is captured by these two quotations, one from Stephanie, a relatively low user of ICT, and one from Helen, a high user. Both of them are talking about forms of play that in principle have much in common – playing with dolls, and playing with virtual pets – but one takes place through the screen and one does not.

Int: Now who's this doll in bed with you? Who's this?
Stephanie: That's Laura. I've had her for years. She's about five. Because I've had her for about five years. I've got proper clothes for her [...] This was my coat, or my cousin's, which is my mum's sister. These clothes here came with her and I got these underclothes which are on her and I got a nappy.
Int: Oh a proper nappy!

Stephanie: Yeah. Because I look after her. I take her round with me
             sometimes […] I walk around with my pram. I've got a pram
             down there in the shed which used to be mine and (my
             sister's), I take her round in that. I walk her and stuff, I dress
             her properly. I look after her quite a lot.
Int: Does she need looking after?
Stephanie: Yeah. Because she's a lovable baby.

                              (Stephanie, aged 10, Saxingham)

Helen: We've got a new game on the computer, it's called Creatures
             2, and that's quite complex. You have a colony of creatures
             that you have to direct around. You can't actually move them
             with the pad. You've got to use the mouse and say 'Come
             here, come here.' And you can teach them how to speak and
             that's really quite hard. They're really sweet. You can name
             them and as soon as you name them they say 'My name is
             … ' […]
Int: Do you think they're kind of like human babies or are they
             more close to, you know, sheep and things like that? What
             do you reckon? Do you think they're anything like real babies
             or not? What do you reckon?
Helen: They're nothing like sheep. They're a lot more intelligent.
             They can talk to you and you can talk to them. You can
             teach them things.

                              (Helen, aged 10, Deanbridge)

Although both of these girls were 10 when we interviewed them about
these activities, it is likely that, through their play, they were getting in
touch with the sorts of feelings and ideas that Turkle says are associated
with children of a younger age. Helen knew perfectly well that her
Creatures were not alive, they only 'lived' on the screen. Nevertheless
the sophisticated programming encouraged her to suspend disbelief and
enter the fantasy that they were real. Stephanie did the same though it is
likely that when playing in this way with Laura, she was getting in touch
with ideas and fantasies that were much stronger when she was younger.

One of the difficulties of comparing 'real' and 'virtual' play is that
software programs vary enormously in the sorts of engagement they
afford. As we have seen time and again in this book, some programs
afford complex forms of interaction, others are more constrained. What
is interesting about Creatures 2 is that it offers a particularly rich
environment where Helen had to breed, feed, nurture and teach her virtual
pets. As the Website for the game says: 'Enjoy playing with the building

blocks of life. Build relationships with the world's most advanced artificial life commercially available today. Breed them. Nurture them. Teach them. Explore with them. They'll make you laugh. They'll make you cry. They'll make you think' (http://www.creatures2.com).

Creatures 2 therefore offered Helen a context in which to play that was quite as rich as the forms of imaginative play engaged in by Stephanie. Where they differed is that the forms of engagement with the screen-based toys are inscribed in the software; the software (and it is particularly rich software) demands certain ways of interacting with it; the range of 'affordances' Creatures 2 offers are challenging and rewarding but strictly defined. If you don't look after the Creatures – feed them, nurture them – they will die. The affordances offered by Laura, Stephanie's doll, on the other hand, were much more open, much more dependent on her engagement, on her own imagination. Which offers the most rewarding form of play is impossible to answer. What we can say is that the quality of play offered by Creatures 2 is in large part determined by the quality of the programming; with Laura, although the clothes, nappy and pram were significant in influencing the nature of her play, much more was left to be determined by Stephanie's own imagination.

There is however one further important difference between these two 'toys' and that is a difference again highlighted by Turkle (1984) in her analysis of screen-based play. Through her engagement with Creatures 2, Helen in a sense 'inscribed' herself in the little animals; she gave them names which they could say, she taught them tricks which they remembered. When she came back to the program later, there was 'a little bit of herself' left on the screen – it was, to use Turkle's (1984) phrase, a 'second self'. It is here, through such forms of 'interactivity', that we find the computer's appeal, its potential power and its significance in children's lives. It is a power that potentially encourages real engagement and sometimes psychological projection. This is not to say that Laura, as a doll, does not encourage engagement too; clearly for Stephanie she did. But playing in an interactive environment where you have the power to influence the course of events, where you find your decisions and actions today influence future play, is, as we discussed in Chapter 5, a powerful incentive to playing – sometimes even obsessively. And a number of our young people did indeed play games obsessively. Faezal for example, loved playing his German war game:

Faezal: Those are soldiers. You have to steal these bombs to blow up the dam. So I have to sneak in. You're going to have to steal this German suit, you're going to have to walk about and do all reconnoiters.

Int: So you have to kill the Germans do you? So what are you trying to do now?

Faezal: I have to hide and get these people to come here. Then we're going to have to shoot them dead [...] Fire a gunshot, people can hear us so they come. And I can just kill them. See this is sights, the (INAUDIBLE) sight, what you can see in the field. He gets alarmed when he sees that man so then he calls for back up. So they all come running [...] After you kill them you can grab them and bury them under the snow so they won't see.

Int: What are you doing now? Giving them all a gun are you?

Faezal: We're all getting the gun so we can shoot them [...] I'm burying myself so they won't see me, I'm camouflaging myself.

Int: Who are you?

Faezal: My name is Green Beret.

(Faezal, aged 12, Pandy)

Throughout this edited description, which originally went on for nearly five minutes, Faezal was watching the screen and was highly animated; there was no question that he identified with his character. The interactivity of the game encouraged him to identify himself with Green Beret and for the moment, while reality was suspended, to live through the screen.

Interacting with virtual environments such as these, where you 'leave a bit of yourself' on the screen, is clearly a powerful form of motivation for playing on the screen. But as Turkle has suggested in her more recent work (1995), a rather different set of motivations and rewards are offered by 'play' which involves the Internet where we communicate with people 'at a distance':

> ... at one level, the computer is a tool. It helps us write, keep track of our accounts and communicate with others. Beyond this, the computer offers us both new models of mind and a new medium on which to project our ideas and fantasies. Most recently, the computer has become even more than a tool and a mirror: We are able to step through the looking glass. We are learning to live in virtual worlds. We may find ourselves alone as we navigate virtual oceans, unravel virtual mysteries, and engineer virtual skyscrapers. But increasingly, when we step through the looking glass, other people are there as well.
>
> (Turkle, 1995, p9)

What such environments give us is the power to decide what and how much of ourselves we reveal to the other person whom we don't know; they give a very particular form of control. As we described earlier in this chapter, David used chat rooms to contact people who were also interested in his then pop idol, Billy. For a rather shy adolescent boy, they gave a controlled form of contact which he valued (the uncontrolled bits – swearing, sexual jokes, propositions – he screened out). Jamilla's friends very much wanted to use chat rooms too but fantasised about rather different purposes.

Int: Have any of you ever asked anybody out over email?

Girl: Well we would love to. That's one of the reasons we've got an email address [...]

Girl: Yeah that's true yeah. Because if you go on the chatlines, you know the one I said there was something dirty on the left hand side, so we really wanted to go on it, but then it was like … she was like 'Go on, get on there, go on.'

Girl: Yeah, there was this, you got this email address, there was this Indian guy who was doing them for like Asians or something and we were going to go on it but then she was like 'Oh I'm too scared!'

Girl: Really we want any chatline to be honest [...] We just want to like talk to someone. Talk to someone that we haven't really … you know, you can make up lies. 'I'm 21, tall, got a degree in this …'

(Interview with Jamilla and friends, aged 13, Pandy)

Playing on the computer can therefore be a psychologically rewarding activity. Virtual environments can give children very powerful forms of feedback; the Internet can give them rewarding communication with others in ways that they can control. As Turkle (1995, pp268–9) says, 'Some are tempted to think of life in cyberspace as insignificant, escape or meaningless diversion. It is not. Our experiences there are serious play. We belittle them at our risk.'

But what is the significance of this play? What does it mean to them? Should we be concerned by forms of play that are often violent, sexist or potentially expose vulnerable young people to unknown others? Certainly many commentators, both popular and academic are concerned about such issues.

For example, in relation to violence in games, Alloway and Gilbert (1998, pp107–8) say:

Better graphics, better technology and the advent of virtual reality offer young men and the few young women players, the opportunity to know, to practice, to play at and to embody gender and sexual politics as suggested through the narrative and semiotic features of games and gaming texts.

Similar concerns are now expressed in relation to the Internet. But the key question is whether through their play young people do 'know, practice, play and embody' the violence or the sexism or whatever other values are embedded in the text. The truth is that research to date has as yet shown us very little about what young people actually project into their screen-based experiences. What research there is,[19] as discussed in some detail in Chapter 5, suggests that what players themselves find most motivating in such games is not the violence *per se*, but the challenges. 'Learning how to advance in the game, overcoming difficult situations, solving problems and competing, something to do with the interactive nature of the games. Essential also is the emotional excitement and immersion that the games give rise to' (von Feilitzen, 2000, p18). Our interpretation, and it is only an interpretation, is that this was the motivation for Faezal and for the several other boys we met who enjoyed similar games.

But even if they do, for the moment of play, project themselves into the violent and sexist characters they manipulate on the screen, we must ask 'does it matter?' Does it matter if Faezal takes pleasure in seeking out and killing the enemy; does it matter if Heather takes pleasure in 'killing off' patients who annoy her in her virtual hospital game; does it matter that the screen affords Jamilla's friends new and enticing opportunities to articulate their sexual fantasies about being older and meeting men? The answer is that it all depends. As Turkle (1995, p205) says in relation to the Internet games environments called 'MUDs' (Multi User Dungeons)

> Life in cyberspace, as elsewhere, is not fair. To the question 'Are MUDs good or bad for psychological growth?' the answer is unreassuringly complicated, just like life. If you come to the games with a self that is healthy enough to be able to grow from relationships, MUDs can be very good. If not, you can be in for trouble.

In conclusion we can say that what these screen environments provided our young people with when they played was a space in which they were allowed and indeed encouraged to experiment. When using computer games, they could 'play' with a range of different identities; with violence and sexism; with nurturing (as with virtual pets); with being an entrepreneur (running Manchester United) or even the architect of a whole civilisation. When engaged on the Internet the opportunities were even broader. But whether the computer became more than this for them; whether, because of this experimentation, it amounted to a 'social laboratory' in which these children were forging a fragmented postmodern personality[20] is less certain. Our evidence would lead us to be cautious about such conclusions. It may have been their age or it may have been because of their stage of technological sophistication but our sense was that even amongst the highest users of ICT, their 'lives on the screen' represented only a relatively small part of their lives as a whole; the influence of the screen, however powerful, remained partial and indeed 'virtual'. Its psychological significance amongst the children we met seemed relatively modest.

Conclusion

What we have tried to do in this chapter is to explore the range of ways in which regular engagement with ICTs *potentially* alters childhood. And we have seen that our research provides plenty of evidence that, potentially, it does. It can increase access to globalised and more commercialised forms of activity; it can encourage more flexible childhood roles (between teaching and learning, between work and play, between producing and consuming) and it can provide a new and potentially potent context for play. What we have not been able to answer, through our small-scale research, is how significant these changes really are. Whether larger scale quantitative research would in fact be able to measure and identify the prevalence of such 'impacts' across a larger group is also, in fact, debatable.

However, such evidence as we have would lead us to be cautious about over-claiming the significance of any of these changes. While we would not deny that some children's lives may indeed be changed fundamentally in all of the ways we have outlined, for the many children we met through our research, this was not the case. As we tried to show in Chapter 7, most children, even those who use the computer a great deal, have other lives, other arenas in which to play and learn, other relationships at home and at school that are untouched by these changes. For the 10–14-year-olds we met, these other dimensions of their lives remained far more powerful than those they accessed through the screen.

Yet on the other hand we should not deny these potentialities. Through the computer, children do gain some insight into new and changed childhood roles, even if in only one small section of their lives; they do have access to an environment that allows and even encourages them to experiment and to play with different sides of personalities; they do have access to forms of entertainment that increase (even further) the penetration of global and commercial culture into their day-to-day lives. Bringing the computer into the home may not, as yet, have *transformed* childhood, but it has to a degree changed it for all children. It may also have changed 'learning', and in the next two chapters we turn our attention to an exploration of children's learning with ICTs, both at home and at school.

Part V

Learning with the computer

Chapter 10

Learning with computers at home

Tools, activity and learning

This chapter is about how and what young people are learning when they use computers at home. Do young people find out about how to use computers on their own or do they learn from friends, from family, from schoolmates? Are they becoming creative learners and playful experimenters through their computer use or merely following rules? And should their learning, even if it is 'for fun', be valued by worlds outside school? In this chapter we will explore the different and diverse learning resources available to young people within their homes and their wider networks and discuss the ways in which they make use of these resources. Centrally, we want to explore how young people's interaction with digital technologies in the home may be transforming their approaches to learning, both on and off the screen.

Learning is at the centre of our humanity and our culture; it defines us as human beings and it is something that we do throughout our lives. We learn to walk and talk before we go to school and we continue to learn many things after we have left: gardening, cooking, DIY, politics. We learn these things through interacting with people and the world which surrounds us, from what the culture values and what gets talked about in our social worlds. Nowadays, however, there is a tendency to forget the ubiquitous nature of learning, and in public discourse at least, the word learning has become almost synonymous with 'education'. In this discourse 'learning' is increasingly coming to mean learning only about what is considered to be important by schools and society. More worryingly, learning is increasingly linked to attainment and external measurements of attainment; even such buzz phrases as 'lifelong learning' are coming to mean lifelong *certification* of learning. As a result, policy makers talk about motivating young people to learn at home without realising that young people are already learning all the time when they are at home. They may be learning about football or playing cards or text messaging, but they are nevertheless learning within all these activities.

Within this chapter we want to step back from a preoccupation with schooling, education and qualifications and look through the lens of our case studies in order to investigate the learning which takes place when young people use computers in the home. Here we draw upon the perspective of socio-cultural psychology in which we view learning as a dynamic process which involves interaction between a person and their social and physical environment and through which a person emerges changed in some way.[1] This change appears as abilities to use 'tools' to produce things, to engage in discourses and act differently in the world. Importantly, when we talk about 'tools' we do not mean only material objects such as a pen, a wordprocessor, or a digital camera, but also symbolic objects such as a map of the world, or a representation of a function in graphical form, with the master tool being recognised as language.[2] This perspective suggests that in order to investigate what young people are learning when they use computers at home, we have to investigate what they actually *do* with them, together with the discourses and practices which surround and contextualise this computer activity.

Any exploration of young people's learning with computers therefore has to consider what sort of 'tool' the modern computer is and what sorts of activities it 'affords'. The term 'affordance' encapsulates not only what a 'tool can do' but relates to what a person *perceives* they can do with it.[3] Most people, for example, perceive that a wordprocessor 'affords' writing, but would they view a wordprocessor as a tool for multimedia production, a tool for producing a dynamic text which embeds video, or a tool for the collaborative production of knowledge? The role of perception with respect to a tool is important, as it necessarily influences what we try to do with it. If we view a spreadsheet as an environment for producing a list of information, for example, then we may not view it as a powerful computational tool for mathematical modelling.

As we have discussed in some detail in the preceding chapters, children's perceptions of computers are shaped by their interests, previous experiences, and the social and cultural resources which surround them, and these influences lead them to use the computer in a variety of different ways. Many of the young people we worked with used the computer to express and communicate their ideas through activities such as desktop publishing, designing artefacts, drawing, image manipulation, word processing and animation. Some used it as a digital encyclopaedia for finding out and manipulating information. A few young people used it as a computational machine, for programming, calculating or working with spreadsheets. Increasingly, numbers of children were using the computer as a communication medium, for engaging with people at a distance. Some used it as a 'teaching machine', to learn a foreign language, to learn about the biology of the body or to revise for school examinations. And almost all young people chose to use the computer for playing games. When using the computer at home, therefore, young people engaged with a wide range of different activities.

Importantly, when children were using the computer at home, it was *they* who actively chose what they wanted to use the computer for. These choices might not always have been entirely 'free', as we discussed in previous chapters; however, the children's decision to use a computer tended to be a decision to use it for an activity that had meaning for them within their day-to-day lives. The significance of this for an understanding of learning at home is profound in that, through our research, we rarely saw children actively choosing to 'learn to use the computer' as an activity in itself (unless, of course, this was seen as an enjoyable and valuable activity for the individual).[4] Rather, learning to use the computer, and learning *from* the computer, were usually 'side-effects' of doing something else that they wanted to do on the computer at home. What and how our children learned from and with the computer, then, was inextricably bound up with the things they chose to do on it.

To summarise, this chapter is based on the view that learning with computers at home relates to what a young person chooses to do with the computer. And what a young person chooses to do relates to what they perceive a computer can be used for, that is, the affordance of this particular tool. Arguably, given the wide diversity of uses described in Chapters 5 and 6, this leads to wide diversity in learning. In turn, this raises the question of whether, indeed, it is possible to make a 'blanket statement' about what young people are learning when they use a computer at home. Unlike the mass marketing campaigns which argue that computers will in principle 'make your children more creative', 'make your children think smarter', we will argue that learning with computers is a much more complex matter, involving an interaction between child, technology and their specific socio-cultural contexts.

In this chapter, then, we begin by discussing what these diverse processes of learning with the computer in the home actually look like; we then go on to discuss what young people might come to learn from using the computer for these different activities.

How do young people learn with computers at home?

> If I want to use something new my dad's always sort of usually in a helpful mood. Or I try and work it out myself. Because we've got a computer and we've got the case of manuals behind us, so if my dad isn't there then I usually sort of like to look it up because I've usually got loads of time to do that and that's how I usually work it out. Or if there's the help thing on the computer I usually go to that as well.
>
> (Karen, aged 9, Pen-y-Bryn)

> If we get a new game I just read the manual about what to do in the game and then put the disk in, go to where I usually go to play this and if it doesn't work that way, call Mum and say 'Mum what must I do.'
>
> (Stephanie, aged 9, Saxingham)

As we have seen throughout this book, young people find very different reasons for wanting to use the computer in the home, but how do they get started? What do they do if they get stuck or don't know something? How do they learn to use the computer as part of their chosen activities? In this section we will be discussing the range of resources and strategies young people draw upon and deploy to support their computer use.

First, we will suggest that the computer 'affords' interaction and that it is this interaction which draws them into engaging with a computer in the first place. Second, that they are surrounded by social resources, that is people, parents, brothers and sisters, grandparents, or neighbours whom they draw upon in informal ways to support their learning. Third, that they make use of material resources such as books and magazines and that increasingly these resources are in digital form, for example 'cheats' for games. However, it seemed to us that the most important factor in supporting children's learning in the home was *time*, and the opportunities this gave for these children to *play*.

Time

Time is probably the most important resource which is available in the home; time for playing, time for exploring, time to become immersed in a process and time to go and ask someone when you don't know. Time affords a way of working which is simply not possible within current school structures, where the pressure of the bell inevitably constrains ways of working.

Boy 1:   School's boring because you're not allowed to …
Boy 2:   School's more limited.
Boy 3:   Yeah. Because they say 'Right, you've got to do this, you're not allowed to do this this and this …'
Boy 1:   And you've got a certain time but … my mum gives me a certain time and I say 'Oh, can't I have 5 minutes more?' and she gives me about 5 minutes and I keep on getting 5 minutes.
            (Interview with Alistair and friends, aged 10, Deanbridge)

In this sense time at home offers the possibility of losing oneself in the moment. Time enables a young person to become engaged in a process, to become immersed with the 'flow'[5] of the activity. An abundance of time somehow removes the pressure of creating a final product; it opens up the space to learn. And we found that our young people had no difficulty in spending substantial amounts of time motivated and engaged in activities which they chose for themselves; an observation that contrasts with a general view that young people nowadays are not able to concentrate for long periods.

Time at home is also important in terms of enabling learning to take place over an extended period. For example, when we met Alistair, he had already spent three years learning to program. When we met Maria, she had already spent six years writing with a computer. For these and other young people, learning took over time. What they produced at any particular moment was often unexceptional. But what was exceptional was the way in which they sustained an interest in their 'chosen' activity over an extensive period of time and the way in which this long-term activity led to serious and substantial learning.

Learning through play, experiment and interactivity

Another feature which characterises out-of-school computer use is play and playfulness. As Downes (1998) has suggested, 'The computer as an environment for learning by doing and exploratory learning emerges from the children's activity of playing games' (p204). In response to the question 'What do you do when you don't know how to do something?' for example, many of the young people told us, 'we play around until we find out.' This exploratory play was illustrated by Maria when she described experimenting with fonts:

Maria: I like sort of curly ones, the fancy ones I like, like the Aristocrats. I don't like the boring ones like Times and Roman.

Int: (LAUGHTER) So do you spend quite a lot of time kind of experimenting? Trying out different sorts of … It's important how it looks is it?

Maria: (LAUGHTER) I printed out all the different fonts, printed them out on the computer.

(Maria, aged 12, Saxingham)

And by Helen when describing how she sorted out problems:

> I fiddled around and pressed Pause and then pressed Back, found out that that didn't work. As soon as I pressed Back it went right to the beginning. So I put the mouse on the box and dragged it back. I found that that worked. And you could play it backwards and forwards, just on a little tiny section. On things like Publisher I'll have a small fiddle around and normally mess up my work completely, then get Mum.

(Helen, aged 9, Deanbridge)

Moreover, as young people explore, play and fiddle around, they are engaging with a digital tool which supports interaction and rapid feedback in various forms. Of course, different software environments enable different sorts of interactions between computer and user (as we discussed in Chapter 6). Importantly, however, rapid feedback on the users' actions is a characteristic of any activity in the digital environment. By feedback, we mean simply a change in representation that enables the user to understand that they have carried out a particular action and, on some occasions, 'diagnostic' feedback that highlights specific actions (as in spell checkers). This feedback, we came to recognise, is an important aspect of their learning.

When writing or producing a multimedia text, for example, there is instant feedback on the representational forms of the document (colour, layout, language), there is also feedback in the form of spell checks and (more rarely used) grammar checks. When searching within a multimedia encyclopaedia there is rapid feedback as you land on a new page of information and feedback as you interact with images, sound and film. When communicating by email there is feedback from another person at a distance, as well as the changing representations on screen as you type. When computer programming there is feedback which lets you know whether or not your computer program works. Feedback in various forms, when combined with what we described in Chapter 5 as the impermanence of the digital environment, allows the user to attempt actions, observe the computer feedback and then *reshape* their actions in response to the feedback. Feedback from the computer is, as Csikszentmihalyi *et al.* (1993) argue: 'timely, unambiguous and effective in precipitating the concrete here-and-now consciousness of flow' (p195).

As such, the interactivity between a person and a computer leads the user to become engaged and enter into the 'flow' of an activity; it is a reciprocal exchange – structured for the user by their interest and purpose, and within the software, by rules of the digital environment. Importantly, the very responsiveness of the medium (through feedback) and the impermanence of inscriptions within this environment, gives the illusion of user control. As we discussed in Chapter 9, this interaction with a computer seems to involve leaving something of yourself on the screen,[6] and this 'something' becomes a powerful medium for externalising and interrogating your own developing ideas and creations. Interaction and feedback are therefore inextricably linked and are, we suggest, the twin characteristics of computer environments which lead young people to become engaged and enter into the 'flow' of an activity.

Learning from other people

Knowledge-creating communities

But digital interaction is not the only resource supporting young people's learning at home. Time and again we noticed that it was feedback from and interaction with *people* that was important in supporting children's learning. It was people who were most likely to have provoked children to get started with an activity in the first place and people they drew upon when they got stuck. To a great extent, we found that the ways in which young people learned with and from other people in the home often resembled an apprenticeship model of learning[7] rather than the pedagogical model which is prevalent in schools. For example, in many families, we observed that young people learned through working with their parents on an activity which could also involve playing together:

> Yeah when I did my Design and Technology project, Dad helped me on that, but when we got Comptons Interactive where you make your own sort of video, if you get voice you can talk into it and talk on it and me and Dad went on that for ages, and we started to make our own sort of film.
>
> (Heather, aged 12, Deanbridge)

Or they learned as they participated alongside a more knowledgeable other:

> I recently watched him install some games and I sort of remembered how to do that.
>
> (Karen, aged 9, Pen-y-Bryn)

But whereas an apprenticeship model suggests a novice/expert divide, learning in the home, as we noted in Chapter 9, often involved a more genuinely collaborative enterprise in which both parent and child were 'co-constructing' knowledge. These social networks could relate to the specificities of learning ICT skills and knowledge or to much wider practices, such as learning to edit a magazine or learning French.

> Alan puts it on, then Karen messes with it and then Alan will mess with it and do a bit more and Karen says, 'No do that with it,' or 'We can do that with it.' They're swapping facts. Karen knows something that Dad doesn't and Dad knows something that Karen doesn't.
>
> (Karen's mum, Pen-y-Bryn)

> I've helped my dad with things like the computer at the moment. In work he's designing a page on the Internet for his job, you know, for his boss. And I've helped with stuff on that, doing Hyperlinks and things like that for the computer, and that's about it basically.
>
> (Joe, Huw's friend, Pen-y-Bryn)

> Yeah, he [grandfather] helped me with my French. And through the computer like I've written letters to my grandad in French to ask them about his swimming pool that he's had put in now, he's having that done now.
>
> (Huw, aged 12, Pen-y-Bryn)

Learning in the home can therefore be conceived of as a *dynamic* participation in activities;[8] individuals actually change their culture as they participate within it. Taking this 'ecological' perspective allows us to see the way in which young people themselves are active agents within the construction of their home culture. It draws attention to the way in which agents (whether species, societies, social groups or persons) adapt to and affect one another and their circumstances.[9]

In this sense the family could be constructed as a potential knowledge-creating community where parents and children are *both* involved in learning how to use and do things together with the computer:

Karen: I sometimes know more than Dad … when there's a problem on Microsoft Publisher and we don't know what to do, I just go into the help thing. Dad doesn't bother, he just plays around with it.

Dad: I'm actually doing some computer courses on a Friday afternoon so that I know more than Karen does, so it's not the other way around.

(Karen, aged 9, and her father, Pen-y-Bryn)

If we imagine humans as living embodiments of their learning and knowledge building, then it also makes sense that knowledge building within the home will inevitably draw on experiences at work or at school.[10]

> When I was learning my Windows, she would show me how to use all the different icons like bold and underline and move things around and delete and backspace and I would call her, 'Oh Heather I'm stuck,' and generally she would know. She obviously was using it in school.
>
> (Heather's mum, Deanbridge)

It is not only close family members, however, who contribute to this process; friends (as we discussed in Chapter 8) can also be an important resource for young people's learning outside school. Groups of friends can in fact be seen as 'knowledge-building communities'. Huw, who was involved in a particularly intense and close-knit group of friends with shared interests in technology, exemplifies this process:

> … a lot of it [I've learned] as well from Joe, my friend. He knows a bit about computers but he doesn't know anything about making a Web page. So sometimes like if I don't know how to do something – … when I first got this computer I didn't have a clue what to do because when it said consult the manuals that came with Windows 98 for the code or something, I looked at the back of the computer, I don't actually read through things, I just say 'Oh find the code,' and then I looked at the back of the computer and it didn't work. So I had to phone Joe …, 'Oh look, it's bla bla bla,' and he tells me, you know, Lotus, I didn't know how to use this when I first had it and he told me how to do it.
>
> (Huw, aged 12, Pen-y-Bryn)

This knowledge building is likely to be part of a reciprocal relationship:

But then when it came to like doing the Web page he phones me and I'll tell him how to do other things, you know, it's like a compromise between the both of us. We both tell each other how to do things.

(Huw, aged 12, Pen-y-Bryn)

Interestingly, some young people also developed support networks with adults outside their immediate family:

Boy: My uncle, he is qualified in IT something and he comes once in a while from Birmingham and teaches me a little bit of stuff.

Faezal: And there was a friend I was going to tell you about who knows more than … like as much as me … about all the hardware and everything, cos his father does his PhD, he works in a university.

(Interview with Faezal and friends, aged 13, Pandy)

To summarise, within the home young people and other family members appear to come together to create a knowledge-building community around particular uses of the computer, and this becomes a powerful support structure for learning. The main feature of such knowledge-building communities we would suggest is a willingness to share knowledge around a common set of activities and a valuing of the members of the community and the expertise which develops. How this knowledge is shared appears to be less important and can involve people watching others as they carry out an activity, people asking others for information, people working together and extended dialogue at a distance around a common focus. In other words these informal knowledge-building communities are not preoccupied by a dogmatic educational agenda. Rather, knowledge-building communities are characterised by participants who actively want to know something and it is this agency and activity which is the source of members' learning.

If, as was the case within Jamilla, Samantha and Faezal's families, parents have no experience in using a computer, then young people themselves have to be active in seeking out their own social networks which extend beyond the family. However, as we saw in Chapter 8, not all the children were either able to, or wanted to, construct networks in which ICT was valued and it is these young people who, we found, were not using and thus not learning with the computer at home. Not having the relevant social support networks, we came to recognise, can be a real barrier to the use of the computer in the home. As we will argue in Chapter 11, schools have an important role here, helping young people to create social networks which support learning and knowledge building.

Learning from texts

Learning in purely oral cultures would rely entirely on the social networks we described in the previous section. However, our culture is a literate culture in which texts also have a role to play. In this sense, books, magazines and encyclopaedias are social resources, developed by communities and cultures as ways of communicating knowledge. Although most of our young people seemed to prefer to use the resources of playing around or asking other people when a need-to-know arose, we found that they also used texts, particularly when these other resources were not adequate. Alistair, probably because neither his family nor his teachers could help him learn about programming, depended almost entirely on paper-based books.

Alistair: Well I was sort of fiddling around with it. I was trying to figure out how it worked but I never succeeded until I got this one book out of the library and at the beginning it gave a small list of a Basic program.

Int: And you put it in did you?

Alistair: Yeah, it sort of told you how to write some text to the screen and how to ask for input from the user. That's what I'd been searching for for ages. And I just know that then I could probably do other things. And from that I could read a bit more in the book, how to use maths in my programming.

(Alistair, aged 9, Deanbridge)

James, as we discussed in Chapter 6, drew on books as models for formatting his writing:

We have to write these things, but they don't tell you where to write in italics, but reading the books I've got you can see where to write it.

(James, aged 10, Saxingham)

Other children would begin a particular line of inquiry on the computer and then switch to searching both digital and paper-based resources:

Sometimes I cycle to the library if I can't find certain things on the computer.

(Tim, aged 9, Pandy)

As we will discuss in the next section, young people are aware that texts can offer an important entry point into a world with which they are unfamiliar or can be used as a resource to support their learning. Through our research we came to recognise that there is an increasing blurring of boundaries between paper-based and digital texts at home, and our young people often engaged with both forms; as in the examples above, their digital experiences often led them to search out paper-based worlds.

Creatively copying

Children use a wide range of social and textual resources in order to learn with the computer; they also simply 'play around' in a way that is often encouraged by the software environment itself. Other strategies we became aware of, however, were copying and the use of templates; strategies which are traditionally frowned upon in schools. Maria, for example, copied the words of popular songs; she listened to them on the radio and then wrote them down.

> I used to copy out the words for songs and stuff on the computer so I could see it better … I listened to them slowly and then I wrote them down and then I copied them onto the computer.
>
> (Maria, aged 12, Saxingham)

Alistair copied a basic program which he found in a book as a way to get started with basic programming. Faezal copied clipart and transformed the images into something of his own. Huw copied from information sources when doing his homework, because he felt confident that these sources were correct.

> Like, if there's research and this was for your own research work, what I do is go to an encyclopaedia and copy it. Don't tell the teachers … I'm the type of person who gets the information that is needed from the quickest available source. And I know that information's right. And no one can contradict it and no one can say that it's spelt wrong, no one can say this, no one can say that.
>
> (Huw, aged 12, Pen-y-Bryn)

And Heather copied from the Web when doing her Art homework:

Heather: This is the one I'm actually drawing […] It's called nudes on a red background. There's nothing dirty about it.

Int: Absolutely not, no […] Right okay. And what do you do with that information?

Heather: I would read it through thoroughly and then put it into my own words and highlight anything that I want to highlight and if I was to copy a sentence down then I would highlight it and see where I got it from.

Int: So how did you decide that you wanted to do that picture then? Was that what you were told? To find a picture?

Heather: I looked through to find a picture and to find some information on the artist, but I looked at all the pictures and I found that one most interesting, so I looked up the artist. There wasn't a lot of writing so I thought well, I'll be able to put some of this in my own words.

(Heather, aged 12, Deanbridge)

The use of templates is also a form of copying with respect to the design of or structuring of a piece of work. These templates are an integral part of many software packages which our case study children were using in the home. Many of the children used templates to begin to design work for school; others, as we discussed in Chapters 6 and 9, used templates to design presents for family members and friends (such as calendars, hats and so on). David and Huw regularly used templates to enable them to 'get started' in designing Web pages. It is possible that the use of templates was a strategy that many of the children had developed to enable them to get started with an activity which they were not able to create from scratch. They provide a way into an unknown world, a way of getting started when the practice is not part of the dominant culture of the young person or their family. Consider the case of Paul, passionately interested in art and design, living in a home with parents whose main interests lay in outdoor sports and scouting activities:

Int: Okay, so then what do you do? So we've got coming up on the screen – just for the tape, do you want to tell me what we've got on the screen?

Paul: It's a net, kind of like a net for a party hat. A template. And it's got the words 'Happy Birthday' on it and it's got sort of swirly things on it and triangles and shapes and stuff. If you go up to where that little camera is and stop it says 'Insert a graphic object' so what you do is go up to that …

Int: How did you find out how that worked?

Paul: Fiddling about with it.

Int: Right. So you choose one of these. So you have to type it all in so that you … to get a selection.

Paul: Up comes a thing then you can reduce the size and stuff. That's to make it slanted but it's very hard to get it back. It makes it look like it's gone like that.

Int: Oh okay. So how do you put it on then? So you pick it up and drag it.

Paul: Move it up to where you want it.

(Paul, aged 12, Saxingham)

What became clear through our research was that copying and using templates were important strategies that young people would use when they wanted to find a way into a practice which may have been relatively alien within their own family situation. In this sense it could be argued that they were 'getting inside the head of the master'. As Davis *et al.* (2000, p204) argue in relation to writing:

> Copying and repetition are valuable and important techniques in the development of complex competencies … getting inside the mind of a master has been espoused by many professional writers. A common writing practice for beginners is to select passages from their favorite [sic] authors and to copy them over and over. Through this repetition, the novice will gradually come to notice particular details of writing, including the 'rhythm' of the writer's thinking.

Disentangling what is 'creative' and what is 'reproductive' in this process is of course complex. Rather, as the New London Group argue, what these children produce is 'variously creative or reproductive in relation to the resources for meaning-making available … but it is neither a simple reproduction (as the myth of standards and transmission pedagogy would have us believe), nor is it simply creative (as the myths of individual originality and personal voice would have us believe)' (New London Group, 1996, p76).

We would argue, then, that copying and using templates are vitally important learning strategies for young people; they are ways in which young people can 'scaffold'[11] themselves into a new world or new practices; in other words, copying can become a self-help tool for learning. However, as young people become progressively more confident within a new domain, they are likely, within the constraints of the software, to make less and less use of copying and increasingly start to create things for themselves.

Learning strategies in the home

Importantly, when we examine how children are learning when using computers in the home, we can see that all these different practices – copying, using templates, using material resources, taking time to explore, interacting with the computer feedback, asking and working alongside family and friends – are driven by children's motivation and interest in an activity they have chosen for themselves. Accordingly, this rich range of strategies is mobilised in the service of the children's particular interests, whether programming (for Alistair), writing (for Maria), designing (for Paul), Web design (for Huw), finding out medical information (for Samantha) and so on. We might then suggest that children's learning with computers in the home could be characterised as 'deep' (along the lines of particular interests) rather than 'broad': the development of a wide range of strategies for learning rather than, necessarily, the uniform acquisition of a wide range of 'content' information. This distinction will be particularly important when we consider the differences between learning with computers at home and at school.

What are children learning from using the computer in the home?

As we pointed out earlier in this chapter and in Chapter 6, what children learn using the computer at home relates directly to the activities they choose to use the computer for; it is highly personalised. It makes no sense, therefore, to attempt to describe each child's 'learning from using the computer' in individual detail. Our research, however, suggests that it is worth here discussing the implications of children's home computer use for literacy and numeracy practices, and also to examine some of the claims made for children's learning with 'educational' software.

Literacy practices

As we saw in Chapter 6, the vast majority of young people use the computer in the home to engage in some form of literacy-related practice which would not have been possible with paper and pencil. Given the current academic and popular moral panic about boys' underachievement, it is interesting and important to note that our surveys suggested that large numbers of boys were now using the computer for literacy-related practices.[12] What was notable, when considering what children were learning with the computer in the home, was not only the development of emerging forms of new literacies, but the ways in which the computer enabled some young people to participate in already existing established literacy practices – writing, looking up information and so on – which previously they may have been excluded from. Huw, for example, whose first language was Welsh, was able to begin enjoying the process of playing with English words; Heather, who was daunted by libraries, was enjoying exploring digital encyclopaedias. While, as we have already discussed in detail in Chapter 6, computers are enabling *new* literacy practices, we should also not overlook the extent to which the availability of these resources in the home may be widening and easing access to traditional literacy practices valued in schools and the workplace.

Numeracy

While literacy practices may be widely in evidence in the home, it was notable in our case studies that numeracy practices with the computer were rare. This is in marked contrast to Papert's early vision that, once computers became ubiquitous in the home, mathematics would be learned effortlessly like a mother tongue through interacting with mathematical-type languages such as Logo (1980, p47):

> Our culture is so mathphobic, so math-fearing, that if I could demon-strate how the computer can bring us into a new relationship to mathematics, I would have a strong foundation for claiming that the computer has the ability to change our relationship to other kinds of learning we might fear.

This was a vision shared by those of us who worked with the Logo pro-gramming language in schools throughout the 1980s.[13] The ScreenPlay project, however, has shown dramatically that the simple introduction of the computer into the home environment is not likely to generate, on its own, such massive transformations. Young people just do not seem to be choosing to engage in numeracy-related activities such as computer programming or building spreadsheets in the home. Interestingly, as we shall discuss in Chapter 11, young people's experience of using spread-sheets in school seems to be putting them off using spreadsheets at home, even though they are readily available on their home computers.

Educational software

As discussed in Chapter 6, the majority of the children in our case studies did not choose to use programs which had been developed explicitly for educational purposes. Instead young people chose either to play mainstream games (as described in Chapter 5), often developed for adults as well as children, or they chose to engage with mainstream software (Chapter 6) which is also part of the adult world. Educational programs usually derive from the early computer aided learning environments and, at the time of writing this book, much of this software was characterised primarily as the acquisition of facts and information; accordingly, the structure of this software was heavily reliant upon explicit challenges and rewards.[14] This educational type of software does not usually afford the activity of play, which we have highlighted as being an important learning resource. Perhaps it is because of this that many young people chose not to use educational software in the home, choosing instead professional environments which, paradoxically, although designed for adults, afford an exploratory and playful approach to learning.

The person-plus

Young people as resourceful learners

> In the world outside school, part of knowing how to learn and solve complex problems involves knowing how to create and exploit social networks and the expertise of others, and to deftly use the features of the physical and media environments to one's advantage.
>
> (Pea, 1993, p75)

We have seen throughout this chapter that when young people are able to exercise choice over what they use the computer for, they are motivated to engage with particular activities and through this process they inevitably learn. This learning may be more incidental than intentional, more deep than broad, but it nevertheless does constitute learning. It is also important to emphasise that many young people choose to engage with literacy-related activities in the home which are for their own pleasure and are not for homework. These activities may not be for school but they often overlap with what teachers are trying to teach, as in the example of David's production of a teenage magazine.

We have also shown that within the informal setting of the home, young people are very resourceful as learners and draw upon the people and things which surround them when solving problems or producing artefacts. In this sense the young person operates as a 'person-plus'.[15] This phrase draws attention to the fact that in authentic learning situations, people work with much more than their own mental powers, they work in person-plus-person mode, or person-plus-book mode, or person-plus-computer mode. This contrasts with schools in which person-solo is the dominant mode of working and where, as we shall discuss in the next chapter, young people are often prevented from following their inclinations to draw on networks of people and things which could support learning.

The ScreenPlay project has provided us with a window onto the rich world of learning which takes place in the home. We captured these dynamic processes at a moment in time and as technology changes young people will inevitably take up the affordances which they perceive in new ICT tools, leading to shifts in the learning which takes place in the home. When we carried out the ScreenPlay study, for example, very few people were using computers to download or make music but we know from our more recent surveys[16] that this situation is changing. Accordingly, as these practices change, young people will be learning new and different things about playing and composing music.

We have also shown that most of these young people seemed to prefer to use the same technologies that are used within the adult world, for example mainstream games, wordprocessors and Powerpoint, as opposed to technologies which have been particularly designed for children, such as edutainment software. They also chose to engage with technologies which overlap with their out-of-school interests and sub-cultures and such packages as databases and spreadsheets, which are widely available in the home, do not seem to offer most young people anything in this respect.

We have argued throughout this chapter that it is impossible to separate the learning about a particular practice from the learning of ICT skills, in the same way that it would not make sense to separate learning to write from learning how to use a pen. The process of using the tool is embodied within the practice itself. However, knowing how to use the computer tool is a valuable currency in the home, where families often recognise that there is much to be learned and where young people and their families readily share their expertise within a knowledge-building community which values learning. We shall argue in the next chapter that schools and policy makers need to take this into account in order to value the learning which takes place in the home. Schools could draw on this resource as opposed to ignoring or suppressing it, but in order for this to happen schools will themselves have to become knowledge-building communities where knowledge is shared, respected and valued.

Chapter 11

Learning with computers in school

Why schools still matter

In the previous chapter we celebrated the rich and substantial learning which takes place at home and rather underplayed the fact that all our case study young people are part of a schooled society. Without schooling, young people would be very unlikely, for example, to be engaging with literacy-related practices at home. Many of us have great-great-grandparents who were illiterate; in the past this was particularly the case for women. These people lived before a time of mass education and it is salutary to remember that what we currently take for granted in terms of literacy is inextricably linked to schooling. In other words, literacy is part of the culture of the masses because schooling is part of this culture. The fact that all of these young people from a range of social backgrounds were choosing to use the home computer to write for pleasure cannot be seen in isolation from the fact that they learn to write at school.

We also argued in Chapter 10 that what young people learn at home is linked to their interests and lives as a whole and that this results in deep rather than broad learning. Alistair, for example, focused on symbolic programming and was not interested in learning about more visual environments. Huw's writing was restricted to analysis and presentation of information – he did not choose to write imaginative stories. Maria chose to write stories and poems but did not choose to work with spreadsheets or databases. Karen chose to engage with educational software which prioritised a particular approach to knowledge acquisition and did not choose to write for pleasure. As we argued in Chapters 6 and 10, it seemed to us that these individual choices related, in complex ways, to the cultural, social, technological and knowledge tools available within the family. But such resources are necessarily highly variable; our argument in this chapter is that schools and teachers are key resources in expanding young people's access to the cultural, social, technological and knowledge tools beyond those available in their homes and immediate cultural contexts; only if schools take on this role can we ensure equality of access for all children to these diverse tools. For example, we noted in the last chapter that the vast majority of young people were not choosing numeracy-related activities at home, yet mathematics *is* part of our culture; it is important for citizens to be numerate and schools and teachers have a crucial role to play in this area.

In addition, some young people, despite access to computers at home, do not participate in social networks which inspire and sustain their interest in computer-based activities. This was well-illustrated by the case of Stephanie (discussed more fully in Chapter 8), whose parents and family networks provided an entry into country life, but were not able to provide an entry into the various digital lives that other young people inhabited. For young people like Stephanie, schools are arguably very important sites for the development of knowledge sharing and knowledge-building communities which would support her engagement with new digital practices.

Finally, a significant minority (12–24 per cent) of young people do not have access to computers at home.[1] These young people are evidently missing out on the experiences of learning with computers at home which were described in Chapter 10. Moreover, there is evidence from the surveys discussed[2] in Chapter 2 that those young people who do not have a computer at home *also* have less access to information and communications technologies (ICT) at school than children with home computers. Young people without computers in the home may, then, be doubly disadvantaged. Given that out-of-school inequalities in access are likely to remain in future it is arguably only through schools that these disadvantages can be overcome.

Schools, then, are vital to this twenty-first century knowledge-building society because they are key sites for creating, communicating and reproducing culture, and because they are a major site within society for engendering cultural diversity and social equity.

In this chapter we discuss young people's perspectives on their experiences of ICT use in school, and attempt to understand it with respect to current policies and practices as we understand them through our other research into school-based ICT use.[3] This then provides a basis for our concluding chapter in which we put forward a vision of the ways in which schools might change to productively draw upon the 'know-how' and 'know-who' which young people are developing at home.

Young people's views about learning with ICT at school

> If the teacher doesn't have too many limitations, you know, say for example you wanted to insert a clipart from a different file and the teacher originally knew, you know, this is the way you should do it, and then you said, 'No I know another way to do it to get better images and stuff.' Then a good teacher like Miss Andrews would let you do this. Okay? And then she would take on your information that you inputted into the lesson. She learns from you and you learn from her. So it's like a two-way system. It's not like some teachers who, you know, pound it into you, try to just get information into you, they don't get anything back, that's a bad teaching manner, I don't like that type of teaching at all when the teacher just gives you information and says, 'Write it down' bla bla bla, 'This is it. Revise from it.' That's not good teaching at all. Good teaching is when the teacher asks for questions from the class and answers the questions that the kids give, you know. That's good teaching. But when they just give you information and that's it, they don't answer questions, they don't let you involve yourself in the lesson, that's not a good type of teaching, that's really bad teaching.
>
> (Huw, aged 12, Pen-y-Bryn)

As the above quotation illustrates, young people are very good at identifying the characteristics of good teaching and they often talk about positive experiences of learning in school. However, they are also able to say what they think is not good teaching and our conversations with young people revealed a considerable amount of negativity around the use, in particular, of ICT in schools. We suggest that it is important to understand these perspectives in order to inform policy makers about ways of better harnessing the considerable investment in ICT in schools[4] for the purposes of teaching and learning.

A step-by-step approach

Many of our case study young people criticised their experiences of teaching with ICT as being over-prescriptive, as lessons in which they were required to follow linear step-by-step instructions, within a narrowly defined focus of activity in which 'ICT skills' rather than authentic practice was prioritised. The young people's criticisms suggested that they experienced this sort of teaching with computers as both tedious and controlling, as Huw's comment highlights:

> The IT teacher says, 'You have to do this first then this, then this' and it's really really boring the way that that is set out to me. But at home I can do it my own way and my own sizes like sometimes he will say, 'It should only be this many pages,' or 'You should have put a page break there,' I don't care, I want to do it my own way, it looks nicer. There you go, but it's wrong to him.
>
> (Huw, aged 12, Pen-y-Bryn)

The emphasis in this lesson seemed to be on control over the very details which can give students a sense of pleasure and ownership of their work. As we described in Chapters 6 and 10, young people care passionately about the look of what they produce with the computer, which seems to relate to their ability to enter into the flow[5] of production. Huw, for example, had developed his own style of presentation through working extensively on written documents at home, and did not need to learn about how to change the font size and where to put a page break. Moreover, the presentation of a digital document can be changed at any time while it is being produced, so an emphasis on teaching these techniques in a dogmatically linear fashion is questionable.

This step-by-step and narrowly focused approach was also in evidence in some of our case study children's experiences of Internet use in school. While the young people in the ScreenPlay study who did not have access to the Internet at home were generally positive about their use of the Internet at school, those who were used to their own access at home were less enthusiastic:

Girl: I like the Internet … I've got it at home, but the one in school's a bit boring.

Int: Why's that?

Girl: Because it isn't as good. Because it hasn't got the actual things … well it has but you've got to go a long long way to find it and click through all these buttons and things and in my one at home you type in the name of what you want and then it comes up on the screen.

Girl: In school we have to stick to one thing and then at home we can do like anything we want.

> (Helen and friends, aged 10, Deanbridge)

This 'sticking to one thing' seems to refer to the narrowness of the activity which is being offered, in which the opportunities of digital hypertext environments to follow a range of different 'threads' of information navigation are seen as a threat to the focus of the activity. In this example, the criticism was also compounded by the fact that for these girls, the Internet was more difficult to access within the school network than it was on their home computers.

And again, in the ubiquitous strategy of using the computer to make a 'neat copy' of handwritten work, we saw children reporting computer use in school emphasising ICT skills and presentation, as opposed to enabling children to transform their practice and capabilities:

Karen: We had to write it out by hand then take it to school and type it out on the computer.

Int: Can you remember something that you did at school that you really enjoyed on a computer at school?

Karen: No I can't … I can't.

> (Karen, aged 9, Pen-y-Bryn)

Generally I would say that it's more teaching you the techniques than doing actual work […] because like with the English project we like wrote it up by hand and then all we did is typed it up on the computers.

> (David, aged 12, Deanbridge)

Consider next Maria's experience of learning to use spreadsheets within an ICT lesson.

Maria: I didn't know about the spreadsheets and everything until last term when we did that at school. Now I can use it, but I don't really like using it that much.

Int: And what did you use that for at school?

Maria: We did this project called 'Boiled Maggots'. We took a survey of all the supermarkets and wrote down how many tins of boiled maggots they sold in five months and then changed all the information so that you just had to sort of change one number and it would automatically change everything. But I never did finish that project, actually, because you're supposed to write a write-up at the end and I didn't do that because I took quite a long time to work out the spreadsheets.

Int: And why didn't you like that so much?
Maria: Well it took a long time to change it. *It would have been good if I'd needed to change some of the numbers.*
Int: And is there a spreadsheet on the one at home, do you know?
Maria: Yeah there is.
Int: And have you used that at all?
Maria: No.

(Maria, aged 12, Saxingham)

The spreadsheet which Maria encountered appears to have been pre-programmed by the teacher for a project evidently intended, but unfortunately failing, to be motivating for the pupils. In reflecting on this lesson, Maria suggested that working with spreadsheets would have been more engaging if she had actually *needed* to change the values of the variables set up in the spreadsheet cells. Importantly, in her comments, she showed awareness of the power of spreadsheets to which she was being denied access, that is their potential to model the dynamic relationship between variables within a practical problem. Despite the fact that we know that young people of all abilities can learn to program spreadsheets in this way,[6] in schools they are often protected from this knowledge. Why do many people think that students should first work on pre-programmed spreadsheets rather than set up a program for themselves? Does it relate to a view about teaching and learning or to issues of classroom control? Does it relate to a view about students' abilities or to the teacher's own confidence and competence with the software?

Maria also described a school project with databases in which she was again presented with a pre-programmed package.

Maria: He'd written out the ingredients for a pizza and the nutrition value and then we had to change the pizza for a vegetarian pizza and keep the fat [...]
Int: So you already had something programmed in there then?
Maria: Yeah.
Int: Was it always like that? It was set up and then you had to change some things. Would you say it was very creative for you?
Maria: Not really. [...] We didn't learn very much from it.
Int: And why not?
Maria: Usually if I don't enjoy a lesson then I don't learn anything, I don't remember anything.

(Maria, aged 12, Saxingham)

It seems that Maria did not enjoy this lesson because she wasn't motivated or challenged by the 'pizza project'. When probed about what she would do if she were the teacher, Maria suggested that students should be able to choose their own projects:

Int: So, if you were in charge of teaching the group ... what would you teach them ... how would you do something that might be different, that might help them to learn?

Maria: I'd let them choose a project that they found interesting.

(Maria, aged 12, Saxingham)

What our young people seemed to be asking for was to be able to work on engaging and challenging projects which gave them the space to do things 'in their own way', space to be creative and space to make some decisions for themselves. What they seemed to be experiencing however was over-directed uses of ICT with too much of a focus on ICT skills as opposed to ICT as a tool for use within authentic and relevant activities. While we acknowledge that our sample is small – only eight schools and interviews with 130 children – and that, moreover, many of the children reported so little computer use in school (often only 3–4 times a year) that their experiences were not themselves based on substantial exposure to school ICT, there is a growing body of school-focused research evidence that these children's negative experiences reflect a nation-wide phenomenon.[7]

No time for questions and play

An inquiring disposition is a central aspect of human learning and so it might be expected that schools would welcome questioning and inquiry. However, many of the children reported that over-controlled and over-prescriptive ICT lessons created an over-dependence on the teacher and left little space for questions.

Girl: Yeah you ask them something, they go, 'Oh, I don't know how to do that. You'll have to go and ask the IT teacher.' I think 'Oh God! I've just spent 15 minutes with my hand up trying to ask you.'

Girl: You'll say, 'What am I doing next?' and they'll say, 'Draw a box with the writing in,' and you'll say, 'Right, how do I do that?' and they'll go, 'I don't know, you just draw the box with the writing in.' So they tell us what to do but they don't know how, we're supposed to use the computer ourselves anyway.

(Interview with Heather and friends, aged 13, Deanbridge)

This scenario of waiting for an answer contrasts starkly with what young people would do if they were at home: that is, find someone to help or play around until they could work something out for themselves. As the same girls went on to say:

Girl: Yeah because at home you don't really have a time limit how long you're on there. You can go on all night if you want to. Apart from your brothers.

Girl: And like one adult can help you and spend like 20 minutes just sorting out one thing. Whereas the teacher has like 2 minutes at the most to spare.

(Interview with Heather and friends, aged 13, Deanbridge)

What we are arguing here is that it is the same young people who would naturally explore for themselves when they are at home, who in school can become trapped into an over-dependence on a teacher. This over-dependence, we would argue, inhibits exploratory and playful activity, the very resources which are central to learning. This way of working may also be leading them to think that there is only one right answer – therefore they would rather wait with their hands up for 15 minutes than get an answer wrong.

Another reason there is little opportunity for play in school is that play is often constructed as being in opposition to work. However, Davis *et al.* (2000) suggest that the opposite of play is actually rigidity or motionlessness and they stress that 'a key quality of all living forms is play – and conversely a likely indicator of an inert form is a lack of play' (p147). At home, as we discussed in Chapter 10, young people recognise that computer environments actually 'afford' play, and that computers are increasingly designed to be playable; within the school setting, however, they are often not able to mobilise this resource.

Time for play is also a necessary (although not sufficient) condition for creativity to develop, and policy makers are beginning to recognise the potential of ICT for supporting creative processes.[8] However, as long as the use of computers is structured around single lessons with little opportunity for sustained work on projects over a period of time, there will be little possibility for young people to enter into the 'flow'[9] of creative production in school.

Copying – cheating or an opportunity to learn?

We saw in Chapter 10 that in the home young people often copy the work of others, whether it is the words of a song, pieces of clipart or some information from the Web. We argued that this copying may be a way of entering a world with which young people are unfamiliar, a way of beginning to master something new. We also argued that we need to look more closely at this practice in order to understand the way in which copying can also involve creative transformation. But we also know that the academic world in general and schools in particular are extremely concerned about copying from the work of others. The following is an extract from an interview with one of our children's primary school teachers:

Int: I know that [copying] has come up as a subject of concern amongst parents and amongst other people about kids getting information from the computer and printing it out and bringing it in.

Teacher: … what I probably don't like about it is the children probably have gone in to the relevant place and they just print it. They haven't read it themselves or scanned it. They don't know what it contains either, other than it's on the subject that we were talking about in history yesterday.

(Primary school teacher)

Within a high-stakes assessment system such as the one which currently dominates British schools, any form of 'copying' is regarded as cheating. However, if a piece of work is not being assessed, then copying could be seen as a process of getting 'into the head of an expert'.[10] As we saw in Chapters 5, 6 and 10, most of what might be considered to be copying actually involves some form of creative transformation or re-representation of the object being copied. Also, young people choose to copy within practices which have nothing to do with school work, such as copying the words of a song. Copying then has to be seen to be a central part of human activity and thus human learning and an aspect which should be explicitly recognised by schools. Copying and progressively transforming an object within a digital environment could be actively encouraged as a creative way of becoming immersed within a new practice on the basis that 'the idea isn't to duplicate what was done, but to participate in a particular way of thinking'.[11]

Control and creativity

From the top down

Given that computers are mostly used by young people at home to open up their approaches to learning and enquiry, why is it that in many schools computers are being used to close down, control and suppress initiative and inquiry? Does this relate to the centrally controlled and increasingly prescriptive National Curriculum in England and Wales? Does it relate to networked computer systems which often operate in much less flexible ways than stand-alone computers? Does it relate to an emphasis on ICT skills? Does it relate to the nature of schooling itself as a system for social control, or to teachers' lack of confidence and knowledge with ICT? Within this section we will examine some of these factors, predominantly focusing on ICT as a separate curriculum subject because this is how the majority of our young people experienced ICT at school.

Certainly lack of confidence amongst teachers was one factor that was identified by our case study pupils and we suggest that a lack of confidence with and knowledge about an area will perhaps inevitably provoke a teacher into being more over-directive than normal because of a very real fear of pupils becoming out of control.

> I find that the teachers aren't that literate in computers. They say, 'Don't do anything apart from what we've told you in case it crashes … because I don't want it on my head …' which basically means, 'I don't know how to undo it.'
>
> (David, aged 12, Deanbridge)

Many teachers, it seems, were only just keeping one step ahead of their pupils, as this primary school teacher explained to us:

> My computer skills are so weak … well I am honest, I literally live sort of from hand to mouth and prior to each visit, if at all possible prior to each visit to the computer room with my class I've got to go down there the night before to make sure that I can at least sort of access the bits I want and I can manipulate the bits and pieces of whatever software I'm using.
>
> (Primary school teacher)

A fear that the technology is not going to work is also likely to provoke a teacher to become more over-directive than normal. Increasingly, in schools, the software which is available is on a system which is centrally controlled either by a local authority or a managed service provider. This practice undoubtedly leads to a lack of control on the part of the teacher which could influence the way in which they behave in the classroom. We recognise that it has not been straightforward for schools to manage networked systems which often work in less than optimal ways. As Andrew Smith, the ICT co-ordinator in one of our secondary schools, explained:

> My main goal initially was, having assessed what the problems were, was to upgrade large chunks of the network. We had a serious problem in the very early stages in that it was very, very unreliable. Three or four times a lesson you could probably guarantee the machines would crash, so I first of all taught myself, I got sent on one course but really taught myself the network operating systems, how networks should be structured by asking questions of contractors [...] The technician left, so I was sort of left with no technical support.
>
> (Andrew Smith, ICT co-ordinator)

Many ICT co-ordinators, however, are not only responsible for managing the hardware and software provision within a school, but also for developing the ICT curriculum. Yet there is little support for these co-ordinators to develop good pedagogical practice with ICT. Indeed, ICT has only been a separate school subject for the last few[12] years and so there is little history of good pedagogical practice linked to ICT as a school subject. As an interim measure, many schools are using CLAIT (computer literacy and information technology)[13] materials to train their teachers and these present a highly prescriptive and potentially problematic step-by-step model of teaching.

In the Staff Training section of the ICT handbook for one of the project schools, for example, the teacher is being asked to work through a sequence of instructions (numbered from 1.1.1 to 1.4.3) related to learning aspects of word processing. The teacher, as student, has not created their own text, has not created their own need for manipulating text and is not being taught about how to find out how to do things for themselves, through exploration of the menus and icons on offer. In fact, this type of training material leaves absolutely no space for the user to play with the icons at the interface of the screen. It may well be that teachers are being influenced by such CLAIT materials, because this model of teaching ICT appears to be very pervasive in schools.

The key problem that this approach raises for ICT use in schools, and indeed elsewhere, is that it emphasises a linear sequential approach to learning 'how to use the computer', rather than an approach which emphasises a flexible development of strategies for 'learning how to learn to use' the computer. Today, powerful computer packages are constantly being developed; as a result, it is never possible for an individual to know everything about every package. Accordingly, it is likely that the ability to explore new interfaces to find out what you need to know, or examine what is on offer, may be the most important 'skill' of all; the ability to learn to learn, rather than learning to 'know' the computer system.

Interestingly the English ICT curriculum[14] does not appear to place an overemphasis on ICT skills. Consider the following Key Stage 2 specifications:

> During key stage 2 pupils use a wider range of ICT tools and information sources to support their work in other subjects. They develop their research skills and decide what information is appropriate for their work. They begin to question the plausibility and quality of information. They learn how to amend their work and present it in a way that suits its audience.

However, the ICT curriculum is specified without a problem context, it is fragmented into 'levels' and it is compulsory. Possibly all these three factors come together to lead many teachers and schools to 'deliver ICT' in a routine as opposed to a creative way. In the world of work and, as we have seen throughout this book, in the home, ICT is always used within a context which has meaning for the user. By contrast, in schools, ICT teachers are having to make up contexts (such as the 'boiled maggots' context described in the spreadsheet example above) and this may be where the problem lies.

From the bottom up

As we saw in Chapter 10, in the home, most young people do not learn about ICT for its own sake; we would therefore not expect many young people to be interested in lessons which focus mainly on learning ICT. But what about Alistair whom we first met at primary school? He was longing to go to secondary school to learn more about computer programming. At home, from the age of seven, he learned to master his computer system. When he went to secondary school he gained pleasure from exploring the bounds of the school computer network.

Alistair: Well I've already managed to sneak a copy of QBasic onto it.
Int: How did you do that?
Alistair: I took it on a floppy disk. I can't believe it. They don't want you to access the rest of their network drives, but they give you access to your one. And so all you have to do is go to the Tools Menu in Windows Explorer and select Go To and then type in another drive. And I found Sonic on their machines.
Int: Found what?
Alistair: Sonic, Sega
Int: So do you play with that at lunchtime?
Alistair: I managed to copy it to one of their network drives. They haven't noticed it yet. It's the only non-educational game they've got.

(Alistair, at age 11, Deanbridge)

However, Alistair never succeeded in finding an outlet for his interests and expertise in school, despite his hopes that the secondary school would provide a computer club which would support him learning Java programming. For family reasons Alistair moved to Scotland in his second year of secondary school and his email to us, after he left the school, reflects his despondency:

> One of the IT staff shouted at me for going into Windows Explorer, everyone used it at Deanbridge to open files and stuff. They had made a custom start menu and there was no desktop, so couldn't they just take it off the start menu ... and he threatened me with 'being kicked off the network for all the time I was at the school such a threat!'

(Alistair at age 12, after relocating to Scotland, email to researcher)

This is an example of bottom-up creativity meeting top-down control. Another example came from Huw; he explains how he and his friends (called computer 'nerds') put 'stuff' in other pupils' files in order to both secretly demonstrate their expertise and to 'get their own back' on the pupils who were calling them nerds:

> ... computer nerds did this, just to spite the people who used to pick on them. Because they thought the people who were the nerds were the inferior people. But then they were shown up and they had their accounts disabled by the administrator because they had stuff in their

file that they shouldn't have that the actual nerds had put on there just to get their own back perhaps.

(Huw, at age 13, Pen-y-Bryn)

In the same interview Huw went on to say:

And we [the computer nerds] were talking to each other, but the thing we forgot to think about is we forgot that the computers aren't connected directly, they all go through the main administrative computer first, which is the network server, and it takes over all functions and the message pops up. Well anyway, so Ashley's clever idea was to send Win Pop-up through the server and we kind of like got caught. We got our accounts disabled, so we had to go then and tell him what it was. He had to delete it then off File Manager itself. But it's still in existence it's just hidden. He doesn't know it's there, we do.

(Huw, at age 13, Pen-y-Bryn)

These two examples from Alistair and Huw illustrate the ways in which, for some young people, creativity and knowledge about ICT systems is being diverted into very clever rule-breaking activity. This powerfully suggests that if within a system there are no natural outlets for an individual's creativity and learning, these natural abilities will manifest themselves in inappropriate places. Moreover, young people are likely to be learning more from these subversive ICT-related activities than from what they are explicitly being taught at school. For both Alistair and Huw, their expertise in managing computer systems was being ignored by their respective schools. Their expertise had not found a voice in the school system although this expertise could be considered to relate to a very high level of the ICT National Curriculum, such as, for example, this Level 8 specification:

Pupils independently select appropriate information sources and ICT tools for specific tasks, taking into account ease of use and suitability. They design successful ways to collect and prepare information for processing. They design and implement systems for others to use. When developing systems that respond to events, they make appropriate use of feedback.[15]

There are many ways in which ICT can be used in schools and we would agree with Trilling and Hood (2001) that computers-as-subject of study fits with an industrial age model of schooling and that computers-as-tool for learning is the model which fits with schools which are readapting to the knowledge age. Maria experienced computers-as-subject in her secondary school in England and she was very demotivated by these experiences; despite her interest and expertise at home, she actively chose not to continue studying ICT after the age of 14. In her previous school in Ghana (her father was Ghanaian), she had clearly experienced the computer-as-tool for learning.

Maria: We could use the games and Encarta and stuff in our free time.
Mum: In Ghana they did a project on slavery and wrote a story, and they did the slaves up to the moment they were captured and then they exchanged it with schools in America.
Maria: We used the Internet in Ghana. We do have it in school here but we're never allowed to use it … there's a whole row of computers and our passwords don't work on any of those computers in that row. I think there's something wrong with them.

(Maria, aged 13, Saxingham)

From the descriptions she gave, Maria's school in Ghana seems to have been more open in its approach to the use of games in free time, more open in the ways in which students accessed computers and also more enlightened in its organisation of student projects. This contrasts with what seems to be the dominant practice in England and Wales which centres around overly controlled, overly prescriptive, overly linear approaches to the use of computers within lessons which are dedicated to teaching ICT. Moreover, we are fearful that the implementation of a compulsory ICT Key Stage 3 Strategy[16] will make the situations which we are describing even worse. We are critical of this new strategy because it appears to leave very little time and space for young people to become engaged in the flow of creative production. It represents an industrial model of schooling with the teacher as knowledge-giver in an area where any one teacher will never be able to know all about the vast knowledge-domains which are being specified. Our evidence would suggest that such curriculum specification might actually push teachers into pretending they know more than they do as opposed to supporting the two-way learning system which Huw so eloquently argued for in the quote at the beginning of this chapter.

Conclusion

> What has not yet been fully understood is that computer-based
> technologies can be powerful pedagogical tools – not just rich sources
> of information, but extensions of human capabilities and contexts for
> social interactions supporting learning. The process of using technology
> to improve learning is never solely a technical matter, concerned only
> with properties of educational hardware and software. Like a textbook
> or any other cultural object, technology resources for education
> function in a social environment, mediated by learning conversations
> with peers and teachers.[17]

We have seen in this chapter that young people are predominantly
encountering the use of computers in schools in England and Wales within
dedicated ICT lessons. This is a practice which contrasts with what is
happening at home, where the use of a computer is usually embedded
within some other activity such as games playing, writing a story,
designing a garden or looking for information about a particular subject.
At home the computer is being harnessed as a tool for all learning, whereas
in schools in England and Wales the focus tends to be on computers-as-
subject of study with a particular emphasis on learning computer skills.
That the computer is more rapidly being made 'at home' in the domestic
context than in the schools context is in evidence in the difference between
the spatial organisation of computers in homes and schools (See pictures
11.1 and 11.2).

This is a difficult phenomenon to understand. The ICT curriculum in
England and Wales emphasises much more than computer skills, and all
national curriculum subjects specify the use of the computer as a tool for
learning. This suggests that it is important to understand the complex
relationship between policy specifications and practices in the classroom
with respect to ICT. There are certainly competing priorities emanating
from policy makers. On the one hand, there is an emphasis on back-to-
basics and traditional numeracies and literacies, which were important
in the industrial age. On the other hand there is a policy agenda to
transform schools for a knowledge-based economy, with visions of young
people learning online, any time, anywhere. Teachers and schools are
left to make sense of these competing agendas and this leaves very little
space for teachers to learn how to incorporate ICT into their teaching in
ways which transform both learning and the knowledge which is being
learned.

There is considerable work to be done in this area, which we can
appreciate through our ongoing project – InterActive Education.[18] This

Picture 11.1 Computer games at home in Heather's bedroom

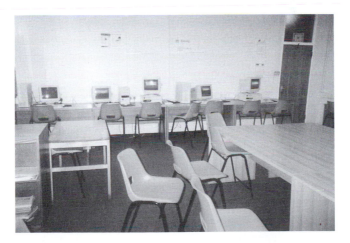

Picture 11.2 The computer lab in one of the secondary schools

project is investigating the ways in which ICT can be used to enhance learning within a wide range of school subjects at both primary and secondary level and shows that within our current structures teachers *can* use ICT to transform learning. In order to do this, however, they need to be part of supportive social networks which prioritise learning about ICT, learning about the relationship between ICT and a particular knowledge domain, learning about teaching, and learning about how children learn. There is, also, increasing evidence from countries outside the UK, that computers can and are being used creatively in schools. For example in Mexico, a developing country, computers are being used by many mathematics teachers in creative and challenging ways in some of the poorest schools in the country.[19] Personal communication with Angela McFarlane also confirms this view; her recent experience of observing children using computers in Chile starkly contrasts with what she oftens finds when she visits schools in England.

In contrast with what many early enthusiasts believed would happen when computers were first introduced to schools,[20] it is absolutely clear that the presence of technology alone will not improve education. In the home, parents, siblings and friends are crucial parts of the social system which support young people to learn. At school teachers need to develop similar social networks to support their own learning in creative and constructive ways. And when we understand better the role of social systems in learning then we will be able to design schools of the future which begin to organise space and time in ways in which people can interact with computer networks in productive ways.

Part VI

Conclusion

Chapter 12

Conclusion

> Professor Bell is convinced that in the near future it will be possible to see by telegraph, so that a couple conversing by telephone can at the same time see each other's faces. Extending the idea, photographs may yet be transmitted by electricity, and if photographs, why not landscape views? Then the stay-at-home can have the whole world brought before his eyes in a panorama without moving from his chair.
>
> (The Industrial Development of Electricity, 1894, quoted in Marvin, 1988, p260)

Humans have always had intimate associations with the devices and technologies they have created and no matter what the technology, contemporary commentators have predicted that the consequences will be socially transformative. Of all the new technologies that are currently available to us, screen-based technologies that provide new forms of access to information and new ways of working with knowledge and with other people have particular social and educational significance. The progressive invasion of the classroom, the living room, and other public and private spaces – bedrooms, shops, arcades – by computers, games consoles, the CD-ROM, the Internet, etc., constitutes, many have argued, a techno-cultural revolution.[1] New forms of information storage and retrieval affect communication patterns which in turn affect social relationships and the psychological construction of the individual. People, it has been argued, are constituted differently in these new communication acts and structures.[2]

For most adults, much of the 'digital ecology'[3] which surrounds us is something that has developed in the course of our lifetimes and to which we have adapted – some of us more readily than others. But young people have been born into it and this has given rise to much speculation about its consequences; much of this speculative literature, as we have noted before, has emphasised the socially transformative nature of the technology. For example, several early Australian studies[4] argued that young people are fundamentally 'culturally positioned' by the pervasiveness of computer-based and media technologies which are resulting in the development of a new 'post-modernist consciousness'. Media, it was suggested, has replaced schooling as the prime 'ideological state apparatus'[5] in the socialisation of the young. This argument was taken further in another Australian study, that of Green and Bigum (1993, p122), who suggested that

> ... a new kind of subjectivity is forming, an entirely new identity formation emerging from the nexus between youth culture and the increasingly global media complex. This we shall describe for the moment and with all due trepidation in terms of post modern subjectivity, understanding by this a particular realisation of social identity and social agency embodied in new forms of human being and becoming.

As a result of this transformation, they argued that there are now 'aliens in the classroom' – young people who are differently motivated, differently designed and differently constructed.

As we indicated in Chapter 1, the starting point for the ScreenPlay project was our considerable scepticism about these sorts of arguments and predictions; about the idea that young people are somehow transformed by their engagement with the new technologies. Such arguments were, we felt, oversimplified, based on 'essentialist' assumptions about children (that all the children of what has been called the 'Y' generation[6] are all the same) and about technology (that it is the technology itself which is determining generational difference). The basis of our scepticism was two-fold. In the first place we were sceptical of the empirical basis of many of the claims being made in the mid-1990s. Much of the writing was self-avowedly speculative rather than based on empirical research. And those empirical studies that did exist were, for the most part, based on relatively flimsy evidence, where there was a tendency for researchers to focus on the 'exotic' activities of a small number of young people rather than look at the commonplace activities of a broad cross-section of the population.

The second source of our scepticism was theoretical. If we are to learn anything from the historical study of the introduction of technologies into our social world[7] it is that the way in which those technologies are accommodated into everyday living has been far more complex than initially predicted. Technologies always enter into already existing socially constructed worlds – a fact routinely recognised by designers who take considerable care to design technologies which are accessible and which resonate with the consumers they are trying to attract.[8] Yet the complexities involved in the 'socialisation' of technology are more than ones of design. Interestingly, such complexities start to emerge if one takes the user (in this case the child) rather than, as so much of the speculative literature has done, the technology, as the centre of analysis.

We also felt it important to recognise that, outside the context of the school, we know very little about how young people actually learn to use such technologies and how they engage with them, how they use them as 'cognitive tools'.[9] Before we could assert that such practices are socially and educationally transformative, we believed that much more careful empirical and theoretical work was needed contrasting learning at home and learning at school. For example, it has been suggested that computer users may well abandon traditional routes to gain knowledge and, in processes which borrow more from experiment and play, acquire skills demanding a more creative approach.[10] But, we wanted to know, is this in reality the case? Important theoretical and empirical questions therefore emerged on the relationship between school and 'non-school' learning. Finally, we felt it was essential to recognise that, however powerful new technologies are, they are only one context amongst many that young people inhabit. As Grossberg (1988, p125) points out, 'if youth lives in post modernity, it also lives in many other places and contexts'. More careful empirical research, we hoped, might help to put into perspective any changes that do come about in young people's lives as a result of engaging with ICTs.

It was with these theoretical and empirical questions in mind that we designed the ScreenPlay project. And as we indicated in Chapter 1, in order to address these questions we considered it necessary to use a range of different empirical strategies. The questions we wished to raise demanded careful, in-depth analysis. Only by 'following the individual child' as he or she engaged with ICTs at home alone, with family members, with friends and at school, could we gain some purchase on the complexity of the issues involved. But we were also concerned to ensure that we worked with an ordinary cross-section of children, from different social and cultural backgrounds and attending ordinary but different types of school. If we were not to fall into the trap of focussing only on the 'exotic', then our case study children needed to be carefully selected from a broader sample. Our initial questionnaire therefore not only provided large scale data on a broad cross-section of children in ordinary schools, it also provided a vitally important sampling frame. In this way we could ensure that our case study children were indeed an ordinary cross-section when judged on a range of key criteria. By combining both survey and case study methodologies in this way, we hoped to overcome some of the more obvious limitations of biased sampling in qualitative research.

But we also recognised that we needed to employ a range of theoretical frameworks too. Like so many educational problems, understanding the role of ICT in children's lives is not a straightforward issue; there was no single theoretical framework available that was sufficiently rich to allow us to 'prise open' all of the complexities that were raised by the questions we wanted to pose. A multi-disciplinary approach, drawing on sociology, media and cultural studies and socio-cultural psychology, was essential. Working as a multi-disciplinary team has been highly productive but not always easy. There is a danger that in wanting to draw broadly on a range of different perspectives, one does not do theoretical justice to any of them. Nevertheless, at the end of the project, we remain convinced that the advantages of this way of working have outweighed the disadvantages; without a multi-disciplinary approach, we could not have addressed many of the 'common sense' issues that concern parents, teachers and policy makers. Such concerns stubbornly refuse to be confined to single disciplines or theoretical frameworks, however sophisticated or fashionable.

But now, at the end of the study, where are we in relation to the questions that we began with? In this concluding chapter we want to address just three key issues that have remained with us throughout our research, reflecting on what we now think we know about them. The three questions are:

- is there a 'digital divide' and if so what form does it take, and is it important in children's lives?
- is there a new 'digital generation' and if so, what does it look like?
- is there 'digital learning' and if so, in what ways is it different from other forms of learning?

We then want to go on to consider the implications of our findings for parents and for educationalists – teachers and policy makers.

Key questions

A digital divide?

What does our research tell us about the much vaunted 'digital divide'? Is there such a divide and if so what form does it take, and is it important in children's lives? The first point is to confirm that there is indeed a 'digital divide'; some children are excluded from the world of ICT by their family circumstances; others exclude themselves because they do not find ICT compatible with the social identity they are constructing for themselves. However, our research would suggest that the divide is more complex and more deep-seated than popular commentators or indeed national policies often recognise. This is because children's exclusion from a full engagement with ICTs takes a number of forms. First, and most obviously, we became aware that a significant minority of children are excluded from home-based access to ICT because of cost; cost is a major feature in the initial purchase of a computer and in ongoing maintenance and upgrading. Cost also continues to be a major factor in influencing children's access to online facilities even when their parents have managed to purchase a computer in the first place. The fact that virtually none of the 855 children in our initial survey had experience of accessing ICTs in places other than the home or school or (mainly for games) in friends' houses suggests that for this age group at least, community-based provision (libraries, youth centres, etc.) offers little in terms of overcoming such disadvantage. This is because the digital divide involves far more than mere physical access.

Becoming an effective user of ICT at home, we suggest, also involves having access to a rich array of learning resources, principally though not exclusively from other people. Parents and other family members who, through work and other educational experiences, bring such technical knowledge, networks and other resources into the home are hugely important in helping young people realise the potential of ICT in their lives. This is not to suggest that children who do not have such support will never become competent with ICTs; some children we met were very resourceful in trying to establish for themselves networks (both real and virtual) to support their learning. Nevertheless it is significant to observe that many of the young people who identified themselves on our initial questionnaire as ambivalent or low users seemed to have less ready access to such support. We also need to remind ourselves that many of these low and ambivalent users were from poorer socio-economic backgrounds; as we saw in Chapter 8, social and financial forms of disadvantage in relation to ICT use are closely interrelated.

But some of our families were more or less advantaged in other ways too. Some had the experience and confidence to engage directly with their children around the computer and, in this way, helped them to realise its 'educational' rather than its 'leisure' potential. This is not to deny that the 'leisure' potential of computers is itself very important; as we saw in Chapter 10, the 'playfulness' that can be learned through playing games is a key learning strategy. Nevertheless, some parents clearly recognised the power of ICT to support quite traditional forms of learning and supported and encouraged their children in doing that. A few others, particularly those with a strong technological background themselves, saw the power of ICT to support new forms of learning, what have been called 'elite literacies',[11] and were able to help their children understand and reflect on this potentiality. Once again, cultural and social differences between families positioned children quite differently in relation to ICT. From this perspective, the 'digital divide' is not between those who have a computer and those who do not; nor is it between those who can gain technical mastery of 'the new basics'[12] and those who can not. Rather it is between those who learn how to realise its educational potential in both new and traditional ways and those who are locked out of such worlds. When looked at from this point of view, many of the children we worked with who had computers and used them regularly were on the wrong side of the divide in terms of making meaningful use of them.

But if there is a 'digital divide', does it really matter? After all, some children exclude themselves from the world of computers; should we therefore be concerned about this? Despite our recognition that children and families must themselves have a right to choose, our conclusion is an unequivocal 'yes'. Children who do not have significant and substantial home-based access to ICT are at a disadvantage compared with those children who do. We come to this conclusion largely as a result of our comparison of homes and schools as contexts for learning and our recognition of the profound limitations of what is currently on offer in the majority of schools. Because of the way schools currently work, children who do not have an effective engagement with ICTs at home are missing out on the experience of playing with the technology; they are missing out on the experience of using multiple resources to support their learning; of working in their own time; of working with their own content in which the boundaries of specific knowledge domains dissolve. They are also missing out on the experience of changing the relationships between work and play, teaching and learning; creating and consuming. Yet our sense is that this is the world that children as they grow older will increasingly be expected to inhabit; a world where they will be expected to be confident in a range of different 'literacies' and the strategies for learning and working that they demand. While our schools remain unable to respond to these changes, those children who do not have access to well-supported experience at home are doubly excluded; they are excluded at home *and* at school since school learning so often fails to provide an adequate entry into this new world of learning.

A digital generation?

As we indicated above, questions about whether there is indeed a digital generation, whether, to use Green and Bigum's (1993) phrase, there are now 'aliens in the classroom', were central to our original research proposal. Frankly, we were sceptical. More recently, Green (1998, pp37–8) has made the following comments on the original discussion of 'aliens':

> … admittedly this (the concept of 'aliens') was always something of a deliberate provocation, a 'thought experiment' so to speak. We were concerned with two things: on the one hand, the notion that kids were being differently constructed, designed as a consequence of growing up immersed in new forms of relation with media technologies of various kinds … and on the other, the sense that teachers were increasingly like strangers in a strange land … This thesis has a certain (melo-) dramatic quality, to be sure and certainly things aren't as clear-cut as images such as these suggest. But even so, I think it has been generative to set such themes loose in the system, like a wave of hopefully benevolent viruses, because it is important – it seems to me – to find other and new ways of doing and thinking in education, in what are very different times and conditions.

Certainly those 'viruses' have been generative for us and we acknowledge the importance of ideas and metaphors which disrupt taken-for-granted assumptions in education. But where do we stand on this issue at the end of our project; are there indeed 'aliens', be they teachers or pupils, in today's classrooms? What our research has shown is that as far as children are concerned, the straightforward thesis of generational change is fundamentally flawed. What our research demonstrates is that, at present, children differ substantially in their engagement with ICTs – what they use them for, how much they use them and how important they are to them. For some of them, using the computer is almost a way of life, the primary medium through which they engage with the world and construct their identities. For others, it is of only moderate significance and for yet others it is an irrelevance or even something to be rejected entirely in the construction of a very different life story. Moreover, even for those who use the computer a great deal, it constitutes only one small part of their lives. Day-to-day relationships with parents, with teachers, with brothers and sisters and engagement with other sorts of work and other sorts of play were, for the children we met, far more significant than their lives on the screen; and importantly, many of these relationships remain unchanged by new technologies. Talk about a fundamental generational shift with the emergence of a new form of childhood – the 'cyberkid' – is not substantiated by our evidence.

But what about teachers; are they now the aliens in their own classrooms? Our work with teachers was much more limited than our work with children and their families. However, our observation is that, for the most part, teachers are not overwhelmed by the changes of a new digital culture. Whether or not they participate in it in their private lives (and as average professional adults there is every chance that they do) there was little evidence that their day-to-day practices in the classroom were fundamentally challenged by having to work with ICT. As became apparent in the last chapter, if anything, classrooms seem to be last bastion against such changes.

But despite our scepticism of the 'aliens' thesis, it is hard to deny that our world is changing; ICTs are now proliferating in almost every domestic, leisure and work setting. Moreover, the majority of young people do now have some regular, if highly variable, engagement with that world and it is hard to deny that this is potentially challenging for schools. While not denying the importance of these changes, our conclusion is that the 'aliens' metaphor is now, and probably always was, unhelpful. What children bring with them into school, albeit in different degrees, is experience of the ordinary world outside, which is increasingly, in key respects, a digitalised world. This is the world that is overtaking us all, not only children, and to reify the notion of a digital generation obscures that important point. Moreover, as we indicated in our discussion of Helen in Chapter 7, as engagement with ICTs becomes more routinised, more domesticated, more part of everyday life, it loses its significance; it becomes 'natural'. Computers in the very near future are likely to be as unmarked, but integrated, into everyday domestic and working life, as telephones, cars, electricity or even the humble pencil. If this is the world that both children and teachers now routinely inhabit in their lives outside of school, then what is 'alien' in the classroom is neither the teachers nor the pupils *per se* but the curriculum and working practices of schools which find it so difficult to accommodate the challenges of the new technologies. This brings us to our third and final question; is learning different?

Digital learning?

In our analysis of learning, we highlighted a number of features that seemed to characterise learning with computers at home as distinct from learning with computers at school. In the home we saw that children control what it is they want to do on the computer: that their 'learning' is incidental, a by-product of their substantive activity; that they control their own time; that they use a wide range of learning resources (playful discovery, asking people, looking things up, using online support); that their expertise is often celebrated by family and peers; and that their learning involves 'depth' rather than 'breadth'. By contrast, learning in school more often involves teachers choosing the activity; learning is the explicit purpose of computer-based activities; there is seldom sufficient time to engage effectively; the learning resources allowed are much more limited and primarily linguistically based (verbal or written instructions); children's expertise is often not recognised or explicitly rejected; and learning involves 'breadth' rather than 'depth'.

Given that these experiences of learning are so different, we must ask if it is ICTs themselves that impose these distinctive ways of working; if that were so, it might explain why schools currently find it so hard to accommodate them within their traditional approaches to teaching and learning. In truth, however, it seems that many of these features are simply those associated with informal rather than formal learning. When we learn a new recipe, when we learn how to repair a broken window, or how to grow tomatoes, our learning has many of the same features that children describe in their learning with ICTs. It is the interest in the substantive topic that drives us forward, learning itself incidental; we use a wide variety of resources to help us learn; we have time to experiment; and our achievements, however modest, are celebrated by our family and friends. As Coffield stated in his final report to the ESRC's Learning Society Programme (Coffield 2000), informal learning is essential and ubiquitous; it constitutes 'the structure below the surface', perhaps accounting for two-thirds of learning but remaining largely unseen. Yet despite its importance, research and theorising on informal learning is substantially underdeveloped though there is at least a growing awareness of the significance of social networks in the process – what some, more hopeful social analysts, have characterised as the dominant form of social organisation emerging in the context of globalisation.[13] Certainly our research would substantiate the importance of social networks in learning with ICTs, though we would place such networks alongside other resources both virtual and real and, in particular, the affordances offered by different technologies.

But does this mean that there is nothing different about learning with computers? Our observation is that there are indeed a number of important and distinctive features of learning with ICT but that these are not the features that emerge by contrasting home and school; this is because they are largely absent from school learning but taken for granted at home. For example, as we have indicated a number of times in this book, the speed and sheer volume of information flow associated with ICTs is unmatched in other contexts; learning how to live with the depth and breadth of information made available by ICTs is a unique feature of learning in this context. Forms of interactivity offered by ICTs are also highly distinctive. Such interactivity can be virtual, as captured by Turkle (1984) in her metaphor suggesting that the screen acts as a 'second self', allowing us to 'leave a little bit of ourselves on the screen'. Increasingly, of course, such interactivity is with other people: through email, through chat rooms and other interactive environments. Again as Turkle (1995) says, as we 'step through the looking glass', there is now often someone else there as well.

Volume and speed of information and different forms of interactivity are central to the nature of ICTs; they are what makes life on the screen different and powerfully engaging. Yet there was little evidence from our research that these were essential features of learning with ICTs at school. This, we would suggest, is because at present in school, computers are seen primarily as a *resource* for learning rather than a *context* for learning. The hope of our national curriculum and much of our day-to-day practice in schools is that, by capturing the power of ICTs, we will be able to teach children to learn what we have always wanted them to learn, but more effectively, and perhaps cheaply, than in the past. The reality of a world saturated by ICTs is that interactivity and the speed and volume of information flow fundamentally transform the content as well as the nature of teaching and learning in the first place. The context *is* different. What has to be learned, and how it has to be learned, is fundamentally changed. Yet, as we saw in Chapter 11, too many schools today still focus on 'skills' and 'methods'. Yet to do so, as Green (1998) argues, 'is not simply a matter of missing the point but, rather, it arguably contributes to and even *constitutes* the very problem itself' (p37). Learning in a digital world is different but that difference has yet to be recognised by our schooling system.

Some policy issues

What then are the implications of our research? In this final section we focus firstly on the implications for parents and then for educationalists – both teachers and policy makers.

Implications for parents

For parents, perhaps one of the first things to state is that having a computer in the home is potentially beneficial to children. If it can be afforded, it is a good investment. However, parents also need to recognise that, in itself, the computer is not necessarily 'educational'; nor is it necessarily good, bad or dangerous. It can be all or none of these things; what matters is how children and also how families including parents engage with it.

In Chapter 3 we used a number of different metaphors to describe how families did indeed engage with the computer; some we said saw it as an 'interloper' and kept it at a distance, others saw it as 'a children's machine', while others seemed to place it 'at the heart of the family'. What is clear is that those families who were able to place the computer 'at the heart of the family' were most effective in helping their children exploit its full potential. This way of looking at the computer was sometimes reflected in its physical location (in public and shared spaces) but more importantly in the ways in which the computer was valued and used by the family. Families that engaged with the computer in this way did not see it as a special object, too sacred or too expensive to be used except on special occasions or under close supervision. Rather it was seen as a valuable resource that everyone could benefit from; that everyone, what ever their experience, could engage with.

Parents in such families found regular opportunities to engage with their children's computer-based activities, celebrating their achievements and encouraging them to recognise the learning as well as the pleasure potential of the technology. Even parents who themselves are not particularly technologically competent can do this. One effective strategy for such engagement is to encourage our children to teach us what they know. As we saw in Chapter 9, developing the skills of being a teacher as well as a learner is a key strategy for participating in an ICT-based world. As knowledge proliferates, expertise becomes more distributed; none of us now can ever know everything. Therefore helping children themselves develop the skills of teaching is valuable in itself; it also provides powerful validation of their knowledge, and gives them an important opportunity to reflect on and articulate what it is they know. The 'meta-cognition' demanded by teaching is a powerful stimulus for learning in itself.

But what messages do we have for parents about particular activities – games, for example? Many parents express concern about their children playing games; our conclusion however is that in principle, games playing is a valuable dimension of computer use. As we described in Chapters 5 and 10, it is through games playing that children develop 'playfulness' in relation to the computer – a key strategy in effective learning. They can also gain a great deal of pleasure from games playing. All but one of our case study children had developed their confidence and enjoyment in computer use, at least in part, by playing games. Parents therefore should not see games as something to be rejected or discouraged nor should they see games playing as somehow opposed to 'serious' computer use; children need to be able to use the computer for a wide range of different sorts of activity including, and perhaps when they are younger even primarily, games.

Our views on commercial forms of 'edutainment' are more ambivalent. Only a minority of our young people engaged with these forms of software and as they grew older and more confident in their computing skills, even this minority seemed to leave them behind. Clearly such software is only as good as the programming behind it; in principle therefore there is no reason why software manufacturers should not develop forms of edutainment that do provide children with valuable and stimulating environments for learning. All we can say is that most of the software that we came across in our work with families was relatively limited. Too often, behind the glossy graphics and the marketing hype, children were being asked to engage with the computer in very restricted ways. As a result, children seemed to derive only limited learning and, interestingly, only limited pleasure from such software. While we would not therefore warn parents off purchasing edutainment software, we would suggest that they should treat cautiously marketing claims that it will significantly enhance their children's learning. Moreover, if children were given a diet of only such software, there is a possibility that their skills and confidence with the computer would be restricted.

And, finally, what of the Internet? Clearly, if edutainment programs provide a learning context that is sometimes too limited to be truly educational, the Internet, with its literally limitless possibilities, is the opposite. It is an immensely powerful resource for work, for leisure and for education and all of us need to find some way of accommodating it in our lives. At the time that we undertook our fieldwork, the Internet was only beginning to have an impact on families; today it presents a major resource but also a major challenge for all parents. Most of the parents we met were relatively reluctant to talk explicitly about what they saw as the dangers of the Internet: access to pornography, violence, dangerous liaisons. Fears, to the extent that they were there, were often expressed in terms of money: 'We limit our children's use because of the cost' was a common response. Nevertheless, behind that response were, we felt, serious concerns.

And indeed parents are right to be concerned about the Internet. Its introduction to the home means that the home is, to a degree, a different place. We would be naïve to suggest that the home is now, or ever has been, an entirely private and secure bastion against the dangers of the world. The introduction of TV, and even the novel, let alone the incidence of domestic violence, means that most homes are anything but safe havens. Nevertheless, the Internet does potentially mark a step change in the ready access to what most parents consider unwanted and unwelcome information and contacts.

But, as parents, how should we respond to such challenges? Should we refuse to subscribe to the Internet; should we police our children closely; or should we trust them? In our research we came across families that adopted each of these positions. Our view is that we have no alternative but to trust our children; the potentiality of the Internet is so significant that to exclude children from it is unhelpful and anyway, with the proliferation of access sites (in public places, in friends' houses), is unlikely to be successful. So too is close monitoring. As we saw on a number of occasions during our research, if children are more technically competent than their parents then close monitoring is easily subverted. The answer for parents is no different from how we deal with any other difficult or dangerous issues, such as sexuality or drugs. We have to trust our children but we also have to educate them about the dangers as well as the possibilities of the online world. That again means engaging with them closely in their ICT-based world, not policing what they do but finding opportunities to work with them as equals and celebrating their achievements. With the domestication of the Internet the metaphor of 'the street' is in some ways now more accurate to describe our homes than the 'safe haven'. The street is an exciting and valuable environment (it can take us places) but it can also be dangerous if we do not know how to use it properly. Just as it is our job as parents to teach our children how to use the street safely and wisely, so it is our job to do the same with the Internet.

Implications for teachers and policy makers – the school of the future

But what are the implications for education? What should the school of the future look like if we are genuinely to capitalise on the benefits of ICT? One of the interesting things about our research is that although it focused mainly on the home, through it we have come to understand just how important schools are in relation to children's ICT education. Schools are vital for a number of different reasons. The first is because, as we have seen, when children engage with ICTs at home, that engagement is often relatively restricted in its focus; their home-based learning is characterised by 'depth' rather than 'breadth'. For example, as we indicated in Chapter 10, very few children at present are using ICT at home to engage in numeracy-related practices. Schools therefore have a vital role to play in ensuring children are exposed to the full range of technology's potential in all subject areas.

But we also noted how at present most of our children and indeed their families were relatively uncritical of what it is they were learning through ICT. In Chapter 9, we gave the example of Samantha who was frustrated because she could not find out about Welsh lovespoons on Encarta. Encarta effectively silenced her cultural heritage but without the intervention of school or other informed adults, neither she nor her family was able to gain a critical perspective on the knowledge that was being presented to her. By using the computer at home, children may well be developing new and more elaborate forms of literacy; they are developing 'implicit' understandings of how and why and when to combine resources, and of the strengths and drawbacks of particular tools. What they may not be developing, however, are the 'critical literacies' that enable them to see these resources as socially and culturally specific products.

As with media studies more generally, it is arguably increasingly important that we recognise that cultural tools, such as particular software packages, are just that – that they are the products of specific times and specific places and specific interests. This is not simply to say that we need children to understand the role of Microsoft within global capitalism (although this would be interesting) but to say that we need a recognition of the partiality of cultural resources, and of differences between them. This is about recognising our own difference from others and attempting to communicate across barriers as much as it is about developing a coherent critique of 'bias' in information.

However, schools, we came to recognise, have another, even more important function in relation to ICT and that concerns the digital divide. As we reminded readers above, the digital divide does exist and involves far more than mere physical access to technology. As we described in Chapter 10, children who have well-supported access to computers at home almost 'naturally' seem to develop the ability to use what we called the 'person-plus' model of learning: they work interactively with the technology; they use multiple learning resources (playful discovery, working with others, modelling, etc.); they learn through the process of doing; they develop the ability to use multiple literacies, often working in more than one software environment at a time. These, we would suggest, are the key skills that young people will need in their future work; they are also the skills they need to be a full and active member of a democratic society in a digital age. Yet what concerns us is that, at present, schools do not seem to be providing these sorts of learning experiences. Children who are currently disadvantaged at home by not having well-supported access remain excluded. Certainly policy makers must continue to explore ways of giving all groups in society physical access to ICT, but physical access is, we have learned, only the beginning of what real access means. If education is to challenge the digital divide then schools themselves have a vitally important role to play.

What then must the schools of tomorrow do if the learning experiences they offer children are to be as good and productive as those experiences in most homes? At one level, the lessons of our comparison of learning at home and at school are simple enough. Schools of the future need to give children more time to engage effectively with ICT; children need time to get into the flow of production, time to get pleasure. As Maria said to us, 'If I don't enjoy something then I don't usually learn.' Teachers also need to find ways of recognising and valuing children's existing skills and knowledge; most importantly, they need to recognise the importance of multiple learning resources including the importance of learning collaboratively, learning from other people, learning by copying and modelling what others do.

But we would suggest that these changes are unlikely to come about until schools and policy makers recognise the limitations of much current practice in schools; limitations which derive at least in part from our centrally driven curriculum and assessment systems. Difficulties in the curriculum arise from the fact that in England and Wales, ICT is currently constructed as a separate subject. The traditional subjects of our national school curriculum such as Mathematics, English or Geography represent areas of knowledge that for generations have demonstrated that they are vital to our society. However, traditional subjects also need to acknowledge that outside school, these domains are being transformed in significant ways by the introduction of digital tools. This implies that these traditional subjects themselves need to be adaptive to change. Yet for years, traditional subjects have been resistant to incorporating the use of the computer as a tool for learning. National curriculum Mathematics has taken scant account of the role of computational environments to change mathematical practices; national curriculum English has taken scant account of the role of digital environments in changing literacy practices. And our case study children recognised this. For example, as David said to us:

> My English teacher stops you doing homework on the computer … she said, 'Unless I tell you, don't do any more homeworks on the computer David'… she claims that the grammar checker cannot possibly work and so I typed up an entire page that was completely wrong grammar and then used the grammar checker. She said, 'You must have done that by hand.' She obviously doesn't like computers … she obviously doesn't want to believe they are good …
>
> (David, aged 12, Deanbridge)

As a result of such attitudes, ICT has been forced to develop as a separate subject in England and Wales and now spans Mathematical Modelling, Design and Technology, Computer Science and Media and Cultural Studies (DfES 2002c). However, like other new 'subjects' – 'problem-solving' and most recently 'creativity' – there is a danger of ICT becoming decontextualised and incoherent. Indeed this was one of the most abiding criticisms made by children of their ICT experience in schools – because it was decontextualised, activities had no meaning. As Maria, whom we quoted in Chapter 10, so tellingly said, using spreadsheets would have been interesting if she had *needed* to use them. Until mainstream subjects recognise and incorporate the challenges and changes to the nature of knowledge instituted by ICT within their particular fields, there is every chance that children will continue to find what they are offered dull and irrelevant.

But it is not only the curriculum that needs to be different in the schools of the future; approaches to teaching and learning also must change. As we indicated above, children at home already operate within what we have characterised as the 'person-plus' mode; they learn by exploiting a wide range of personal and technological resources and this strategy is central to all of our learning lives. Yet as Perkins (1993) has suggested, at present schools do not operate in this way; indeed they mount a persistent campaign to turn learning from 'person-plus' into 'person-solo': 'Person plus pencil, paper, text, almanac, encyclopaedia and so on is fine for studying but the target performance is typically person plus paper and pencil'.[14] Teaching in schools too often involves children being expected to function on their own or at best with only a limited range of resources (verbal instructions; written instructions); 'modelling' is called copying and frowned upon; children are only rarely allowed to collaborate and almost never to consult sources of information and expertise beyond the school.

But perhaps most significant of all in maintaining the artificial 'person-solo' model of teaching and learning is our high stakes assessment system. As both teachers and parents are only too well aware, in England and Wales, assessment has come to dominate our children's school lives with public assessment points at 5, 7, 11, 14, 16, 17 and 18. In every case, what is assessed is their performance in terms of 'person-solo'; it is based on a highly individualised model of learning. Given that it is individualised, given that it is so high stakes for teachers' personal careers and for their schools' competitive position in the marketplace, then it is not surprising that they adopt this individualised model of learning. With an entirely centralised curriculum and individualised forms of assessment, there is little space for the 'person-plus' model of teaching and learning that we believe is central for using ICTs effectively.

We are not arguing against any form of assessment in schools. There are creative alternatives which focus on the works produced by young people, and ICT can be used to make these alternative approaches possible. For example, it is possible to put extended pieces of writing or extended pieces of mathematics online for critical appraisal by communities outside school. As our research with children at home has so powerfully shown, creating authentic work for authentic audiences is highly motivating for all learners and whereas we fully understand that it is not easy to create the conditions for these practices in schools, we are particularly disturbed by the fact that the very potential of using ICT for these purposes is being inhibited by current educational policies in England and Wales.

In conclusion, our research would lead us to agree with Scardamalia (2001) that the schools of the future need to move to becoming knowledge-creating as opposed to knowledge-reproducing communities.

> Knowledge creators and expert learners alike deal directly with ideas. In contrast, most school learning situations, whether didactic or child-centred kinds, focus on something other than ideas – producing an essay, doing assigned exercises, carrying out a prescribed experiment, or undertaking a student-designed project … It is as if schools are designed to promote learning by any means as long as it does not involve work with knowledge. The challenge is to bring knowledge into the center of students' (and teachers') attention.[15]

That is what was so different in children's learning at home; their learning was authentic in that it was involved, albeit in different degrees, with knowledge creation. Within schools, it is crucially important for teachers to find ways of supporting reciprocal knowledge-building activity and, in order to do this, ways have to be found to make the knowledge-creation process more transparent. ICT tools can be used to support this process: the interactive whiteboard can be used collectively to build and interact with knowledge, as could an informal email link between members of a class who were engaged with particular learning. A virtual learning environment could also be explicitly constructed for this purpose. And if collective knowledge-building and knowledge-sharing were to become part of a culture of a school, then new tools will be developed to support this process, as illustrated so powerfully by the work of Scardamalia and Bereiter (2000).

We believe that the skills associated with knowledge creation are central to learning in the information age and this is the challenge that children who are already computer literate are posing for the education system. But the implications of such an approach are profound. They challenge us to recognise that we can no longer control the curriculum in traditional ways; they challenge the growing temptation on the part of a whole range of different bodies – from governments to software manufacturers – to define what good teaching is; and, probably most importantly, they challenge us all to find new ways of assessing and valuing children's capabilities themselves as knowledge producers.

Notes

---

1 The ScreenPlay project

1 Hertz, JC cited in Prensky (2001).
2 Green and Bigum (1993).
3 Sefton-Green (1998).
4 Silverstone and Hirsch (1992).
5 Wheelock (1992).
6 Hirsch (1992).
7 Skelton and Valentine (eds) (1998).
8 Livingstone and Bovill (1999).
9 Lupton (1995); Valentine and McKendrick (1997); Bingham and Valentine (1999).
10 Wertsch (1991).
11 Gibson (1979).
12 Pea (1993); Perkins (1993).
13 There were in fact 16 families as our 18 young people included two sets of twins.
14 We note that one family was only able to participate in the first three interviews of the study as the boy's mother sadly died during the course of the project. We continue to extend our thanks to them for their part in this study.

2 Setting the scene

1 BECTA (2001) and BECTA (2002).
2 Facer (2001).
3 DfES (2002a).
4 MORI (1997).
5 The wording on the questionnaire reflected the relative infancy of the Internet at that time and, in fact, we would treat the 25 per cent figure reported with some caution.
6 DfES (2002a), p7.
7 The Interactive and ScreenPlay surveys both draw on postcode data to determine the socio-economic make-up of the areas in which individual children lived. Children cannot be said necessarily to come from a 'high income' or 'low income' household, but from areas in which there is a high penetration of households with high income and education, or low income and education. We

used the MOSAIC mapping method for this process, which categorises postcodes into one of 52 different categories, and which can be interrogated for income and education variables. This technique is currently being used by HEFCE to determine backgrounds of University applicants.

8 DfES (2002a), p8.
9 DfES (2002a), p8.
10 DfES (2002a), p15.
11 DfES (2002a), p15.

3 Computer histories, computer roles in the home

1 Green and Bigum (1993); Tapscott (1988); Prensky (2001).
2 Haddon (1992).
3 Murdock (1992); Nixon (1998).
4 'Through the idea of incorporation we want to focus attention on the ways in which objects, especially technologies, are used. Technologies are functional. [...] To become functional a technology has to find a place within the moral economy of the household, specifically in terms of its incorporation into the routines of daily life' (Silverstone and Hirsch, 1992, p24).

4 The computer in family life

1 Morley and Robins (1995); Silverstone and Hirsch (1992).
2 See Livingstone and Bovill (1999); Holloway and Valentine (2003).
3 Early studies of the introduction of radio into the home saw the radio incorporated into the role of the family 'hearth' around which the family would gather for warmth and conversation. See Frith (1983).
4 In this family Steven is acting, in Michel de Certeau's (1992) terms, 'tactically' in relation to the computer, grasping an opportunity to access it as and when it presents itself. This means of acquiring access to a computer may be particularly significant amongst young people, many of whom may not be able to claim 'ownership' of the technology but who, nevertheless, want to assert their right to use it in competition with others: 'The place of a tactic belongs to the other. A tactic insinuates itself into the other's place fragmentarily, without taking it over in its entirety [...] Because it does not have a place, a tactic depends on time – it is always on the watch for opportunities that must be seized "on the wing". "Whatever it wins it does not keep"' (De Certeau, 1992, p23).
5 Murdock (1989); Nixon (1998).
6 See Holloway and Valentine (2003) for similar observation.

5 The digital landscape

1 Virilio (1987); Poster (1990).
2 Prensky (2001).
3 See Buckingham and Scanlon (2003) and Livingstone and Bovill (1999) for a discussion of different forms of 'interactivity'. Friedman (1995) also provides a useful framework within which to discuss different types of interactivity across a range of computer game genres. These critiques and frameworks are notably

more trenchant than the marketing discourses surrounding new media, in which 'interactive' is usually used in an uncritical manner to denote total user control over experiences and outcomes within the digital environment. It is this latter perspective that we will challenge within this chapter.

4 Gillespie (1995); Furlong (1995).
5 Greenfield (1984); Prensky (2001).
6 For a fuller discussion of these 'communities of learning' around computer games, see Williamson and Facer (2002).
7 As Eilola again argues: 'Games [and information resources] such as these provide environments for learning postmodernist approaches to communication and knowledge: navigation, constructive problem-solving, dynamic goal-construction' (Eilola, 1998, p188).
8 Green (1988).
9 Snyder (2001).
10 Much of this theoretical work is based on an understanding developed during the 1980s and 1990s that 'literacy': 'needs to be conceived within a broader social order, what Street and others have called a "new communicative order" (Kress and van Leeuwen, 1996; Lankshear, 1997; Street, 1998). […] The NLS reject the view of literacy as a "neutral" technical skill, conceptualising it instead as an "ideological practice, implicated in power relations and embedded in specific cultural meanings and practices"' (Street, 1995, p1), (Snyder, 2001, p118).

6 Writing, designing and making

1 See Heath (1983); Street (1984); Michaels (1986); Moss (2001); Snyder (1998); Snyder (2001).
2 See Prensky (2001) for a 'checklist' of characteristics of the literacy of the 'new digital generation'.
3 Moss (2001), p146.
4 As Buckingham and Sefton-Green (1998) have argued, for example, the application of pre-existing notions of what might constitute 'creativity' to the analysis of children's media production in the home may blind the researcher to the subtleties of children's interactions with digital resources.
5 Facer (2001) InterActive Education Survey Report.
6 See discussion of this field in Snyder (1994); Snyder (2001).
7 Balestri (1988), p14.
8 Facer (2001) InterActive Education Survey Report.
9 Buckingham and Sefton-Green (1998) and Haddon (1992).
10 In the InterActive 2001 survey, 19 per cent of children with home computers reported using the computer to make or record music and 11 per cent reported using the computer to work with moving images (Facer, 2001).
11 See Sinker (2000) for a discussion of the critique of children's multi-media production on the computer.
12 See Downes (1998) for the origination of the terms 'everyday' and 'exotic' in relation to children's computer use in the home.
13 Buckingham and Sefton-Green (1998) and Haddon (1992).
14 Facer (2001) InterActive Education Survey Report.
15 See BECTA (2002) Digital Divide report, which argues the case for children as producers of Web-based resources as well as consumers. See also Lachs (2000).

16 Levi-Strauss (1966); de Certeau (1992).

7 Computers, consumption and identity

1 Green and Bigum (1993); Howard (1998); Tapscott (1998); Turkle (1995).
2 For example, Kline (1993).
3 For example, Seiter (1995).
4 Featherstone (1991).
5 De Certeau (1988); Levi-Strauss (1966).
6 Green and Bigum (1993); Howard (1998); Tapscott (1998); Turkle (1995)
7 Brah (1993) argues that, traditionally, Asian women are seen as 'caught between' two cultures – a view which denies the agency of the young women themselves. Dwyer (1998) suggests that some of the young women she worked with in her research openly resisted dominant ways of being female while others used clothes 'strategically' in different places in order to escape parental approbation or to safely negotiate particular spaces such as the 'public spaces' of the streets. She argues that for these young women, 'dress style is a highly significant marker of cultural identity which is constantly negotiated' (p58).
8 As Haddon (1992) notes, even highly technologically competent girl's classroom conversation is dominated by non-technical concerns and is more likely to be about general school gossip than computers.

8 Computers, gender and class

1 There is a rich literature on gender and the computer. See, for example, Spender (1995); Haraway (1985); Gilbert (2001); Wajcmann (1991) Plant (2000); Springer (2000); Squires (2000). In addition there is a strong literature on children, gender and the computer: Shashaani (1993); Reinen and Plomp (1997); Brosnan (1998); Opie (1998); Alloway and Gilbert (1998).
2 Facer (2001) InterActive Project Report, June 2001, n = 1,818 (children aged between 8 and 17).
3 Ibid.
4 See, for example, Holloway and Valentine (2003).
5 For a critical discussion of the role of such games in the construction of masculinity, see Alloway and Gilbert (1998).
6 Cassell and Jenkins (1998), p2.
7 Thorne (1993) describes the increased competition and gender distinctions that boys and girls often engage in when they come to occupy the same place and space as 'borderwork'. Through such emphasised behaviour and banter, they maintain the 'borders' of gendered identities.
8 Shilling (1991), for example, describes the role of boys' sexist behaviour as an important dimension in playground and classroom culture.
9 McNamee (1998a), for example, argues that as boys have deserted the street for the home, competition between boys and girls around the computer has increased.
10 See also McNamee (1998a); Kenway and Bullen (2001); Holloway and Valentine (2003).
11 Holloway and Valentine (2003), for example, assert that there are such gender markings of particular computer activities.

12   Relatively little has been written about the relationship between children's actual use of ICT at home and social class. An important exception is Snyder *et al.* (2002).
13   DfES (2002a), p7.
14   Facer (2001), p26).
15   As Gorard *et al.* (2002) have highlighted, a recent large scale national survey of adults has shown that currently only 17 per cent of the economically most disadvantaged groups (social groups D and E) have access to the Internet while 67 per cent of those in social classes A and B have access.
16   There would seem to be a similarity here with what Gee *et al.* (1996) call 'elite literacies' – higher order, scientific and symbolic literacies.

9 Digital childhood

1   For example, Graham and Marvin (1996); Tapscott (1998); Valentine and Holloway (2003).
2   Kenway and Bullen (2001); Steinberg and Kincheloe (1997).
3   Lee and Liebenau (2000).
4   Green and Bigum (1993); Turkle (1984, 1995).
5   Skelton and Valentine (1998); Holloway and Valentine (2000); Holloway and Valentine (2003).
6   McNamee (1998a).
7   Whether the growth of ICTs in the home is a cause or a consequence of such changes is hard to determine. Jenkins argues that they are primarily a consequence; children spend far more time on the screen because families and external social and economic pressures mean that there are now fewer and fewer places for them safely to inhabit outside the home. ICTs 'did not make backyard play spaces disappear; rather they offer children some way to respond to domestic confinement' (Jenkins, 1998, p266). Several of the parents in our study, particularly parents of 'high using' boys, such as David or Huw, took a different view. While they admired and celebrated their sons' technological competence, they sometimes wished that they would have a more 'balanced' existence. Visions of computer 'addiction', though seldom articulated or defined, clearly hovered in the background.
8   See, for example, the United Nations Educational, Scientific and Cultural Organisation (UNESCO) review (von Feilitzen and Carlsson, 2000) of the impact of 'new media' on children's exposure to violence and pornography.
9   Kenway and Bullen (2001); Montgomery (2000); Steinberg and Kincheloe (1997).
10   Green (1988).
11   Ibid.
12   The extent to which the school will continue to be able to claim ownership of 'legitimate knowledge' may, however, be limited, if emerging views that computer games support the increasingly valued attributes of 'thinking skills' continue to gain ground (Prensky, 2001).
13   Lee and Liebenau (2000). Historically, of course the delineation between home as site of leisure and home as site of work is only true of particular classes and of particular historical periods.
14   See Downes (1998); Haddon (1992); Nixon (1998).

15 For a discussion of these 'new literacies' see Snyder (1998); Lankshear *et al.* (2000); Snyder (2002a).
16 Hard fun (Papert, S cited in Thompson, 2003).
17 See Prensky for a full discussion of the expectations of the work environment from children used to 'playing' on the computer (2001).
18 For other evidence on 'displacement' see also Livingstone and Bovill (1999); and Holloway and Valentine (2003).
19 See, for example, the recent UNESCO Yearbook on children and media, von Feilitzen and Carlsson (2000). Also Malone (1980) and Prensky (2001).
20 Turkle (1995), p205.

10 Learning with computers at home

1 See, for example, Wertsch (1991); Säljo (1999).
2 Cole and Engestrom (1993).
3 Gibson (1979).
4 Both Huw and Alistair, for example, enjoyed exploring the boundaries of their computer knowledge as a 'fun' activity in itself.
5 See Chapter 5 for a longer discussion of Csikszentmihalyi's definitions of 'flow'.
6 Turkle (1995).
7 Lave and Wenger (1991).
8 Rogoff (1998).
9 Davis *et al.* (2000).
10 See Chapters 2 and 9 for a further discussion of the links between parents' work experiences and learning with ICT in the home.
11 Wood *et al.* (1976).
12 Ninety-three per cent of boys with a home computer used a computer to write; 14 per cent of boys with a home computer used a computer to write every day (Facer, 2001, InterActive Survey).
13 Hoyles and Sutherland (1989).
14 Facer *et al.* (2002).
15 Perkins (1993).
16 Facer (2001) InterActive survey.

11 Learning with computers in school

1 As discussed in Chapter 2, the percentage of children reporting home computer ownership ranges from 76 per cent (DFES, 2002b) to 88 per cent (Facer, 2001).
2 See Facer (2001); BECTA (2001).
3 See, for example, further research carried out by the authors into ICT use in school: BECTA (2001), BECTA (2002) and the ongoing InterActive Education project, funded by the ESRC (Sutherland *et al.*). See also reports on current ICT practice in school such as the IMPACT 2 report (DfES, 2002c).
4 The ScreenPlay study took place in a period which coincided with the UK government's commitment to increasing the educational use of ICT in schools (DfEE, 1997). During this period, ICT was specified as a curriculum subject for students from age six to 16. ICT was also incorporated into curriculum specifications within many subject areas, although this became more explicit within the new Curriculum 2000 specifications. At the same time, a major teacher

training initiative (NOF training) was introduced to train teachers to incorporate ICT into their subject teaching. In 2002 a Key Stage 3 ICT strategy was put forward, in line with the numeracy and literacy strategy (DfES, 2002b).

5   Csikszentmihalyi (1990).
6   Healy and Sutherland (1990); Sutherland and Rojano (1993).
7   See, for example, further research carried out by the authors into ICT use in school: BECTA (2001), BECTA (2002) and the ongoing InterActive Education project, funded by the ESRC. See also reports on current ICT practice in school such as the IMPACT 2 report (DfES, 2002c).
8   NACCCE (1999). The QCA is also currently working on a draft framework for 'ICT and Creativity'.
9   For more discussion of the idea of flow see Chapters 5, 6 and 10.
10   This idea draws from the writing of Davis *et al.* (2000).
11   Davis *et al.*, 2000, p204.
12   IT was specified as a compulsory curriculum subject in 1989.
13   CLAIT is a suite of qualifications designed to provide a range of opportunities for candidates to gain recognition for their computer skills (http:// www.clait.org.uk/).
14   http://www.nc.uk.net/nc/contents/ICT-2—POS.html.
15   http://www.nc.uk.net/nc/contents/ICT—ATT.htm.
16   DfES (2002b).
17   Bransford *et al.* (1999), p218.
18   Sutherland *et al.* (1999).
19   More information about this is available from the report which Rosamund Sutherland wrote for the Mexican EMAT project after visiting several schools in Guadalahara in December 2002.
20   Papert (1990); Hoyles and Sutherland (1989).

12   Conclusion

1   Robins (1995).
2   Poster (1990).
3   Virilio (1991).
4   Smith *et al.* (1988); Smith *et al.* (1995).
5   Althusser (1971).
6   Tapscott (1998).
7   Marvin (1988); Furlong (1995); Morley (1992).
8   Forty (1986); Walker (1989).
9   Wertsch (1991); Salomon (1993).
10   Turkle and Papert (1990).
11   Gee *et al.* (1996).
12   Gee *et al.* (1996).
13   See, for example, Castells (1989) and Giddens (2000).
14   Perkins (1993), p95.
15   Scardamalia (2000), p5.

Bibliography

Abbot, C (1998) 'Making connections: young people and the internet', in Sefton-Green, J (ed.) *Digital Diversions: Youth Culture in the Age of Multi-Media*, London: UCL Press.

Alloway, N and Gilbert, P (1998) 'Video game culture: playing with masculinity, violence and pleasure', in Howard, S (1998) (ed.) *Wired-up: Young People and the Electronic Media*, London: UCL Press.

Althusser, L (1971) 'Ideology and ideological state apparatuses', in Althusser, L *Lenin and Philosophy*, London: New Left Books.

Balestri, D (1988) 'Softcopy and hard wordprocessing and writing process', *Academic Computing*, February, pp14–17 and pp41–5.

Battle, J (1997) Cited in HANSARD, Information Society Debate, 22/7/97.

Beavis, C (1998) 'Computer games, culture and curriculum', in Snyder, I (ed.) *Page to Screen: Taking Literacy into the Electronic Age*, London: Routledge.

Beavis, C (2002) 'Reading, writing and role-playing computer games', in Snyder, I (ed.) *Silicon literacies; Communication, Innovation and Education in the Electronic Era*, London: Routledge.

BECTA (2001) NGfL Pathfinders – Preliminary Report (DfES/0813/2001, BECTA 2001) www.becta.org.uk/research/reports/ict_re.html.

BECTA (2002) NGfL Pathfinders – Synoptic Report (DfES/0743/2002, BECTA 2002) www.becta.org.uk/research/reports/ict_re.html.

Bernstein, B B (1977) 'Class, codes and control', vol 1, *Theoretical Studies Towards a Sociology of Language*, 2nd edn, London: Routledge and Kegan Paul.

Bigum, C (2002) 'Design sensibilities, schools and the new computing and communication technologies', in Snyder, I (ed.) *Silicon Literacies: Communication, Innovation and Education in the Electronic Era*, London: Routledge.

Bingham, N and Valentine, G (1999) 'Where do you want to go tomorrow? Connecting children and the internet', *Environment and Planning D: Society and Space*, vol 17, pp655–72.

Bourdieu, P (1986) *Distinction: A Social Critique of the Judgement of Taste*, London: Routledge.

Bourdieu, P (1990) *In Other Words: Essays Towards a Reflexive Sociology* (trans. Adamson, M), Stanford, CA: Stanford University Press (Original work published 1982, 1987).

Brah, A (1993) ' "Race" and "culture" in the gendering of labour markets. South Asian women and the labour market', *New Community*, vol 19(3), pp44–58.

Bransford, J, Brown, A and Cocking, R (1999) *How People Learn: Brain, Mind, Experience, and School*, Washington: National Academy Press.

Bromley, H and Shutkin, D (1999) 'Refusing to choose: dilemmas of dissenting technology educators', paper presented to American Educational Research Association annual meeting April 1999, Montreal.

Brosnan, M (1998) *Technophobia: The Psychological Impact of Information Technology*, London: Routledge.

Buckingham, D and Scanlon, N (2003) *Education, Entertainment and Learning in the Home*, Milton Keynes: Open University Press.

Cassell, J and Jenkins, H (1998) *From Barbie to Mortal Kombat: Gender and Computer Games*, Cambridge, MA: MIT Press.

Castells, M (1989) *The Informational City: Information Technology, Economic Restructuring and the Urban–Regional Process*, Oxford: Basil Blackwell.

Coffield, F (2000) (ed.) *Differing Visions of a Learning Society, Research Findings*, vol 2, Bristol: Policy Press.

Cole, M and Engestrom, Y (1993) 'A cultural-historical approach to distributed cognition', in Salomon, G (ed.) *Distributed Cognition*, Cambridge: Cambridge University Press.

Csikszentmihalyi, M (1990) *Flow: The Psychology of Optimal Experience*, New York: Harper & Row.

Csikszentmihalyi, M, Rathunde, K and Whalen, S (1993) *Talented Teenagers*, New York: Cambridge University Press.

Davis, B, Dennis, S and Luce-Kapler, R (2000) *Engaging Minds: Learning and Teaching in a Complex World*, London: Lawrence Erlbaum Publishers.

De Certeau, M (1992) *The Practice of Everyday Life*, Berkeley: University of California Press.

DfEE (1999) *All Our Futures, Creativity, Culture and Education*, London: HMSO.

DfES (2002a) *Young People and ICT*, by Taylor Nelson-Sofres, London: HMSO, www.becta.org.uk/youngpeopleict.

DfES (2002b) *Framework for Teaching ICT Capability: Years 7, 8 and 9*, Standards and Effectiveness Unit, London: Department for Education and Skills.

DfES (2002c) 'ImpaCT2: the impact of information and communication technologies on pupil learning and attainment', London: Department for Education and Skills.

Donzelot, M (1980) *The Policing of Families*, London: Hutchinson.

Downes, T (1998) 'Children's Use of Computers in their Homes', unpublished DPhil thesis, University of Western Sydney Macarthur.

Dwyer, C (1998) 'Contested identities; challenging dominant representations of young British Muslim women', in Skelton, T and Valentine, G (1998) (eds) *Cool Places: Geographies of Youth Cultures*, London: Routledge.

Eilola, J J (1998) 'Living on the surface: learning in the age of global communication networks', in Snyder, I (ed.) *Page to Screen: Taking Literacy into the Electronic Age*, London: Routledge.

Facer, K (2001) 'Children's out-of-school uses of computers', report for the InterActive Education Project, available on http://www.interactive education. ac.uk/school.pdf.

Facer, K and Furlong, R (2001) 'Beyond the myth of the cyberkid: young people at the margins of the information revolution', *Journal of Youth Studies*, vol 4 (4) pp451–69.

Facer, K, Furlong, J, Furlong, R and Sutherland, R (2001a) 'Constructing the child computer user: from public policy to private practices', *British Journal of Sociology of Education*, vol 22(1) pp91–108.

Facer, K, Furlong, J, Furlong, R and Sutherland, R (2001b) 'What's the point of using computers: the development of young people's computer expertise in the home', *New Media and Society*, vol 3(2) pp199–219.

Facer, K, Furlong, J, Furlong, R and Sutherland, R (2001c) 'Home is where the hardware is: young people, the domestic environment and "access" to new technologies', in Hutchby, I and Moran-Ellis, J (eds) *Children, Technology and Culture*, London: Falmer.

Facer, K, Sutherland, R, Furlong, J and Furlong, R (2002) ' "Edutainment" software: a site for cultures in conflict?', in Sutherland, R. Claxton, G and Pollard, A (eds) *Teaching and Learning where Worldviews Meet*, Stoke on Trent: Trentham.

Featherstone, M (1991) *Consumer Culture and Postmodernism*, London: Sage.

Forty, A (1986) *Objects of Desire: Design and Society 1750–1980*, London: Thames and Hudson.

Friedman, T (1995) 'Making sense of software: computer games and interactive textuality', in Jones, S (ed.) *Cybersociety*, London: Sage.

Frith, S (1983) 'The pleasures of the hearth', in Donald, J (ed.) *Formations of Pleasure*, London: Routledge.

Furlong, J, Furlong, R, Sutherland, R and Facer, K (2000*)* 'The national grid for learning: a curriculum without walls?', *Cambridge Journal of Education*, Spring 2000, vol 30 (1), pp91–110.

Furlong, R (1995) 'There's no place like home', in Lister, M (ed.) *The Photographic Image in Digital Culture*, London: Comedia, Routledge.

Gee, J P, Hull, G and Lankashear, C (1996) *The New World Order; Behind the Language of the New Capitalism*, St Leonards, NSW: Allen and Unwin.

Giacquinta, J, Bauer, J and Levin, J (1993) *Beyond Technology's Promise: An Examination of Children's Educational Computing at Home*, Cambridge: Cambridge University Press.

Gibson, J J (1979) *The Ecological Approach to Visual Perception*, Boston: Houghton Mifflin.

Giddens, A (1984) *The Constitution of Society: Outline of the Theory of Structuration*, Cambridge: Polity Press.

Giddens, A (1991) *Modernity and Self Identity; Self and Society in the Late Modern Age*, Cambridge: Polity Press.

Giddens, A (2000) *The Third Way and its Critics*, Cambridge: Polity Press.

Gilbert, P (2001) 'Refining gender issues for the twenty-first century; Putting girls' education back on the agenda', *Curriculum Perspectives*, vol 21(1), pp1–8.

Gillespie, M (1995) *Television, Ethnicity and Cultural Change*, London: Routledge.

Gorard, S, Selwyn, N, Madden, L and Furlong, J (2002) 'Technology and lifelong learning: are we cutting it?', Cardiff University School of Social Sciences, paper presented to the 'All-Wales Education Research' Conference, University of Wales Conference Centre, Gregynog, 3–5 July 2002.

Graham, S and Marvin, S (1996) *Telecommunications and the City*, New York: Routledge.

Gray, A (1992) *Video Playtime: The Gendering of a Leisure Technology*, London: Comedia, Routledge.

Green, B (1988) 'Subject specific literacy and school learning: a focus on writing', *Australian Journal of Education*, vol 32(2), pp156–79.

Green, B (1998) 'The new literacy challenge', *Literacy Learning: Secondary Thoughts*, vol 7(1), pp36–46.

Green, B and Bigum, C (1993) 'Aliens in the classroom', *Australian Journal of Education*, vol 37(2), pp119–41.

Greenfield, P M (1984) *Of Mind and Media: The effects of television, video games and computers*, New York: Fontana.

Greenfield, P and Cocking, R (eds) (1996) *Mind and Media: The Effects of Television, Video Games and Computers*, Mahwah, NJ: Erlbaum.

Grossberg, L (1988) 'Rockin' with Reagan, or the mainstreaming of postmodernity', *Cultural Critique*, vol 10, pp123–49.

Haddon, L (1992) 'Explaining ICT consumption: the case of the home computer', in Silverstone, R and Hirsh, E (eds) *Consuming Technologies: Media and Information in Domestic Space*, London: Routledge.

Hall, S (1992) 'New ethnicites', in Donald, J and Rattansi, A (eds) *'Race', Culture and Difference*, London: Sage.

Haraway, D (1985) 'Manifesto for Cyborgs: Science, Technology, and Socialist Feminism in the 1980s', *Socialist Review*, vol 80, pp65–106.

Healy, L and Sutherland, R (1990) *Exploring Mathematics with Spreadsheets*, Hemel Hempstead: Simon & Schuster.

Heath, S B (1983) *Ways with Words*, Cambridge: Cambridge University Press.

Heath, S B (1984) 'What no bedtime story means: narrative skills at home and school', *Language and Society*, vol 11, pp19–76.

Hirsch, E (1992) 'The long term and the short term of domestic consumption: an ethnographic case study', in Silverstone, R and Hirsch, E (eds) *Consuming Technologies: Media and Information in Domestic Spaces*, London: Routledge.

Holloway, S and Valentine, G (2000) 'Speciality and the new social studies of childhood', *Sociology*, vol 34(4), pp763–83.

Holloway, S and Valentine, G (2003) *Cyberkids: Children in the Information Age*, London: Routledge.

Howard, S (1998) (ed.) *Wired up: Young People and the Electronic Media*, London: UCL Press.

Hoyles, C and Sutherland R (1989) *Logo Mathematics in the Classroom*, London: Routledge.

Huizinga, J (1938) 'Nature and significance of play', in Reichard, J (ed.) *Play Orbit*, London: Studio International.

Jameson, F (1984) 'Postmodernism, or the cultural logic of late capitalism', *New Left Review*, vol 145, pp53–92.

Jenkins (1999) 'Complete freedom of movement: video games as gendered play spaces', in Cassell, J and Jenkins, H (eds) *From Barbie to Mortal Kombat; Gender and Computer Games*, Cambridge, MA: MIT Press.

Katz, J (1997) 'The rights of kids in the digital age', http://www.wired.com/wired/4.07/features/kids.html (accessed August 1999).

Kenway J and Bullen E (2001) *Consuming Children: Education – Entertainment – Advertising*, London: Routledge.

Kline, S (1993) *Out of the Garden: Toys, TV and Children's Culture in the Age of Marketing*, London: Verso.

Kress, G (1998) 'Visual and verbal modes of representation in electronically mediated communication: the potentials of new forms of text', in Snyder, I (ed.) *Page to Screen: Taking Literacy into the Electronic Age*, London: Routledge.

Kress, G and van Leeuwen, T (1996) *Reading Images: The Grammar of Visual Design*, London: Routledge.

Lachs, V (2000) *Making Multimedia in the Classroom*, London:Routledge.

Lajoe, S and Derry, S (eds) (1993) *Computers as Cognitive Tools*, Hillsdale, NJ: LEA.

Lankshear, C (1997) *Changing Literacies*, Buckingham: Open University Press.

Lankshear, C, Snyder, I and Green, B (2000) *Teachers and Techno-literacy; Managing Literacy, Technology and Learning in School*, Sydney: Allen and Unwin.

Lave, D, Bruner, J S and Ross, G (1979) 'The role of tutoring in problem solving', *Journal of Child Psychology and Psychiatry*, vol 17, pp89–100.

Lave, J and Wenger, E (1991) *Situated Learning: Legitimate Peripheral Participation*, Cambridge: Cambridge University Press.

Lee, H and Liebenau, J (2000) 'Time and the internet at the turn of the millennium', *Time and Society*, vol 9, pp43–56.

Lee, N (2001) 'The extensions of childhood: technologies, children and independence', in Hutchby, I and Moran-Ellis, J (eds) *Children, Technology and Culture: The impacts of Technologies in Children's Everyday Lives*, London: Routledge.

Levi-Strauss, C (1966) *Totenism* (trans. Needham, R), London: Merlin Press.

Livingstone, S and Bovill, M (1999) *Young People, New Media*, London: LSE/ICT.

Livingstone, S, Gaskell, G and Bovill, M (1997) 'Europäische Fernseh-Kinder in veränderten Medienwelten', *Television*, vol 10, pp4–12.

Lupton, D (1995) 'The embodied computer user', in Featherstone, M and Burrows, R (eds) *Cyberspace, Cyberbodies, Cyberpunk: Cultures of Technological Embodiment*, London: Sage.

Lury, C (1996) *Consumer Culture*, Cambridge: Polity Press.

McNamee, S (1998) 'Youth gender and video games: power and control in the home', in Skelton, T and Valentine, G (eds) *Cool Places: Geographies of Youth Cultures*, London: Routledge.

Malone, T (1980) *What Makes Things Fun to Learn? A study of Intrinsically Motivating Computer Games*, Palo Alto: Xerox.

Marvin, C (1988) *When Old Technologies Were New*, Oxford: Oxford University Press.

Massey, D (1998) 'The spatial construction of youth cultures', in Skelton, T and Valentine, G (eds) *Cool Places: Geographies of Youth Cultures*, London: Routledge.

Michaels, S (1986) 'Narrative presentation: an oral preparation for literacy with 1st grades', in Cook-Gumperz J (ed.) *The Social Construction of Literacy*, Cambridge: Cambridge University Press.

Mitchell, D (1995) *City of Bits*, Cambridge, MA: MIT Press.

Montgomery, K (2000) 'Children's media culture in the new millennium; mapping the digital landscape', *The Future of Children and Computer Technology*, vol 10(2), pp145–67, http://www.futureofchildren.org.

Morgan, D (1999) 'Risk and family practices: accounting for change and the fluidity in family life', in Silva, E B and Smart, C (eds) *The New Family*, London: Sage.

MORI (1997), *The British and Technology*, Basingstoke: Motorola .

Morley, D (1992) *Television, Audiences and Cultural Studies*, London: Routledge.

Morley, D and Robins, K (1995) *Spaces of Identity: Global Media, Electronic Landscapes and Cultural Boundaries*, London: Routledge.

Moss, G (2001) 'On literacy and the social organisation of knowledge inside and outside school', *Language and Education*, vol 15(2&3), pp146–61.

Murdock, G (1989) 'Critical inquiry and audience activity', in Deruin, B, Grossberg, L, O'Ceefe, B and Wartella, E (eds) *Rethinking Communication*, vol 2, London: Sage.

Murdock, G, Hartman, P and Gray, P (1992) 'Contextualising home computing: resources and practices', in Silverstone, R and Hirsch, E (eds) *Consuming Technologies: Media and Information in Domestic Spaces*, London: Routledge.

NACCCE (1999) *All our Futures, Creativity, Culture and Education*, London: DfEE Publications.

New London Group (1996) 'A pedagogy of multiliteracies: designing social futures', *Harvard Educational Review*, vol 66(1), pp60–92.

Nixon, H (1998) 'Fun and games are serious business', in Sefton-Green, J (ed) *Digital Diversions: Youth Culture in the Age of Multi-Media*, London: UCL Press.

Opie, C (1998) 'Whose turn next? Gender issues in information technology', in Clark, A and Millard, E (eds) *Gender in the Secondary Curriculum: Balancing the Books*, London: Routledge.

Papert, S (1980) *Mindstorms: Children, Computers, and Powerful Ideas*, Brighton: The Harverster Press.

Papert, S (1993) *The Children's Machine: Rethinking School in the Age of the Computer*, New York: Basic Books.

Pea, R (1993) 'Practices of distributed intelligence and designs for education', in Salomon G (ed.) *Distributed Cognitions, Psychological and Educational Considerations*, Cambridge: Cambridge University Press.

Perkins, D (1993) 'Person-plus: a distributed view of thinking and learning', in Salomon, G (ed.) *Distributed Cognitions, Psychological and Educational Considerations*, Cambridge: Cambridge University Press.

Plant, S (2000) 'On the matrix: cyberfeminist solutions', in Bell, D and Kennedy, B (eds) *The Cybercultures Reader*, London: Routledge.

Poster, M (1990) *The Mode of Information: Post-Structuralism and Social Context*, Cambridge: Polity Press.

Prensky, M (2001) *Digital Game-Based Learning*, New York: McGraw-Hill.

Provenzo, E F (1991) *Video Kids: Making Sense of Nintendo*, Cambridge, MA: Harvard University Press.

Reinen, I J and Plomp, T (1997) 'Information technology and gender equality: a contradiction in terminis?', *Computers in Education*, vol 28, pp65–78.

Robins, K (1995) 'Will image move us still?', in Lister, M (ed.) *The Photographic Image in Digital Culture*, London: Comedia, Routledge.

Rogoff, B (1998) 'Cognition as Collaborative Process, in Kuhn, D and Siegler, R S (eds) *Cognition, Perception and Language*, vol 2, Handbook of Child Psychology (5th Edn) New York: John Wiley.

Rogoff, B, Goodman, C, Turkanis, C and Bartlett, L (2001) *Learning Together. Children and Adults in a School Community*, Oxford: Oxford University Press.

Såljo, R (1999) 'Learning as the use of tools: a sociocultural perspective on the human-technology link', in Littleton, K and Light, P (eds) *Learning with Computers: Analysing Productive Interaction,* London: Routledge.

Salomon, G (1993a) *Distributed Cognitions, Psychological and Educational Considerations*, Cambridge: Cambridge University Press.

Salomon, G (1993b) 'On the nature of pedagogic computer tools: the case of a writing partner', in Lajoe, S and Derry, S (eds) *Computers as Cognitive Tools*, Hillsdale, NJ: LEA.

Scardamalia, M (2001) 'Can schools enter a knowledge society?', in Selinger, M and Wynn, J (eds) *Educational Technology and the Impact on Teaching and Learning*. Proccedings of an International Research Forum at BETT 2000, RM Plc, Oxford.

Scardamalia, M and Bereiter, C (2000) 'Engaging students in a knowledge society', in Scardamalia, M and Bereiter, C (eds) *On Technological Learning*, San Francisco, CA: Jossey-Bass.

Scardamalia, M, Beireter, C and Lamon, M (1995) 'The CSILE Project: trying to bring the classroom into world 3', in McGilly, K (ed.) *Classroom Lessons: Integrating Cognitive Theory and Classroom Practice*, Cambridge, MA: MIT Press.

Sefton-Green, J (ed. (1998) *Digital Diversions: Youth Culture in the Age of Multi-Media*, London: UCL.

Sefton-Green, J and Buckingham, D (1998) 'Digital visions: children's "creative" uses of multimedia technologies', in Sefton-Green, J (ed.) *Digital Diversions: Youth Culture in the Age of Multi-Media*, London: UCL Press.

Sefton-Green, J and Sinker, R (eds) (2000) *Evaluating Creativity: Making and Learning by Young People*, London: Routledge.

Seiter, E (1995) *Sold Separately: Parents and Children in Consumer Culture*, Piscataway, NJ: Rutgers University Press.

Selwyn, N (2002) *Literature Review of Citizenship, Technology and Learning*, Bristol: NESTA Futurelab Series, Report 3.

Shashaani, L (1993) 'Gender-based differences in attitudes towards computers', *Computers in Education*, vol 20, pp169–81.

Shilling, C (1991) 'Social space, gender inequalities and educational differentiation', *British Journal of Sociology of Education*, vol 12, pp23–44.

Silverstone, R and Hirsch, E (eds) (1992) *Consuming Technologies: Media and Information in Domestic Spaces*, London: Routledge.

Silverstone, R, Hirsch, E and Morley D (1992) 'Information and communication technologies in the moral economy of the household', in Silverstone, R and Hirsch, E (eds) *Consuming Technologies: Media and Information in Domestic Spaces*, London: Routledge.

Sinker, R (2000) 'Making Multimedia: evauating young people's multi-media production', in Sefton-Green, J and Sinker, R (eds) (2000) *Evaluating Creativity: Making and Learning by Young People*, London: Routledge.

Skelton, T and Valentine, G (eds) (1998) *Cool Places; Geographies of Youth Cultures*, London: Routledge.

Smith, R, Curtin, P and Newman, L (1995) 'Kids in the "kitchen": the social implications for schooling in the age of advanced computer technology', paper presented at the Australian Association for Research in Education Conference, Hobart.

Smith, R, Sachs, J M and Chant, D (1988) 'Use of information technology by young people in Australia and Sweden', *Nordicom Review* (of Nordic Mass Communication Research), vol 2, pp37–9.

Snyder, I (1994) 'Reinventing writing with computers', *Australian Journal of Language and Literacy*, vol 17(3), pp182–97.

Snyder, I (ed.) (1998) *Page to Screen: Taking Literacy into the Electronic Age*, London: Routledge.

Snyder, I (2001) 'A new communication order: researching literacy practices in the network society', *Language and Education*, vol 15(2&3), pp117–61.

Snyder, I (2002a) (ed) *Silicon Literacies: Communication, Innovation and Education in the Electronic Era*, London: Routledge.

Snyder, I (2002b) 'Introduction', in Snyder, I (2002) (ed.) *Silicon Literacies: Communication, Innovation and Education in the Electronic Era*, London: Routledge.

Snyder, I, Angus, L and Sutherland-Smith, W (2002) 'Building equitable literate futures: home and school computer-mediated literacy practices and disadvantage', *Cambridge Journal of Education*, vol 32(3), pp367–83.

Spender, D (1995) *Nattering on the Net*, Australia: Spinifex Press.

Springer, C (2000) 'Digital rage', in Bell, D and Kennedy, B (eds) *The Cyber-cultures Reader*, London: Routledge.

Squires, J (2000) 'Fabulous feminist futures and the lure of cyberculture', in Bell, D and Kennedy, B (eds) *The Cybercultures Reader*, London: Routledge.

Steinberg, S and Kincheloe, J (1997) *Kinderculture: The Corporate Construction of Childhood*, Oxford: Westview Press.

Strathern, M (1992) 'Foreword', in Silverstone, R and Hirsch, E (eds) *Consuming Technologies: Media and Information in Domestic Spaces*, London: Routledge.

Street, B (1984) *Literacy in Theory and Practice*, Cambridge: Cambridge University Press.

Street, B (1987) 'Models of computer literacy', in Finnegan, R, Salaman, G and Thompson, K (eds) *Information Technology: Social Issues*, Milton Keynes: Oxford University Press.

Street, B (1995) *Social Literacies: Critical Approaches to Literacy in Development, Ethnography and Education*, London: Longman.

Street, B (1998) 'New literacies in theory and practice: what are the implications for language in education?', *Linguistics and Education*, vol 10(1), pp1–24.

Sutherland, R, Facer, K, Furlong, J and Furlong, R (2000) 'A new environment for education? The computer in the home', *Computers and Education, Special Edition*, vol 34, pp195–212.

Sutherland, R, Facer, K, Furlong, R and Furlong, J (2001) 'A window on learning with computers in the home', in Selinger, M and Wynn, J (eds) *Educational Technology and the Impact on Teaching and Learning*, Abingdon: RM.

Sutherland, R, Robertson, S and John, P (1999) InterActive Education: Teaching and Learning in the Information Age. Project funded by the ESRC Teaching and Learning Research Programme, Award no L139251060, www.interactive education.ac.uk.

Sutherland, R and Rojano, T (1993) 'A spreadsheet approach to solving algebra problems', *Jounal of Mathematical Behaviour*, vol 12(4), pp351–83.

Tapscott, D (1998) *Growing up Digital*, New York: McGraw Hill.

Thompson, J (2003) 'Computer games and learning', http://www.johnhenry1, com/hardfun.1.html, accessed 14 May 2003.

Thorne, B (1993) *Gender Play: Girls and Boys in School*, New Brunswick: Rutgers University Press.

Tobin, J (1998) 'An America "otaku": (or a boy's virtual life on the net)', in Sefton-Green, J (ed.) *Digital Diversions: Youth Culture in the Age of Multi-Media*, London: UCL Press.

Trilling, B and Hood, P (2001) 'Learning technology and educational reform in the knowledge age', in Paechter, C (ed.) *Learning Space and Identity*, London: Paul Chapman.

Turkle, S (1984) *The Second Self: Computers and the Human Spirit*, New York: Simon & Schuster.

Turkle, S (1995) *Life on the Screen: Identity in the Age of the Internet*, New York: Simon & Schuster.

Turkle, S and Papert, S (1990) 'Epistemological pluralism: styles and voices within the computer culture', *Signs*, vol 16(1), pp345–77.

Valentine, G and McKendrick, J (1997) 'Children's outdoor play: exploring parental concerns about children's safety and the changing nature of childhood', *Geoforum*, vol 28(2), pp219–35.

Virilio, P (1991) *The Aesthetics of Disappearance*, New York: Autonomedia.

von Feilitzen, C (2000) 'Electronic games, pornography, perceptions', in von Feilitzen, C and Carlsson, U (eds) *Children in the New Media Landscape: Games, Pornography, Perceptions*, Gotenborg: Unesco International Clearinghouse on Children and Violence on the Screen.

von Feilitzen, C and Carlsson, U (2000) (eds) *Children in the New Media Landscape: Games, Pornography, Perceptions*, Gotenborg: Unesco International Clearinghouse on Children and Violence on the Screen.

Wajcmann, J (1991) *Feminism Confronts Technology*, Cambridge: Polity Press.

Walker, J (1989) *Design History and the History of Design*, London: Pluto.

Wells, H G (1913) 'The beginnings of modern little warfare', in Reichard, J (ed.) (1969) *Play Orbit*, London: Studio International.

Wertsch, J (1991) *Voices of the Mind: A Sociocultural Approach to Mediated Action*, London: Harvester.

Wheelock, J (1992) 'Personal computers, gender and an institutional model of the household', in Silverstone, R and Hirsch, E (eds) *Consuming Technologies: Media and Information in Domestic Spaces*, London: Routledge.

Williamson, B and Facer, K (2002) 'School bans computer games: developing learning communities around games', paper presented at the 'Game On' Conference, Edinburgh, November 2002, available at www.nestafuturelab.org.

Wood, D, Bruner, J S, and Ross, G (1976) 'The role of tutoring in problem solving', *Journal of Child Psychology and Psychiatry*, vol 17, pp89–100.

Index

Note: Tables in the text are indicated by (*Table*) after the page number, e.g. 24(*Table 2.26*), and pictures by (*Pic.*), e.g. 42(*Pic. 3.2*).